THIN BLUE LIE

THIN BLUE LIE

THE FAILURE OF
HIGH-TECH POLICING

MATT STROUD

METROPOLITAN BOOKS

HENRY HOLT AND COMPANY   NEW YORK

Metropolitan Books
Henry Holt and Company
Publishers since 1866
175 Fifth Avenue
New York, New York 10010
www.henryholt.com

Metropolitan Books® and m® are registered trademarks of
Macmillan Publishing Group, LLC.

Some reporting in this book first appeared in *The Verge, The Incercept,* and *Public Source.*

Library of Congress Cataloging-in-Publication Data

Names: Stroud, Matt, author.
Title: Thin blue lie : the failure of high-tech policing / Matt Stroud.
Description: First edition. | New York : Metropolitan Books/ Henry Holt and Company,
    [2018] | Includes bibliographical references and index.
Identifiers: LCCN 2018038059 | ISBN 9781250108296 (hardcover)
Subjects: LCSH: Police—United States. | Police—Technological innovations—United States. |
    Police-community relations—United States. | Police administration—United States.
Classification: LCC HV8139 .S89 2018 | DDC 363.2/30973—dc23
LC record available at https://lccn.loc.gov/2018038059

Our books may be purchased in bulk for promotional, educational, or business use. Please contact
your local bookseller or the Macmillan Corporate and Premium Sales Department at
(800) 221-7945, extension 5442, or by e-mail at MacmillanSpecialMarkets@macmillan.com.

First Edition 2019

Designed by Kelly S. Too

Printed in the United States of America

1 3 5 7 9 10 8 6 4 2

To Kylie, Evy, Cori, and Charlie

Police work is largely a game of bluff.

— Jacob Riis, *The Making of an American*, 1901

CONTENTS

THIN BLUE LIE

You hear a click, like the sound of a light switch or a pencil being snapped.

You're facing away from it, looking straight ahead, just as instructed. The click and the searing pain you feel are nearly instantaneous, but your mind tricks you into thinking that there's a distinct period between the click and your first realization that something's gone very wrong. Maybe that's because your shooter—friendly and supportive, congratulatory, even, somehow impressed that you were dumb enough to have volunteered for this—has prepared you for it, warned you that a pain like no other is about to strike you.

So you just stand there, waiting for it, on the wrong side of target practice.

When it hits you, no matter how much you expect it, it comes as a surprise—a literal shock, like a baseball bat swung hard and squarely into the small of your back. That sensation, which is actually two sharp steel barbs piercing your skin and shooting electricity into your central nervous system, is followed by the harshest, most violent spasm you can imagine coursing through your entire body. Needles everywhere, overwhelming you. With the pain comes the terrifying awareness that you are completely helpless. You cannot move. You lose control of almost everything and the only place you can go is down, face first to the floor.

THE WHOLE THING lasted five seconds—but it felt like an eternity.

I had just spent several hours interviewing employees in the Scottsdale, Arizona, headquarters of the wildly successful, publicly traded company that makes Tasers, the black-and-yellow electroshock devices. At the time, the company was called Taser International. Just a few years earlier, Tasers had become Internet famous when a college student was filmed shouting "Don't taze me, bro!" at a university police officer in 2007. Like many who saw that viral video, I hadn't taken the weapons very seriously.

But on my way out of the building, the company's main press officer asked me, "Do you want to take a ride?"

He was asking if I would voluntarily subject myself to being shocked by the company's signature product. It was "typical," he claimed, for anyone visiting Taser International's massive, futuristic desert compound to "get a taste of what Taser's all about."

Maybe it was the hot desert air. Maybe it was the fact that I'd never read or heard a good explanation of what it feels like to be shocked with a Taser. Whatever the reason, I agreed to play along.

AS SOON AS it was over, I began to ask myself for the first time: Is a weapon this powerful really necessary for police to do their work safely?

Many cops would say yes, of course: the purpose of Tasers is to disable and immobilize unruly suspects. Tasers give police another option that is less likely to kill someone than a gun. Tasers make police *safer*.

But as I looked deeper into Taser International, this reasoning seemed flimsier and flimsier.

I soon came to see that this was just one example of many in which police put their total faith in technology, expecting it to solve the massive, seemingly intractable problems inherent to their work. We've seen this same kind of blind optimism concerning body cameras, Compstat, predictive policing, cell phone trackers, and even surveillance cameras. Leaving aside the important privacy concerns that have been raised about some of these technologies, in many cases they simply don't do what they're supposed to do. And more often than not, the technologies have turned out to be expensive stopgaps that give the police a sheen of forward-thinking pragmatism while in fact steering them away from the kinds of fundamental reforms that could make a real difference. How did police come to trust technology so fervently? And what role has technology played in pitting them against the communities they're supposed to serve and protect?

WHEN PUBLIC ORDER BREAKS DOWN

Everyone remembers Ferguson. The small municipality in Missouri, located ten miles northwest of St. Louis, with a mostly black population of about twenty-one thousand, was the setting of a shocking police killing in 2014 that captured the nation's attention.[1] The city's population, however, also represented a much broader trend—the culmination of a cycle of white flight that had been playing out all over the country for decades. In the 1950s and '60s, as blacks moved in massive numbers from the South to large northern cities like St. Louis, white families fled those cities for the suburbs. By the 1980s, some blacks had accumulated enough wealth to move to the suburbs, too, and when they did many whites fled again to exurban communities even farther out. This trend created intensely segregated and often impoverished suburbs[2]—which Ferguson perfectly exemplified: between 1980 and 2010, Ferguson's white population decreased from 85 to 29 percent while its black population increased from 14 to 67 percent.[3] All the while, the number of black police officers in Ferguson remained extremely low: by 2014, only three of the city's fifty-three police officers were black.[4] Like so many other communities in the United States, Ferguson had become a majority-black city policed almost entirely by white officers.

Just before noon on a hot Saturday, August 9, 2014, one of those officers, Darren Wilson, got an alert on his radio to be on the lookout for two young black men who had just left the Ferguson Market & Liquor convenience store, where they'd allegedly stolen cigarillos. Minutes later, Wilson, driving an SUV patrol car, spotted two black teenagers walking in the street in a low-traffic area of Ferguson near the Canfield Green Apartments complex less than a half mile from the store. Wilson approached them in his SUV and ordered them to move onto the sidewalk so he could question them. The young men, according to Wilson, refused, and one of them, eighteen-year-old Michael Brown, approached the vehicle. In less than a minute, Brown would be dead.[5]

As shocking as the incident was, it easily could have remained a local story. It's a sad fact of life in America that police killings happen all the time, all around the country. But this case was different. First, it happened in the middle of the day, in the sunny heat, within yards of a populated apartment complex where a number of bystanders watched from a distance. It was immediately heartbreaking, too: Brown lived in the complex, and the first person to identify the young man lying dead on the ground was his grandmother, who fell to her knees and wept. Furthermore, Brown was unarmed during the incident, and people on the scene claimed that he had been holding up his hands in a gesture of surrender when the officer opened fire.[6] Brown was black, and the officer was white. The timing was important, too: less than a month earlier, Eric Garner, a black man in New York City, had been killed as police officers attempted to arrest him using a controversial chokehold, setting off massive protests around the country.[7] To the millions nationwide who had taken to the streets, Brown's killing represented yet another—perhaps an even more flagrant—example of police brutality inflicted upon a black man.

Would an unarmed white man in Brown's situation have faced the same fate?

After Brown's killing, the U.S. Department of Justice commissioned a report on the incident. It found that Wilson was part of a police department made up of mostly white officers who—whether they meant to or not—essentially terrorized the mostly black communities they served. According to the report, Ferguson police officers went to extraordinary lengths to generate revenue, issuing an enormous number of tickets and fines for minor civil offenses. They also targeted black people much more frequently and aggressively than white people: between 2012 and 2014, 85 percent of people stopped by the Ferguson Police Department and 93 percent of those arrested were black, despite blacks making up just 67 percent of the population. Ninety-five percent of Ferguson's jaywalking tickets went to blacks, and 94 percent of its "failure to comply" offenses—a charge for not immediately following an officer's command—went to blacks, as well.[8]

These tickets weren't insignificant expenses for people living in Ferguson's impoverished neighborhoods. The city's unemployment rate had shot up in recent years to a high of more than 13 percent in 2012[9] as household earnings fell by one-third and the population living below the poverty line doubled. These citations, in other words, added up to a form of wealth extraction, a system that sucked money from the already poor to fund the operations of an increasingly overextended police force. In many cases, people would find themselves unable to pay a fine for an arguably meaningless nonviolent offense and end up in jail as a result. Worse still, there was a perverse incentive encouraging officers to continue these practices: Ferguson police officers were given promotions based on what was euphemistically called "productivity"— which in reality meant the amount of money an officer brought in.[10] Indeed, the City of Ferguson relied on cops writing tickets and issuing fines to keep its budget balanced.

The Ferguson report's findings bore a striking similarity to another report issued nearly a half century earlier. Titled "The Challenge of

Crime in a Free Society," this 1967 report was commissioned by President Lyndon B. Johnson's administration in response to what were, at the time, some of the most destructive riots the country had ever seen, the Watts uprising of 1965. In presenting the report to Congress, President Johnson issued a statement of his own on the importance of responsible law enforcement. "When public order breaks down, when men and women are afraid to use the public streets, their confidence is seriously shaken," he wrote. "When hundreds of thousands of young people enter adulthood carrying the burden of police records, when contempt and mistrust too often characterize public attitudes toward lawful authority, all—young and old, private citizens and public officials—suffer the consequences."[11] The report itself proposed a wide range of ideas for improving the ways that society responds to crime,[12] including more than two hundred specific policy changes within the Department of Justice, state governments, civic organizations, religious institutions, and business groups—even employment agencies and government programs employing social workers. Calling for "a revolution in the way America thinks about crime," the report didn't just make recommendations about how police departments and prisons should operate; it proposed improving options for affordable housing to ensure people wouldn't have to scrounge and resort to crime to make ends meet and establishing citizen advisory commissions in "minority group neighborhoods" to help improve relationships between police and communities. The report, unlike many other analyses at the time, seemed to truly understand the circumstances that made policing such fraught work. "It is hard to overstate the intimacy of the contact between the police and the community," the report explained.

> Policemen deal with people when they are both most threatening and most vulnerable, when they are angry, when they are frightened, when they are desperate, when they are drunk, when they are violent, or when they are ashamed. . . . Every police action can affect

in some way someone's dignity, or self-respect, or sense of privacy, or constitutional rights.[13]

The report acknowledged that while police "have been well trained to perform such procedures as searching a person for weapons, transporting a suspect to the stationhouse, taking fingerprints, writing arrest reports, and testifying in court," they had received almost no guidance when it came to handling "intricate, intimate human situations." Police training, the report went on, is

focused almost entirely on the apprehension and prosecution of criminals. What a policeman does, or should do, instead of making an arrest or in order to avoid making an arrest, or in a situation in which he may not make an arrest, is rarely discussed. The peace-keeping and service activities, which consume the majority of police time, receive too little consideration.[14]

The report recommended specific steps that departments could take to help alleviate these problems: Police leaders should strive to be more engaged and visible in their communities by attending local meetings and events as well as participating in community discussions. They should deal more openly with complaints, and train new hires to use force only when absolutely necessary. Police departments in communities with substantial minority populations should recruit "minority-group officers, and deploy and promote them fairly." Furthermore, departments should address citizen grievances fairly, explain clearly to citizens what police are and are not permitted to do under the law, hire people with college degrees, and stress abilities over seniority for promotions. Finally, the report suggested that every department, regardless of size, should have a comprehensive program to identify and weed out bad cops.[15]

These were important, necessary recommendations—yet half a century later, in Ferguson, few of them had been implemented in any meaningful way. Money was a large part of the reason. The Johnson administration's report estimated that state and local governments around the country were already spending approximately $2.8 billion annually—the equivalent of about $21 billion today—on policing alone.[16] And its recommendations, had they been followed, surely would have driven that number even higher. Coming up with the necessary funds to retrain officers, hire new ones, and restructure how the criminal justice system worked would have been a massive undertaking. Eventually, it was hoped, those costs would pay for themselves by making law enforcement more efficient and addressing the root causes of crime. Police would have fewer arrests to carry out, fewer people to incarcerate, and would need fewer resources for active patrols. But the up-front investment required was just too great. And so the changes never took off.

The underlying problems that had brought crime to such high levels in the first place soon worsened as a recession hit the United States in the 1970s. As the slowing economy deprived government agencies of resources, the idea of making a substantial new investment to transform law enforcement seemed increasingly impossible.

The spikes in both poverty and crime persisted into the 1980s, creating a demanding, demoralizing situation. Police commanders and the politicians overseeing their work simply did not have the capacity—or the willingness—to consider the recommendations of "The Challenge of Crime in a Free Society" in the years that followed. Instead, they tightened budgets and doubled down on what they already knew—more aggressive policing and more arrests.

As the recession ended and the 1980s became the 1990s, police budgets started growing once again. But rather than putting that money toward substantive reforms, police leaders turned to the cultural fascination of the moment: technology. Rather than investing, for example, in training to help cops manage stressful encounters with the mentally ill, police leaders spent the money on high-tech crime mapping tools, electroshock weapons, and surveillance equipment. Rather than more closely embedding officers into communities, leaders invested in computer software to help carry out arrests more efficiently. In short, policing became an industry.

And as is the case with many burgeoning industries, companies were falling over themselves to get in on the action. Before long, these companies, especially the ones that got in early, were raking in astounding profits and taking steps to block out competitors, cozying up to police departments and in some cases arranging to keep their contracts secret.

Between 1981 and 2012, the amount of tax money spent on police ballooned from about $16.8 billion[17] to $126.4 billion,[18] an increase of almost 200 percent, adjusted for inflation. By 2014, when Michael Brown was killed, this spending surge—which could be described as a police industrial complex—had changed American policing so radically that many observers jumped immediately to discussing which technologies might have helped to avoid the tragic conclusion rather than asking about underlying, institutional problems within the police force.

Indeed, as weeks turned to months after Brown's killing, many observers asked why Wilson hadn't been equipped with a body camera[19] or a Taser.[20] Wouldn't a video recording of what happened between Darren Wilson and Michael Brown have defused the unrest before it turned violent? And wouldn't a nonlethal weapon with the ability to incapacitate someone from a distance negate the need for guns like the one that killed Michael Brown?

The answer to the former question is impossible to know.

The answer to the latter, it turns out, was probably not. After studying 36,112 use-of-force incidents, University of Chicago researchers determined in 2018 that Tasers do not reduce police use of firearms in any significant way. The company that produces Tasers did its own study and came to a similar conclusion, although it claims this is by design; in a 2018 interview, the company's spokesman Steve Tuttle told CNBC, "We did not provide Tasers to replace firearms."[21] Yet the promise of cutting down on fatal encounters between civilians and police was clearly a large part of their appeal.

In the end, the hype won out. By the end of 2015, the U.S. Department of Justice awarded tens of millions of dollars in grants to help police departments purchase body cameras—a program created specifically in response to the controversy over Brown's death.[22]

Today, the fundamentals of policing have been co-opted by industry—by a corporatized approach to law enforcement that increasingly relies on weapons, software, and covert surveillance. According to this school of reform, technological solutions are always preferable to others. At the same time, community leaders, lawmakers, and some police chiefs have pushed for deeper, more old-fashioned reforms—the kind that are focused on closing the gap between police and communities. But instead law enforcement agencies have maintained a singular focus on the promise of technology.

To understand how we ended up with such a misguided system, we have to look back more than a century, to one of the pioneers of modern policing, a man named August Vollmer.

CHAPTER 1

CONFRONT AND COMMAND

In 1905, August Vollmer had recently returned from a yearlong stint fighting with the army in the Philippine-American War and was working as a fireman while also running his own business in Berkeley, California. That same year, at age twenty-nine, he successfully ran for Berkeley's town marshal position on an anticorruption platform.[1]

Berkeley had no police department at the time, so the town marshal was responsible for enforcing vice laws, dealing with riots, overseeing the town's jail (with the help of a small group of paid deputies), issuing business licenses, and generally maintaining public safety.[2]

Despite not technically being in charge of a police department, Vollmer would become one of the most influential voices in modern policing. On April 18, 1906—only a few months after Vollmer became town marshal—a massive earthquake hit San Francisco, causing destructive fires and killing as many as three thousand people at a time when the city's population numbered just a few hundred thousand.[3] It was one of the most devastating natural disasters to ever hit the United States. "Not in history has a modern imperial city been so

completely destroyed," the novelist Jack London wrote that year.
"San Francisco is gone."[4] In the aftermath, many San Franciscans
fled the city and a sizable number of them landed across the San
Francisco Bay in Berkeley. With nowhere to live, more than fifteen
thousand of these displaced people built a sprawling, makeshift
encampment on Berkeley's outskirts. Overnight, Vollmer found himself in charge of keeping the peace in this new, improvised city,
where problems such as theft and food hoarding were rampant.[5]

To manage such a demanding task, he knew he would need additional manpower, so Vollmer placed a newspaper ad calling for former soldiers (including many who had fought alongside him in the
same Philippine-American War) to apply for a new taskforce that
would maintain order in the encampment. Vollmer received an overwhelming response to the ad, and, in short order, deployed as many
as sixteen hundred of these veterans, using them like an occupying
force and imposing martial law. With strong-arm tactics and brute
force, he managed to quickly drive down crime. He later recalled an
incident in which he threatened to execute a group of thieves in the
encampment—he didn't follow through but, according to Vollmer's
telling, word of his ruthlessness quickly spread.[6]

Before long, his reputation became a source of fascination in the
local media. San Francisco was in the midst of a newspaper boom at
the time, and reporters from across the bay—as well as others from
around the country—flocked to Berkeley to report on the aftermath
of the earthquake and the no-nonsense town marshal who had gone
from overseeing three people to overseeing sixteen hundred in a matter
of days. Vollmer was a phenomenon. He befriended reporters and
became known for providing "good copy." This helped to elevate a relatively small Bay Area town—with only a small crew of men in charge
of normal law enforcement duties—into the national spotlight. Most
of those who sought shelter in the encampment eventually abandoned
Berkeley, but many stayed—and within the span of about a year, the
city saw its permanent population double.[7]

Meanwhile, across the bay, San Francisco found itself engulfed in another disaster—this one man-made. Around that time, the federal criminal court in San Francisco had brought corruption and bribery charges against members of the city's Board of Supervisors, its mayor, and their attorney Abraham "Boss" Ruef. This triggered what would eventually be called the San Francisco Graft Trials, where it was revealed that the city's government and police were deeply enmeshed in organized crime. Prosecutors alleged that owners of illegal businesses such as brothels and unsanctioned casinos would pay off police to allow their continued operation. City politicians had apparently supported and even encouraged this bribery, taking cuts of the proceeds for themselves. Perhaps most alarmingly, it came to light that members of the Board of Supervisors had conspired with police to rig the board's elections.[8]

All of this was ongoing when, in 1909, Berkeley's leaders decided to officially incorporate as a city, forming a police department and establishing a municipal government led by a mayor and overseen by a city council. Vollmer was appointed police chief, and capitalizing on widespread anger over the abuses in San Francisco he made anticorruption a centerpiece of his new department's goals. He also started doing things that no other police chief had done before, pioneering a number of groundbreaking reforms. He took steps to ensure that the department's operations would be timely and efficient, purchasing bicycles for his full-time officers, which allowed them to respond to emergencies faster, and lobbying the city to install a new alarm system of flashing red lights stationed at intersections that would alert officers about reported crimes.[9]

Perhaps Vollmer's most significant contribution to the future of American policing, however, was his invention of a new system of classifying clues and offenders—essentially a database of criminal records with names, the nature of accusations, and mug shots. As Vollmer saw it, police departments had long been crippled by their own disorganization and lack of recordkeeping; if they tracked all charges and kept as much information as possible on criminals, they would be better able to solve crimes and stop repeat offenders. He called this the Modus Operandi system.[10]

To Vollmer, crime and crime fighting were subjects of great importance that demanded intense and continual reevaluation. It was because of this conviction that, within a few years of becoming Berkeley's police chief, he founded the country's first criminology program at the nearby University of California. During his time as police chief, Vollmer became a prominent voice in the policing community and soon joined the International Association of Chiefs of Police—a burgeoning organization of police leaders that would meet semiannually to trade ideas and discuss strategy. The IACP elected Vollmer president in 1921, and he did not hesitate to use the influence of the position to spread his ideas about the importance of organization and technology in law enforcement. Above all, Vollmer prized intelligence, pushing to hire more cops with bachelor's degrees and requiring new recruits to take IQ tests before they could be hired. Once they were hired, he encouraged his cops to pursue classwork in criminology studies. "Why should not the cream of the nation be perfectly willing to devote their lives to the cause of service providing that service is dignified, socialized, and professionalized," he would later write.[11]

Eventually, as Vollmer's ideas took hold in police departments across the country, they evolved into an ethos of professionalism that valued recordkeeping, science, and technology.

ONE OF VOLLMER'S most controversial—and consequential—accomplishments was his pioneering use of lie detectors. As he saw it, figuring out how to discern when someone was telling the truth was one of the most important and fundamental questions in law enforcement. In 1921, one of Vollmer's new recruits in the Berkeley Police Department came to him with a request. The recruit, twenty-nine-year-old John Larson, had just received his doctorate in physiology from the University of California. He was intrigued by an academic article he'd read about experiments that tested whether using a machine to measure a person's heart rate, respiratory rate, and other factors could help determine if they were lying. He asked Vollmer for approval to build a lie-detecting machine of his own and to test it on suspects brought into the police department. Vollmer assented. Larson initially called his new invention "the apparatus," and, by 1923, he and Vollmer had tested it on 861 subjects, determining that more than 200 of them were guilty—at least according to the apparatus.[12]

That year, Larson moved to Chicago to pursue a medical degree and continue his experiments with the apparatus. Vollmer also left Berkeley around the same time, in his case to take a job overseeing the Los Angeles Police Department, where he touted the apparatus to anyone who would listen—including the press, his colleagues at the IACP, and criminologists he'd met through his academic work.

Larson, meanwhile, was pressing forward with his tests in Chicago—and the results were not encouraging. After experimenting on hundreds of people, he found that the rate of accuracy for lie detection was somewhere around 40 percent. He later wrote:

> I originally hoped that . . . lie detection would become a legitimate part of professional police science. It is little more than a racket. The lie detector, as used in many places, is nothing more than a psychological third-degree* aimed at extorting confessions as the old physical beatings were. At times I'm sorry I ever had any part in its development.[14]

---

* It's not clear where or how this phrase originated, but the "third degree" was a common tactic born of the widespread police corruption in the late nineteenth and early twentieth centuries: if a cop wanted a confession, he'd beat it out of a suspect—"give them the third degree." The Wickersham Commission—a committee established under the Herbert Hoover administration as the first ever to investigate law enforcement tactics nationwide—found that "the use of physical brutality or other forms of cruelty to obtain involuntary confessions" was "widespread" and that "physical brutality, illegal detention, and refusal to allow access of counsel to the prisoner is common."[13]

But by the time Larson had completed this tests, it was too late.Press reports referred to the invention as a "lie detector," and before long it became a tool of police departments throughout the country.

The following years saw the continued proliferation of Vollmer's ideas. By 1929, the Eighteenth Amendment had been in place for nine years, and police across the country were now responsible for enforcing a ban on producing, selling, importing, and transporting alcohol. To help police with this responsibility, local and state governments drastically increased law enforcement budgets, allowing departments to hire more officers, while the federal government expanded its own role in enforcement.

Altogether, law enforcement expenditures increased fivefold between 1920 and 1930 and, by the time Prohibition was repealed in 1933, it had cost taxpayers about $300 million, the equivalent of more than $4.3 billion today.[15] That expense was widely understood to have been a colossal waste.[16] But the effects of this financial boost to the institution of policing would be felt long after alcohol was again legalized. Policing had grown exponentially as a result, and the expansion helped to spread some of Vollmer's innovations. In a matter of years, his practice of recording criminal data in a central database would develop into the Uniform Crime Reporting system,[17] a nationwide statistical database of crime data reported by jurisdictions all over the country. His idea of putting Berkeley officers on bicycles eventually led to the use of police cruisers.

By the time the United States joined World War II, police departments had evolved into forces that closely mirrored the military—professional and structured, funded by local, state, and federal governments—operating on the streets of just about every community in the country.

DESPITE THE MANY modernizing reforms that Vollmer brought to policing, there was one huge problem that he did nothing to solve— and in fact contributed to: the way that police treated communities of color and especially African American communities. It goes with- out saying that American law enforcement, from its very beginnings in the nineteenth century, had reflected the attitudes and priorities of a profoundly racist society.

One reform that Vollmer believed was essential to improving law enforcement was getting police to integrate with the communities where they worked—walking the streets, getting to know neighbors and business owners, and staying informed about residents' concerns. But it's almost certain that Vollmer wanted to see police officers inte- grating themselves only within white communities. First of all, polic- ing black neighborhoods just wasn't something that occupied much of his time; as in much of the western United States, Berkeley's black population was astoundingly low. According to U.S. Census figures, black people made up less than 1 percent of the city's population in 1920.[18] Even so, Vollmer made clear in his writings that he felt African Americans were dangerous and that their mere presence contributed to crime. In one instance, he observed that southern cities both con- tained large black populations and had high murder rates, conclud- ing that "the Negro contributes enormously to this unbelievably high murder rate."[19]

In short, American policing may have become more professional- ized, efficient, and humane under Vollmer's influence, but its racism remained potent. This disconnect bears a distinct resemblance to law enforcement's current focus on sophisticated new equipment over efforts to address fundamental, systemic, problems. Then, as now, reforms focusing on efficiency, organization, and technology could do little good unless deeper faults were addressed first.

———

DURING WORLD WAR II, because of labor shortages and an urgent
need for weapons and supplies, there was a great demand for workers
to fill hundreds of thousands of industrial jobs, and increasingly African Americans began to take those jobs. Of course, this was a matter
of necessity, not a sign of an increasingly tolerant society; pushback
against such integration was swift and vigorous. Fearing race riots,
President Franklin D. Roosevelt issued an executive order in June 1941
committing to a national project of inclusion.

> I do hereby reaffirm the policy of the United States that there shall
> be no discrimination in the employment of workers in defense
> industries or government because of race, creed, color, or national
> origin, and I do hereby declare that it is the duty of employers and
> of labor organizations, in furtherance of said policy and of this
> Order, to provide for the full and equitable participation of all work-
> ers in defense industries, without discrimination because of race,
> creed, color, or national origin.[20]

The order technically stated nothing new, simply reaffirming the
language and spirit spelled out in the country's founding documents.
Of course, the United States had not lived up to that spirit, and the
integration required by Roosevelt's executive order would in fact con-
stitute a radical departure from the way things stood. The process of
implementing the changes was arduous and bitterly contested.

In Detroit, for example, high-paying jobs at automakers such as
General Motors and Ford Motor Company attracted workers of all
races and origins during the war, a great number of them from southern states. Mostly adhering to the executive order, companies hired
vast numbers of blacks—though they were kept separated from their
white counterparts.

In the two years following Roosevelt's order, Detroit's overall
population increased by about 25 percent, and its black population
increased even faster, by about one-third over the same period. The

city grew denser, and racial groups that had previously been completely segregated were forced to interact with one another more frequently both on the street and in the workplace. One-off fights would occur in factories; skirmishes would play out in housing developments. Then, in June 1943, the situation reached a breaking point.[21]

That month, the Packard Motor Car Company, which had previously employed black workers but kept them segregated, promoted three of them from unskilled positions to skilled jobs—which until then had been held exclusively by whites—on the manufacturing floor of a facility that produced fighter planes.[22] As many as twenty-five thousand whites walked off the job in protest.

Then, on a warm Sunday, June 20, fights broke out between blacks and whites on Belle Isle, an island city park in the Detroit River, which is connected to Detroit's mainland by the Douglas MacArthur Bridge, which extends nearly a half mile at 2,193 feet. While much of the city remained segregated at the time, Belle Isle was a mostly integrated public property—it was therefore one of the few public places where blacks and whites would intermingle. The fights developed into a full-scale riot, taking over huge swaths of the city and lasting hours. Police responded in force and seemed to break up the melee, declaring it over by midnight.[23] In fact, the conflict had only begun.

In the early morning hours of June 21, fights erupted in mainland Detroit, and amid the confusion unfounded rumors began to spread—that a group of white men had tossed an African American woman off the bridge, and that black men had raped and murdered a white woman in the chaos of the day—fueling new violence. Hours passed and pandemonium reigned. Gangs of white men drove around the city looking for black men to attack; as daylight broke, white people attacked blacks who were on their way to work. White and black mobs assaulted one another, beating innocent motorists and pedestrians, and burning cars, homes, and businesses.[24]

The situation completely overwhelmed the Detroit Police Department, which had committed all two thousand of its officers, working alongside one hundred fifty state troopers, to stem the tide of destruction. They simply didn't have the numbers to confront disruptions of such massive proportions. They were also, clearly, more inclined to help one side of the dispute than the other. A retrospective in the *Detroit News* about the riots explained that at one point, cops considered any black people standing in a certain area northwest of downtown to be looters and reportedly told them to "run and not look back" before opening fire, shooting some in the back as they fled.[25]

President Roosevelt eventually sent in federal troops with armored vehicles and automatic weapons to restore order, bringing the thirty-six hours of rioting to an end, but not before a remarkable number of people had been beaten, arrested, or slain: in the end, thirty-four people were killed, twenty-five of them black, seventeen of whom were killed by police officers. No whites were killed by police. Approximately eighteen hundred people were arrested, most of them black.[26] Of the six hundred people injured in the riots, more than three-quarters of them were black.

Thurgood Marshall, then a young lawyer working for the National Association for the Advancement of Colored People (NAACP), sharply criticized the stark contrast between the way in which police had treated white and black rioters in Detroit. "They used 'persuasion' rather than firm action with white rioters, while against Negroes they used the ultimate in force: night sticks, revolvers, riot guns, submachine guns, and deer guns," Marshall wrote in an article for the NAACP's magazine *The Crisis*. "The entire record, both of the riot killings and of previous disturbances, reads like the story of the Nazi gestapo."[27]

Detroit mayor Edward Jeffries, however, was satisfied with the police department's performance, proclaiming that police did their best in an unbelievably difficult situation and expressing that he was "rapidly losing" patience with "Negro leaders who insist that their people do not and will not trust policemen." Mayor Jeffries did relent on two important points: the Detroit Police Department was almost entirely white, he acknowledged, and its segregated ranks may have contributed to its inability to deal with a race riot. Shortly thereafter, Jeffries agreed to initiate a search for two hundred qualified African Americans to join the Detroit police force.[28]

Mayor Jeffries's willingness, despite his retrograde views about the riots themselves, to bring more blacks into the police department reflected a much larger pressure that had begun to mount on police leadership. But years would pass before serious efforts to integrate took place.

AS THE GREAT Migration continued to bring blacks and whites into closer proximity than ever before, racism in other northern and particularly midwestern cities began to spark violence more frequently. As was the case in Detroit, police leaders in those cities were not equitable in their responses, and did not hesitate to confront black protesters with brutal violence—with, as Marshall put it, "the ultimate in force." One of the first suggestions that a different path was necessary came in the form of a 1944 report by the Chicago-based International City Managers' Association entitled "The Police and Minority Groups: A Program to Prevent Disorder and to Improve Relations Between Different Racial, Religious, and National Groups." The report was short, just twenty pages, and began by describing the unenviable position of police officers during a time of racial strife and general unrest.

"It is almost impossible to handle a riot 'successfully.' Deaths and injuries, extensive property destruction, and severe damage to public morale are virtually inevitable in any large-scale disorder," wrote Clarence E. Ridley, executive director of the International City Managers' Association, in a preface to the report.[29] "Although the police are usually blamed if trouble breaks out, they cannot control or solve the basic causes of antagonism between groups." The authors of the report recommended two relatively simple approaches to ensuring fairness in such a situation: first, mediating community disputes to eliminate misconceptions in an effort to defuse violent unrest before it breaks out; and second, maintaining a professional, calm, nonviolent, and dispassionate demeanor in confronting protests and riots if and when they did begin. The report praised police chiefs in five cities including Washington, D.C., Houston, and Flint, Michigan, where police had succeeded as peacekeepers. The report praised the New York Police Department in particular for its role in confronting race-based fighting in Harlem during the summer of 1943.[30]

On the first day of August that year, a woman named Margie Polite was arguing with a clerk in the lobby of the Braddock Hotel in Harlem, where she was unsatisfied with her room and seeking a refund. A white police officer, James Collins, who had been working in the lobby, eventually confronted Polite and arrested her for disorderly conduct. A black army soldier, Robert Bandy, witnessed the commotion and asked Collins to let her go. While accounts of the incident vary, it's clear that, after some escalating back-and-forth, Collins eventually shot Bandy in the shoulder. Even though Bandy's injury hadn't been fatal, a rumor soon spread through Harlem that a white police officer had shot and killed a black soldier. Soon the streets of Harlem swarmed with angry protesters, including some who were violent. The situation easily could have spiraled out of control as it had in Detroit, but the police, according to the International City Managers' Association report, were able to de-escalate the situation with a calm, professional manner: "All of the police who helped to quell the Harlem riot were given strict instructions directly by Mayor La Guardia and Commissioner Valentine to use no more force than was absolutely necessary and to be impersonal, matter of fact, and diplomatic in their efforts to break up the street mobs," the report read.[31]

In an article for the *New Republic*, the NAACP's president at the time, Walter White, commended the police for their restraint and relative sensitivity: "Thousands of police poured into the twenty-eighth precinct straight from eight hours of duty," he wrote. "During all those troubled hours, I heard not one word about 'niggers' . . . nor was there any other manifestation of racial animosity. They were out to do a job of restoring order, and it was all in the day's work."[32]

The International City Managers' Association report continued:

[The police in Harlem] did not attempt, by a display or use of over-powering force, to make frontal attacks on the mobs which by this time were breaking store windows and beginning to loot merchandise. Neither riot guns nor tear gas were used . . . Instead, the police prevented newcomers from joining the mobs and at the same time concentrated on dividing the mobs that were already active and dispersing the small segments they split off.[33]

Another important factor in the NYPD's ability to de-escalate the strife in Harlem that summer was its inclusion of hundreds of African American police officers on its staff, which helped it avoid being perceived as an occupying force. The report suggested that more police departments should make an effort to include nonwhite officers in their ranks, emphasizing that many members of "minority groups" would "gladly accept police jobs if they knew their services were acceptable and desired." Police leaders should also, according to the report, teach all recruits about "racial similarities and differences," including "that scientists have found that no group has biological or racial tendencies toward criminality or delinquency," and that "social and economic conditions" play a large role in "determining the behavior of different racial, national, and religious groups."[34] Police should, in other words, work to educate themselves about the people and communities they were policing.

BY 1960, DESPITE the many reports, committees, and commissions, policing had changed very little since the Detroit riots of 1943 and police leaders showed little interest in addressing the root causes of their deficiencies. When they did support reform, it was most often the kinds of reforms that Vollmer had championed—better organization and more technology.[35] Meanwhile, protests continued to erupt in major cities such as New York City, Philadelphia, Jersey City, and Chicago. Race underscored it all; African Americans were fed up with the way they were treated by police and society at large, and they were increasingly willing to engage in civil disobedience in order to effect change.

A major incident in Los Angeles would soon show just how little progress had been made. The city's population had increased by more than 500 percent between 1920 and 1960, and its racial makeup had shifted dramatically, changing from a population made up of mostly Caucasians to one of the most racially diverse populations in the United States.[36] Nevertheless, Los Angeles's police force remained, as one *New Yorker* reporter would later put it, "glaringly white."[37]

The Los Angeles Police Department in 1960 served more than six million people, employed tens of thousands of officers,[38] and oversaw a jurisdiction of more than four hundred square miles. The city included neighborhoods as disparate as upscale Brentwood, with its almost uniformly white population, and crime-ridden Harvard Park, with its mostly African American and Latino households. In an effort to turn the LAPD into a "world-class" police force, its police chief at the time, William H. Parker, who had been hailed as a reformer for his work rooting out corruption inside the department, instituted a strategy that he called "confront-and-command."[39] Wounded at D-day, Parker had served in the army before joining the police, and his new strategy was informed by the lessons and habits he had learned there, bringing aggressive, military-style operations to the force.

The idea was that if police were stricter on the streets—enforcing laws more rigidly and aggressively pursuing even petty offenders—civilians would treat them with more respect. By carrying out such a crackdown as a department-wide strategy, Parker thought, he could rebuild the LAPD as an active, uncompromising force that would command respect and intimidate criminals. Backing down from an encounter was not something many LAPD officers would do under Parker's watch. Nearby law enforcement agencies such as the California Highway Patrol and the Los Angeles County Sheriff's Department followed Parker's and the LAPD's lead. But in communities of color, their strategies looked more like targeted racism, with swarms of white cops invading black neighborhoods to make violent arrests.[40]

On Wednesday evening, August 11, 1965, a young man named Marquette Frye—a high school dropout trying to get by in one of the huge city's poorest neighborhoods—was driving his 1955 Buick Special into Watts, one of only two districts in Los Angeles where the city's racially restrictive mid-twentieth-century housing covenants allowed black people to live. An officer with the California Highway Patrol pulled Frye over for speeding and began questioning him. The interaction was peaceful at first. The officer suspected that Frye had perhaps been drinking and put him through the hopping and nose-touching drill of a field sobriety test. Frye was jovial as this went on; he joked with the officer, who laughed along with an obviously drunk Frye. The officer even played along as Frye bantered with residents who'd come from their front porches to see what the commotion was about.[41]

But the mood soon changed. Frye's mother, who lived a couple of blocks away, arrived on the scene with Frye's brother. They began berating Frye for being drunk. Humiliated, he became resistant. When the officer tried to arrest him, he was no longer jovial; he lashed out at the officer, claiming that the arrest was "bullshit" and shouting to leave him alone. More people emerged from nearby residences to observe. As many as four hundred people were on the scene at that point.

In retrospect, it is easy to see how precarious the situation had become—the officer would have been wise to let Frye off the hook with a warning and move along. But instead, following Parker's "confront and command" doctrine, the officer called for backup. He wasn't going to let this go.[42]

As more cops arrived and more residents emerged from their homes, Frye attempted to sneak away. One officer hit him with a baton in the forehead, and other officers went about arresting his mother and brother. The family all resisted, according to reports at the time, and chaos soon ensued. As officers fled with Frye's family in cruisers, residents began throwing rocks and glass bottles at white motorists driving through the neighborhood. A revolt had begun.[43]

It mushroomed into a full-scale insurrection—a riot that completely engulfed the area. It was not confined to any specific street. It was widespread and uncontrollable, stretching throughout the fifty square miles or so that encompassed Watts. LAPD's confront-and-command strategy was worse than useless in response. Officers would descend on certain areas and attempt to make mass arrests in the hopes that those nearby would leave the scene. Instead, those arrests only sparked more anger. Eventually, more than four thousand National Guardsmen had to be called in. Entire blocks were burned to the ground. Charred cars were overturned and left abandoned on the streets. Over the course of five days, thirty-four people died. More than a thousand were injured. Nearly thirty-five hundred were arrested.[44] The riots caused as much as $40 million in property damage.

The Watts riots may have been unprecedented, and the causes may have seemed obvious, but Bill Parker signaled almost immediately that he had no interest in addressing the racial divisions that had set them into motion. Several weeks after the riots ended, he said on NBC's *Meet the Press* that the unrest had simply been an example of "people [giving] vent to their emotions on a hot night when the temperature didn't get below 72 degrees." And if there were any questions about how he viewed Los Angeles's African American population at the time, he put those to rest. "It is estimated that by 1970, 45 percent of the metropolitan area of Los Angeles will be Negro. If you want any protection for your home . . . you're going to have to get in and support a strong police department. If you don't, come 1970, God help you."[45]

Chief Parker had been invited to speak on *Meet the Press* because the Watts riots were unlike anything Los Angeles had seen before, but he was also asked to speak on such a national platform because the strains of racial discord that precipitated the Watts riots were playing out all over the country. How would the nation address this issue? With a larger and more aggressive police force, as Parker suggested? With new organizational systems and equipment, as Vollmer argued? Or with deeper and more substantial changes?

CHAPTER 2

A MAN OF IDEAS

The Johnson administration's report "The Challenge of Crime in a Free Society" included more than two hundred proposals designed to transform the criminal justice system and tackle the underlying problems that allowed crimes to happen in the first place—such as poverty, degraded social services, and widespread distrust of the police. But despite this seemingly holistic approach, the report's recommendations were, for the most part, much more attuned to the needs and concerns of police than to those of the community. It introduced the possibility of a new nonlethal weapon, for example, not by citing police brutality or police killings, but rather by citing the number of police killed in the line of duty.

"A patrol officer, in meeting the diverse criminal situations he must face, has a limited range of weaponry—either the short-range nightstick or the potentially lethal handgun," the report read. "If an officer feels that his life is threatened, he may have to shoot, with the attendant risk that the suspect or innocent bystanders may be killed. If a suitable nonlethal weapon were made available, it could supplement the officer's present arsenal and possibly serve as a replacement for the handgun."[1] In retrospect, it is easy for us to imagine the types of weapons that would eventually come about, but at the time, the proposal struck many as a vague and questionable stab in the dark. The report didn't provide much in the way of specifics—it simply described the qualities that its authors believed would make an ideal nonlethal weapon: "For a nonlethal weapon to be an acceptable replacement for a handgun, it would have to incapacitate its victim at least as fast as a gun.

"The qualities that must be sought in a general purpose nonlethal weapon," the report went on, "are almost immediate incapacitation and little risk of permanent injury to the individual who is the target." It discussed "a wide range of possibilities" that had, until that point, failed. "For example, darts have been used to inject tranquilizing drugs into animals," it said. "However, the drugs presently available offer too great a risk, because of the close correspondence between the dose required to incapacitate quickly and a lethal dose." The report concluded that "no nonlethal weapon is presently available that could serve as a replacement for the handgun, but a continuing effort to achieve such a weapon should be pursued."[2]

It is not clear how inventor Jack Cover discovered the report or why it crossed his desk, but somehow it did. When Cover read about this call for new technology, he must have felt as though he were being personally invited to submit an idea. He even had one in mind.

BORN IN NEW York City in 1920, John Higson "Jack" Cover Jr. grew up in Chicago with academic parents—an accomplished economics professor father and a mathematician mother with a master's degree from the University of Chicago.[3] He spent his youth immersed in books. Among his favorites was a series of Victor Appleton novels about a fictional teenage inventor named Tom Swift. Modeled after autodidact American innovators such as Thomas Edison and Henry Ford, Tom Swift was a problem solver and adventurer whose stories, published in five separate series beginning in 1910, often featured his inventions, which would inevitably save lives and help him to outsmart his adversaries. The stories inspired Cover. Swift accomplished incredible feats simply by designing and building new tools—by inventing. Cover wanted to be an inventor, too.

After graduating from the University of Chicago in 1941 with a degree in applied physics, Cover entered the U.S. Air Force. Serving as an officer, he flew fighter jets and bombers for five years, through World War II. Between 1944 and 1946, Cover was essentially an air force inventor; he designed improved radar systems and developed new techniques to help pilots shoot more accurately. Like Tom Swift, Cover wanted to be defined by his inventions. The way to do that, he figured, was to become an entrepreneur—to build products not just under the auspices of the military, but for himself, and for people everywhere.

During his final years in the air force, and then at the University of Chicago, where he took graduate-level physics courses from 1946 through 1948, Cover tinkered. In his spare time, he toyed with old inventions, trying to improve them, and even attempted to create some entirely new ones. Sometimes he aimed big—sending unsolicited aircraft designs to a major corporation or dreaming up a new kind of missile. And sometimes he aimed small—experimenting with ways to cook foods faster or creating an electric toothbrush years before the idea hit the mainstream. His professional résumé began typically enough, with a page of work and educational experience, but then continued over multiple pages detailing dozens of "developments and inventions" and concept summaries. Cover saw himself as a man of ideas.

Unfortunately, he didn't have much success selling his ideas—at least not right away. But his ambition was palpable, and he was constantly working to improve the concepts around him and find new problems that needed solving.[4] He searched tirelessly for that single, elusive idea whose importance and success would define him.

In the meantime, Cover married and, with his first wife, moved to Southern California. Before long, they had a mortgage and four children. Cover settled into the life of a corporate manager. Building upon his military experience, he helped teams at the aerospace manufacturer North American Aviation to develop missile defense systems and to land a contract to work on NASA's Apollo program. In the decades that followed, he took jobs with IBM and the Hughes Aircraft Company.[5] In his spare time, he still pursued his own inventions, scratching out designs on graph paper, tinkering in his garage.

His breakthrough came during the racial unrest of the mid-1960s.

"I started thinking about it during the Watts riots," Cover said. Then, "a few days later, I read a story in the *Los Angeles Times* about a man who had harmlessly gotten stuck on an electric cattle fence for three hours." Cover started thinking about the electric fence as a kind of armed guard, one that could incapacitate without killing. What if it were portable?[6]

Cover thought back to his childhood, to the Tom Swift books—particularly to one in which Tom Swift and his friends fended off dangerous animals with a gun that shot electricity. The book was called *Tom Swift and His Electric Rifle*.

Cover resolved to make the weapon a reality. The name he chose for it was an homage to the Tom Swift book, an acronym for *Tom Swift and His Electric Rifle*: TSER.

Now he needed to figure out how this TSER would work—and how to ensure it wouldn't kill anyone.

It seemed obvious to Cover that a low-power current applied to the skin would cause an involuntary muscle contraction—this, he figured, was what had happened to the man he read about in the *Los Angeles Times* who had gotten stuck on the electric fence. Cover confirmed as much in his home garage: with a little bit of electricity, he could give himself a mild muscle spasm.[7] Could that same technique incapacitate someone completely—causing a full-body spasm?

Cover was motivated, but he still had a day job. Nights and weekends he could tinker, and he did, but without much urgency. Two years after the release of "The Challenge of Crime in a Free Society," though, Cover had another fateful encounter. "In 1969, my family was attacked by five men who started throwing stones through our windows," he told the *Washington Post*. "I got out my .32 and pointed it through one of the windows and they ran away. That's when I decided to go full speed ahead on the Taser."[8]

Cover dug up research from 1939 that used experiments on dogs and rats—and, unbelievably, children—to help estimate what level of electric shock would send mammalian hearts into an irregular beat, or fibrillation.[9] Fibrillation can lead to cardiac arrest, which can lead to death—exactly what Jack Cover wanted to avoid.

He was walking a fine line. His weapon had to shock enough to incapacitate, but without causing lasting negative effects. He also knew that he was experimenting under ideal conditions that would never be found outside a lab. He needed to account for real-world variables; if his weapon didn't make direct skin contact, for example, it still needed to incapacitate through thick clothing. So he overestimated—he increased the power just slightly. He figured that a total of three watts would do the trick.[10]

After another year of development, Cover had a prototype: a flashlight-size wooden tool with a white plastic switch that, when flipped, ignited gunpowder to launch a pair of wire-trailing metal darts.

Jack Cover's TSER was born.

WHEN DISCUSSING NONLETHAL weapons, the authors of "The Challenge of Crime in a Free Society" dismissed many of the obvious

nonlethal weapons—including riot control gases and service batons—
arguing that they could be only "supplemental," for use "in circumstances in which an officer's life was not threatened."[11]

Would-be inventors delivered ideas such as the so-called airfoil
grenade,[12] a thin ring about the size of a flattened soda can that dis-
penses riot control gas and can be fired from a gunlike device. Other
ideas included brass knuckles with a steel blade, specialized nunchakus[13]
redesigned specifically for law enforcement, and an electrified nightstick similar to a cattle prod.

Cover's invention, though, wasn't a modified version of an existing weapon; it was totally new. And it offered a potential solution to
the growing problem of police brutality. The only question was how
to get it into officers' hands.

By the late 1960s, Jack Cover was approaching fifty. He'd served
his time as a corporate drone and had decades of accomplishments
under his belt. He was on his second marriage; his four children and
two stepchildren were nearly grown. He decided to take the risk: in
1970, he left his job with Hughes, striking out on his own as a true
entrepreneur. He hitched his fate to the success of his invention, which
he soon gave an easier-to-pronounce name: Taser. His new company
would be called Taser Systems.[14]

Thanks to contacts he had made in the military and during his
career in the private sector, Cover was able to arrange demonstrations
of his invention before representatives of the military and the FBI. He
even pitched the CIA, perhaps thinking the Taser might be useful for
agents abroad. His sons often assisted in these demonstrations, even
volunteering to be shocked by the Taser to demonstrate the weapon's
effectiveness.[15]

Cover also identified the major airlines and the U.S. Marshals Service as potential customers. Just as Taser Systems was getting started in
the early 1970s, America saw a rash of high-profile skyjackings; at its
height, commercial jets were being hijacked nearly once a week.[16] Tasers offered an attractive alternative to arming pilots and sky marshals

with guns, which carried the risk of wounding passengers or rupturing the aircraft's fuselage. Within a year, Cover landed tentative orders or letters of intent with Trans World, Eastern, and United Airlines.[17]

Without the necessary capital to fill those orders, Cover needed help. So in early 1971, he sold a significant portion of Taser Systems to a larger company, Advanced Chemical Technology, Inc., staying on to help develop and market his invention.[18] With the backing of ACT, Taser Systems was able to fulfill the airlines' orders, but the company soon encountered the first of several regulatory challenges: when the Bureau of Alcohol, Tobacco, and Firearms examined Cover's design and discovered that the device used gunpowder to discharge the Taser's electrified darts, it declared the Taser a Title I firearm—the equivalent of a pistol. Airline executives—whose main goal in working with Cover was to avoid arming its pilots with guns—balked. The tentative orders dried up.

Cover decided to try the police instead. Again, he faced challenges. The flashlight-shaped model that Cover tried to sell to cops—the "Public Defender"—struck many officers as too bulky to carry on their belts.[19] Cover also put a model for civilians (the "TF1") on the market, and for a short time it sold relatively well, but before it could really take off the National Rifle Association began lobbying lawmakers against it. (Cover later claimed this was because the organization saw Tasers as a threat to gun sales.)[20] The NRA's lobbying successfully convinced the ATF to reclassify Tasers from a Title I to a Title II firearm—the equivalent of a machine gun. Initially undeterred, Cover tried to make the best of the situation by embracing the idea that Tasers were a serious weapon comparable to an automatic rifle. He soon unveiled a new model, the TF-76, which was shaped like a handgun rather than a flashlight, boasting seven watts of power. But the shift in marketing wasn't enough to make the company profitable.

Occasional police orders trickled in, but police chiefs remained largely skeptical of the weapon. And because of the ATF's new classification, civilians, for the most part, shied away. Cover made moves to sell his invention abroad, pitching to potential buyers in the Philippines and the People's Republic of China, among other countries. There, too, the Taser ran into regulatory trouble. When Cover tried to ship orders to these countries, the U.S. Department of State stepped in, categorizing the Taser as a "controlled munition," subject to approval before it could be exported. This significantly delayed shipments and discouraged international purchases.[21]

As Cover's sporadic sales to individuals and police departments in the United States piqued interest among journalists, Tasers began to receive some media attention. Politicians in several states were quick to draft legislation banning the devices. By 1979, Taser Systems' parent company, ACT, had invested millions in an effort to get Tasers to market—and nearly all of it had been lost.[22] It seemed the Taser had reached the end of its road.

THEN CAME THE tragedy of Eula Love.

Love, thirty-nine, who lived in the Harbor Gateway neighborhood just west of Watts, had refused to pay her natural gas bill, disputing the charges. On January 3, 1979, a pair of bill collectors arrived at Love's home; she told them to leave. Instead, they called the LAPD. When officers arrived, Love was outside holding a butcher knife. According to eyewitness accounts, she threw the knife in the officers' direction. Trained to meet lethal force with lethal force, the officers unholstered their firearms. Two minutes and twenty-seven seconds after they arrived on scene, they emptied their service revolvers at Love. She suffered eight gunshot wounds and was pronounced dead on the scene.[23]

Love's killing received national attention. The community's response wasn't as immediate and overwhelming as it had been nearly fourteen years earlier during the riots that erupted in Watts after Marquette Frye's drunk-driving arrest, but law enforcement were still sensitive to the possibility of another such incident. In an effort to be proactive—or to at least appear that way—Los Angeles's city council and mayor ordered an investigation of the incident to be carried out by the Board of Police Commissioners, a five-member civilian oversight board. After interviewing witnesses and gathering information about Eula Love's death, the board changed some procedures and made recommendations ostensibly designed to improve relations between the police and the community.[24] One of the recommendations was to acquire and start using some kind of nonlethal weapon.

Jack Cover had already pitched the LAPD brass a number of times over the past decade, but he'd always been rebuffed on the grounds that the Taser was too weak for cops to depend on. But Eula Love's death and the city's fear of another Watts-magnitude uprising were enough to prompt a change in thinking. As the LAPD began to reconsider its tactics, a young officer named Greg Meyer found himself charged with researching potential alternatives to firearms.

MEYER WAS A Vietnam War veteran who had specialized in intercepting cryptographic communications for the U.S. Army. After finishing his service, he enrolled in journalism school in California, but he didn't gravitate toward the ink-stained life of a reporter. He wanted to be a cop. He signed up as an unpaid volunteer reserve officer for the LAPD in 1976 and was hired full-time two years later.[25]

When Eula Love was shot in January 1979, Meyer explained, that was all any LAPD officer was talking about. "This was front page news," he said. The *Los Angeles Herald-Examiner* did in fact run a front-page story the day after the incident, emphasizing that Love had carried only a kitchen knife, which she threw harmlessly at the officers.[26] At the time, Meyer was in the process of transferring from a street beat to the Planning and Research Division, a group dedicated to solving the department's toughest problems with unconventional solutions.[27] Several weeks after Meyer's arrival in the division, his commanding officer told him he would be serving as a nonlethal-weapons researcher. Meyer was puzzled; he knew virtually nothing about nonlethal weapons and couldn't imagine why he would be placed in charge of selecting which ones the department should purchase.

In those days, Meyer estimated, LAPD officers were involved in about one hundred police shootings per year—he had to guess because the department didn't keep track. Of those shootings, he guessed that perhaps sixty were fatal. Meyer said he was completely oblivious when it came to nonlethal weapons. "We'd heard of Tasers," he recalled. "But we were thinking they're like phasers from *Star Trek*. We really had no idea."

On the first day of his new assignment, Meyer arrived at his desk with his supervisor, who showed him a four-drawer filing cabinet holding all the department's research on nonlethal weapons. Meyer's task was to digest the materials and make sense of what had already been tried, what shortcomings had been identified, and what might be worth a second look. His supervisor mentioned the Taser in particular, saying they'd looked at it years back and found it wanting. "But technology moves along," he continued. "See what's going on with those things now. You know, see if they're getting better."

There were plenty of options beyond the Taser. In the wake of Eula Love's death, Meyer said, "people from all over the world . . . were writing in with suggestions to the police department." Meyer was tasked with sifting through the suggestions and determining whether any of them might actually work. Over several months in mid- to late 1979, he tested thirteen different nonlethal weapons, he said, some of them already on the market, some still just prototypes.

Unaware that the idea had already been researched and dismissed in "The Challenge of Crime in a Free Society," Meyer initially thought tranquilizer darts seemed like a promising option. Then he visited a local zoo and spent the day talking to veterinarians. There were two problems. The first was that police could never know the complete medical history of suspects they needed to subdue and thus couldn't know how to safely drug them. Second, he said, "The media never seems to report what the veterinarian told me, which is that they kill half the animals they shoot."

Then there was something called the action chain control. Two officers would hold "batons with chains crisscrossed in the middle of them," and try to "wrap the guy up while [another officer] with [a] big baton would push him down," Meyer said. "We actually did a demonstration in front of the police commission, and had to take a guy down." Another officer would spray the suspect with a fire extinguisher, while fifth and sixth officers would then immobilize him with a net. "Everybody was like, 'Oh yeah, this is going to be great,'" Meyer said. "Well it wasn't so great."

One problem was the device's complexity—which seemed certain to generate bumbling chaos. Another was the number of officers needed to use this method. "Random officers respond to emergencies based on where they are at a particular time," Meyer said. Rarely would six officers be on the scene, let alone six trained in the fine art of the action chain control.

Most of the suggestions Meyer received either had already been tried and discarded or were just slightly too impractical. There were rubber bullets and gases; there were injectable drug cocktails and nets; there were mace-squirting nightsticks. There was a kind of fire extinguisher to be sprayed in the face of anyone resisting arrest. One man wrote a letter from Australia, Meyer said, suggesting that LAPD cops use ropes with weighted ends to entangle a suspect's legs. Meyer narrowed the field.

He took the job very seriously, he said; in addition to situations like the one involving Eula Love, LAPD cops were, at the time, also increasingly concerned with a new brand of suspect: "dusters"—users of a new drug called phencyclidine, also known as PCP. They were out of control, Meyer said—a danger to police, and every cop knew it.

"We were dealing with them just about every day," he continued, recalling his two years on the streets before joining the Planning and Research Division. "It was ugly." The uproar over Eula Love's killing may have been what spurred the LAPD's leadership to pursue non-lethal weapons, but for ordinary cops patrolling the streets, it was the danger of PCP and other drugs like it that demonstrated the need for a new kind of weapon.

PHENCYCLIDINE, CREATED BY street chemists, first emerged in San Francisco's Haight-Ashbury district, where it was known as the PeaCe Pill, or PCP, and soon after appeared in similar bohemian enclaves in New York and Philadelphia. The drug was sold as a white powder that looked similar to cocaine. If someone took a little bump, they'd feel drunk or numb. If they took a lot, they'd hallucinate, and feel euphoric and powerful. If they took too much, they would experience convulsions and might die. But that sweet spot—that euphoric dose between drunk and dead—made phencyclidine popular[28] beyond the hippie community. Soon, it was known by a multitude of different names: elephant juice, rocket fuel, and the name that stuck most—angel dust.

To Meyer's bosses, PCP represented a serious threat. It also offered an explanation they'd been searching for—the root cause behind what had become a disturbingly common type of police encounter.

According to Meyer, the interactions would go like this: LAPD officers would get a call about a suspect acting erratically. Officers would show up and find themselves faced with a person drenched in sweat, unable to communicate, either in a rage or in a trance, and often completely nude. (Two effects of PCP are elevated blood pressure and body temperature—hence the sweat and the impulse to disrobe.) They were seldom armed, but they were nevertheless uncontrollable; they possessed what Meyer called "superhuman strength." Officers had no idea how to respond. They tried using chokeholds, but the sweat was an issue; getting a grip on the suspect's neck was nearly impossible. A great number of cops would end up on the scene trying to bring one suspect to the ground. Often the incidents would end with the suspect killed by police gunfire. Cops felt an urgent need to devise some new way of dealing with them.

Meyer pored over information about each of the nonlethal weapons available to the LAPD and eventually concluded that only pepper spray and Tasers were capable of helping a single officer immobilize someone high on PCP. By the spring of 1980, he had recommended these weapons to his higher-ups and arranged for Tasers and Chemical Mace (a tear gas developed and sold by a division of firearm manufacturer Smith & Wesson)[29] to be tested by LAPD officers on the streets of South Central Los Angeles—an epicenter, Meyer said, of PCP use.

Meyer believed that the Taser, in particular, would solve the problem police were having with PCP. Cover's company, Taser Systems, was by that time based in City of Industry, California—less than twenty miles from LAPD headquarters. Meyer personally visited Cover and worked with him to get all twelve of the sergeants in South Central Los Angeles equipped with Tasers as part of a test that would compare the effectiveness of Tasers and Chemical Mace spray. Meyer surmised—to Cover, and apparently to anyone else who would listen—that the Taser had an advantage over Chemical Mace when it came to dealing with PCP suspects: the sweat on a "duster" would act as a conductor for the Taser's electrical charge, Meyer said. Where chokeholds and batons had failed, he figured, Cover's electroshock weapon just might succeed.

So it was a great disappointment when reports started coming back from the field that the Tasers were proving ineffective against people who were high on PCP.

"Not everything's gonna work all the time, but this wasn't working on these PCP suspects at all," Meyer said. Before long, he took the Tasers off the streets, put them in a box, and returned them to Jack Cover. A few days later, Cover called him and said, "OK, I'm gonna give 'em back to you, try these." Meyer asked what Cover had done to them. "Well, we tuned 'em up," Cover said. "We upped the power." The first set of Tasers that the LAPD had tested were TF-76s, each with seven watts of power. But now, Meyer said, Cover "cranked up" the power. "I don't know how you do it. You change some kinda parts in it—capacitors, transistors, resistors . . . whatever little power module it is. And he cranked it up to 11."

So Meyer tried again—he handed out six Tasers each to the same two divisions in South Central Los Angeles.

This time: "Immediate success," Meyer said. The first night that officers took the cranked-up Tasers on duty, he continued, there were two successful encounters in one hour: "they both knocked down violent PCP suspects with [Tasers]. Complete knockdown and inca-pacitation."

One of Meyer's colleagues at the time, Dan Watson, spent twenty-eight years with the LAPD and was one of the first sergeants to be issued a Taser during this first testing period. Tasers became an object of fascination among LAPD officers, Watson said—and a source of amusing war stories. More important, by Watson's and Meyer's accounts, they virtually eliminated the threat from PCP suspects.[30]

Watson recounted an incident from 1980 in which officers called for backup in a ground-floor apartment. A suspect was uncooperative and had locked himself in a bathroom. The tub was full of water and overflowing. The suspect was, Watson said, large and muscular and black—and high on PCP. Watson unsheathed his Taser and forced open the bathroom door.

"So I said, 'Put up your hands!'" Watson recounted. "He starts to take a step forward"—which Watson perceived as a threat.

"And there's no way for anyone to get inside the bathroom except me, so I zap him from about three feet," Watson went on. "Good con-nection in his chest. . . . He falls into the full bathtub. Of course water splashes out. He starts screaming like crazy. Flopping like a tuna fish. And sparks are flying out of the water. I mean, the whole tub is sparking."

Watson continued to engage the Taser—which surged power as he held the trigger. "He's not cooperating, so I kept that thing on for at least five seconds. I look outside the window and I see an officer, and I can see his eyes are this big—he'd never seen anything like this."

Watson thought the worst initially. "He goes silent and stops moving, and I thought, *I killed the guy.*" But then the suspect opened his eyes, came to life. "I said, 'Stand up!' And he says, 'Yessir!' I said, 'Put your hands up!' 'Yessir!'—puts his hands up. And the wires were still connected to him, so I could still activate it. I told him to walk out, lay down, put your hands behind your back. He completely cooperated without any resistance. And when they put the handcuffs on, man, I gave the biggest sigh of relief."

Stories like this convinced cops right away of the usefulness of Tasers.

"All of a sudden, the cops love 'em, the community loves 'em, injuries are tremendously reduced," Meyer recalled. "I mean, we used to beat the hell out of these guys, and they used to try to beat the hell out of us. It was amazing. Now everybody wants one. And no one wants to confront a violent PCP suspect—or a violent anybody else— unless there's a Taser there."

It wasn't long before LAPD Chief Daryl Gates put in an order for a total of seven hundred Tasers from Cover's fledgling company.[31]

JACK COVER CONSIDERED himself an inventor above all else, and he wanted to be known for an important, successful idea. But he also wanted to be rich.

His first Taser prototypes may have been built with police in mind, but he never gave up on putting his weapon into civilian hands, too— instead of, or in addition to, firearms. As a businessman, he thought this seemed obvious: the civilian self-defense market dwarfed the law enforcement market in sheer numbers alone. There were hundreds of thousands of cops spread throughout thousands of police departments, but how many civilians purchased—or showed interest in purchasing—weapons for self-protection? It wasn't a stretch to think there could be tens of millions in the United States alone. A large part of the reason Advanced Chemical Technology, Inc., decided to buy into Taser Systems in the first place—and then pour millions into clearing regulatory hurdles to make Tasers legal—was the potential size of the civilian market. ACT's executives expected a return on their investment—and it wasn't going to happen, they believed, if Cover sold only to cops.

By 1982, ACT was sold to Plant Industries, Inc., a company that produced concentrated fruit juices[32] before expanding into the shipping and storage of chemicals. Electrical weapons didn't exactly align with Plant's business, and Cover wanted more control over his product anyway—so executives didn't object when he orchestrated a sale of the Taser division to a group of outside investors—people he knew from his years of pitching Tasers around the country. Cover became the founding chief executive officer, and his investors took their new company public, selling stock on the NASDAQ.[33] The flagship product of Taser Industries, Inc., would be the eleven-watt version of the Taser TF-76—the one Cover had redesigned for the LAPD. The idea was to rebrand it for 1983 as the "Police Special," or PS-83, and sell it to police departments around the country[34]—then make a play for the civilian market based on the credibility those law enforcement sales would bring.[35] The LAPD offered an implicit endorsement, and Greg Meyer was even listed as a sales contact on company marketing materials.

But the plan would fall apart almost immediately. One reason: a new competitor took a more pragmatic approach.

In 1983, a company called Nova USA, based in Austin, Texas, began selling its own version of Cover's Taser design,[36] but with an important difference: it did not shoot darts. The company's founders, Daniel Dowell and Bill Votaw, heard from police officers that the Taser darts were difficult to aim, rendering them effective only about half the time. So Dowell and Votaw skipped the darts and gunpowder altogether.[37]

Their revision, adapted from Cover's patent without initially paying a license fee, was called the Nova XR-5000 Stun Gun. Rather than using darts, the device delivered the charge directly to the skin through a pair of barbs; it therefore required physical contact with its target. But again, police were dissatisfied with the accuracy of the Taser's darts, so this could be seen as an advantage for Nova.

Nova's model was cheaper, too.

The Taser's fifteen-foot range, which some police saw as crucial for incapacitating naked and sweaty PCP users, also made it more expensive to produce. Tasers sold for around $300 per unit in 1983; a Nova stun gun cost $29.[38]

Cover's plan to focus on selling to police departments wasn't working well, either. He was, by then, in his sixties, married for the third time, and gravitating toward retirement. And while he went from one department to the next dressed in a shirt and tie, with the mentality and sales strategies of a corporate executive, Nova had discovered a better way to sell to cops. They hired other cops.

JIM SCROGGINS WAS introduced to Nova by happenstance. A detective and SWAT team member with the Travis County Sheriff's Department—the law enforcement agency for the area surrounding Austin—Scroggins attended a SWAT team seminar in Houston in 1983. It was there that he first heard about a company that was working on electronic weapons. Nova was small at the time—maybe four or five employees—but from what Scroggins heard, it was scrappy and upcoming, a police company for the future.[39]

After the seminar, Scroggins decided to cold-call Nova, and he soon found himself on the phone with its owner and CEO, Dan Dowell. According to Scroggins, Dowell was trying to sell his products to the general public right away—he saw the stun gun as an alternative to a can of mace, and he hoped that people would carry it around in their pocket or purse for self-protection. Scroggins saw potential in selling to cops, too. "You need to get this into police departments," he recalled telling Dowell.

To Dowell, Scroggins was just a stranger on the phone, but he was nevertheless immediately convinced, and offered Scroggins a job as Nova's vice president in charge of law enforcement sales. Scroggins accepted. "He told me how much he'd pay me and that was it," Scroggins said. He left the sheriff's department and joined the company.

Instead of sending salespeople with corporate experience to pitch Nova's stun guns to police departments, Scroggins hired cops and former cops. These were people who would be able to commiserate with police leaders, show empathy for policing concerns, and express why a low-cost Nova stun gun was a perfectly acceptable alternative to an expensive Taser. Nova also hired two cops to create training classes in which they would teach cops to use the stun gun—this became an effective method of marketing the weapons directly to police departments. Soon, police department orders were flooding in, and civilian sales followed. Cover and his Tasers had the LAPD's endorsement and a proven track record combating dusters—but Nova had support from a larger number of police departments and a price within reach of both cops and civilians.

Nova grew rapidly. The company was making money hand over fist, Scroggins said, and quickly drawing attention. Nova produced infomercials to push its weapons, and landed positive coverage in such mainstream news magazines as *Time* and *Newsweek*.[40]

"We were on TV shows, newspapers—it really hit in the early 1980s," Scroggins recalled. Meanwhile, Taser Industries was floundering.

Nova's co-founder Dowell cashed out in 1984, selling the company to Scroggins and two international investors. Right around that time, Scroggins said, Cover contacted him, offering him rights to his

Taser patent. He wanted $50,000 for it. Scroggins didn't see any reason to accept.

"We were doing well, and Taser was not doing well," Scroggins said. Beyond that, Nova was working on its own weapon that could incapacitate someone from a distance—an electroshock weapon that would use water instead of wires to incapacitate suspects. Investing in a wired product—let alone one that wasn't selling as well as Nova's own product—didn't make much sense to Scroggins at the time.

Scroggins rejected Cover's offer—a decision he would soon regret.

WHAT COVER HADN'T explicitly said to Scroggins was that there was an implied ultimatum attached to his offer. Cover believed that Nova had stolen his idea; by offering Scroggins the patent for $50,000, he was, as he saw it, extending to his rival one last opportunity to do the right thing. When Scroggins turned him down, Cover sued Nova, claiming not only that Nova had stolen the intellectual property underlying Taser Industries' flagship product, but that Nova had actually taken credit for its success.[41] Cover's most significant accomplishment in his decade-long career in the nonlethal weapons industry was his sale to the LAPD. It took him years to broker, and he was rewarded with prestige and prominence. Hundreds of other departments purchased Tasers—his weapons, not Nova's—in the early 1980s based on the LAPD's implicit endorsement, he claimed. Yet according to Cover's lawsuit, Nova falsely claimed in brochures that Taser Industries' success was really its own—that Nova weapons were "currently in use by over 400 progressive agencies and correctional facilities worldwide."[42] That was a lie, Cover said.

According to Scroggins, Nova was eventually hit with a $300,000 default judgment for patent infringement—six times the amount for which Cover had offered to sell the intellectual property—and ordered to pay a percentage of future sales to Cover. Nevertheless, Scroggins was convinced Nova could persevere. And he was right—by 1985,

Nova was outselling Taser Industries at least ten to one, in large part due to civilian sales.[43] Tasers were still categorized as firearms at this point—meaning that civilian sales were limited to gun shops. Nova's weapons, on the other hand, were not considered firearms, and could be sold virtually anywhere.

Nova had gotten over its first major litigation hurdle—and seemingly captured the market for electroshock weapons. But there was a lot more it would need to overcome.

AS MORE AND more police departments around the country chose Nova stun guns, media reports began to scrutinize how exactly officers were using them. One case, involving the eighteen-year-old Mark Davidson, brought this discussion to the national stage.

As Davidson described the encounter to the *New York Times*, six NYPD officers apprehended him as he was walking down a street in Queens. They took him to the local precinct station—the 106th—and began questioning him about drugs. The officers insisted that Davidson had recently sold $10 worth of marijuana to an undercover cop, and they pressured him to admit to the crime.[44] When Davidson refused, the officers devised a new strategy to extract a confession: one officer held him down while another took out a Nova stun gun and zapped him repeatedly.

Nova stun guns were smaller than Tasers, about the size of "a pocket calculator," as one 1985 *Washington Post* article described them.[45] But they left behind a telltale sign. When twin triggers on the side of the device were pressed, a visible blue bolt of electricity would sizzle between two probes. When those electrified probes contacted skin, they'd leave red burn marks.

Under normal circumstances, an eighteen-year-old might have trouble getting others to believe his story of being tortured at the hands of six police officers—indeed, the police probably counted on this. But

Davidson had concrete evidence to corroborate his account—in the form of more than forty burn marks all over his body. Soon after he came forward, three other men made similar claims. In the end, five officers were charged with assault and four were convicted; charges were dismissed against a fifth.

Other stories of inappropriate and indiscriminate use of stun guns soon emerged all over the country. A private security guard in San Diego in 1985 admitted to using the stun gun on "transients." In San Antonio, a deputy sheriff shocked a handcuffed prisoner with a stun gun and found himself serving a two-year probationary sentence.[46] LAPD officers reportedly used Tasers to shock an underage Latino boy "in an attempt to force him to confess to stealing stereo parts."[47] After the Queens incident, one Nova official even attempted to spin Davidson's story, telling the *Washington Post* that it showed just how safe Nova's weapons were.

"I don't think you can name another time when somebody has been abused by law enforcement 42 times and doesn't suffer any severe injuries," he said.[48]

THIS WAS ALL clearly a nightmare for Nova's public image. But Taser Industries would soon be dealing with its own publicity crisis—one that would be even more damaging.

Around 11:00 p.m. on August 10, 1983, LAPD officers found a twenty-seven-year-old Hispanic man, Vincent Alvarez, acting strangely on the streets of Los Angeles's Lincoln Heights neighborhood. They reported that Alvarez was clutching a telephone pole and shaking uncontrollably. The officers concluded he was "dusted"—high on PCP. Alvarez was unwilling to answer questions about who he was and why he was there, so officers forced him to the ground, handcuffed him, bound his feet, and then shoved him into the backseat of a patrol car.[49]

According to a police account given to United Press International, Alvarez "managed to loosen his foot restraints and began banging his head on a window and demonstrating exceptional physical strength." An LAPD "Taser expert" soon arrived (presumably a sergeant issued a Taser and on call for just such a situation) and shocked Alvarez in the back. Soon after, Alvarez was taken to a nearby jail ward, where he went into cardiac arrest and died.

The LAPD brass immediately knew Alvarez's death would cause a stir. They had just spent tens of thousands of dollars equipping the force with Tasers, which would replace the newly banned chokeholds as a supposedly safer alternative. Now the weapons that they'd been assured were "nonlethal" appeared to have killed a man. An LAPD spokesman resisted that conclusion, telling UPI it was "premature to assume that Taser darts were responsible for, caused, or contributed" to Alvarez's death.

But as the months passed, a number of strikingly similar cases began to emerge, both in Los Angeles and in other areas where police had adopted Tasers.[50]

Five months later, on January 22, 1984, LAPD officers arrested a thirty-year-old Hispanic tire shop employee, Raul Guevara Jr., under suspicion of receiving stolen property. After making a phone call from the Van Nuys jail, Guevara allegedly tore the receiver and cord from the phone and began struggling with officers when they approached him. In order to subdue him, officers shocked Guevara with a Taser and used a chokehold. Before long, he stopped moving completely. As the officers loaded him onto a gurney, they realized he was no longer breathing. He was pronounced dead at a local hospital.[51]

On August 17, 1984, a thirty-two-year-old black man, Larry Donnell Gardner, was walking along the streets of Waynesboro, Georgia, about thirty miles south of Augusta, when Burke County Sheriff's Office deputies spotted him. Gardner had outstanding warrants at the time for shoplifting and distributing marijuana. A chase ensued, but it didn't last long. When the deputies finally caught up to Gardner, he resisted arrest, so one of them used a Taser to shock him. They cuffed him and took him to the county jail, where he began complaining that he felt hot and that he was short of breath. The deputies called an ambulance, but by the time it arrived it was too late— Gardner was already dead.

Late at night on April 11, 1985, a thirty-five-year-old black man, Cornelius Garland Smith, was found dancing in the street near Locke High School in the Watts neighborhood of Los Angeles. Officers shocked him almost immediately after arriving at the scene. Smith collapsed, and was taken by officers to the nearby Martin Luther King Jr./ Drew Medical Center. The two darts from the Taser were still in his body, according to a UPI story from the next day. He was pronounced dead at the hospital.

On October 13, 1985, LAPD officers responded to a call about a man acting strangely in the Rampart neighborhood of Los Angeles, just northwest of the city's Financial District. There, they found a white man, thirty-five-year-old Lannie Stanley McCoy, who was stabbing at the ground outside the front of his apartment with a screwdriver and a knife.[52] When he ignored orders to drop the implements, the officers shocked McCoy a total of three times with a Taser. Hours later, while a psychologist interviewed him at a local medical center, McCoy collapsed and died.

Before the end of 1985, six people had died of some form of heart failure shortly after police had shocked them with a Taser.

In four of these six incidents, medical examiners didn't even mention the Taser as a possible cause of death. In the cases of Alvarez and Smith, they cited exertion under the influence of PCP as a primary cause of death. In Guevara's case, a medical examiner blamed heart disease. In Gardner's case, death was supposedly caused by "hyperthermia associated with sickle cell crisis"—a dangerously high body temperature brought about by a genetic blood disorder that disproportionately affects people of African descent. The obfuscating nature of that conclusion, and its not-so-subtle racial overtones, drew almost immediate condemnation from a local chapter of the NAACP. "Gross civil rights violations may have occurred," the chapter leader said, calling the Taser "an electric cattle-prod-type device" and excoriating the officers for applying it "to Gardner's wet body, contributing to his deteriorating condition."

The Tasers didn't completely escape blame. In Smith's case, the medical examiner cited exertion while high on PCP as the primary contributing factor to his demise, but his death certificate listed the electrical stimulation of the Taser as a contributing factor.

Jack Cover considered himself a physicist as much as an entrepreneur. To him, there was obviously some risk in using a Taser, and he'd never claimed otherwise. In fact, a report he submitted to the U.S. Consumer Product Safety Commission stated that his own studies showed Tasers could be dangerous. "TASER is nonlethal at the design output to normally healthy people," he wrote.

> However, it must be emphasized that neither this feature nor the noninjury or no-harmful-after-effect aspect can ever be guaranteed. There is no weapon, technique or procedure for subduing, constraining or dispersing that does not involve some risk of injury to healthy persons or of death especially if the individual has a heart ailment.[53]

Paradoxically, however, as the years passed and the deaths mounted, this warning morphed into an afterthought, even among medical professionals. Soon, doctors at Martin Luther King Jr. hospital in South Central Los Angeles were defending Tasers: in a review of Taser cases, the doctors compared 22 gunshot incidents with 218 Taser incidents. By comparing gunshots to Tasers, the doctors came to an easy conclusion: Tasers were less lethal than guns.[54] "I would say that, of the people who were Tasered, it probably saved their lives," one of the doctors said.

———

RIGHT AROUND THE time that Nova was going out of business, in 1985, the Supreme Court issued a landmark decision in the case of *Tennessee v. Garner* that would force police departments to take non-lethal weapons more seriously. The case concerned an incident from eleven years earlier. Responding to a nighttime burglary call, Memphis police officer Elton Hymon chased a fifteen-year-old African American boy, Edward Garner, into a backyard. Hymon was reasonably sure that Garner was unarmed, and he shouted for the boy to stand still. When Garner attempted to climb a six-feet-high chain-link fence behind him, Hymon opened fire. One shot struck Garner in the back of the head and killed him. When Hymon and his partner searched Garner's lifeless body, they found a wallet holding $10.[55]

At the time, a Tennessee statute allowed—and implicitly encouraged—officers in pursuit of a suspect to use deadly force "if, after notice of the intention to arrest the defendant, he either flees or forcibly resists." Garner's father brought a civil case against the police department and the officers on the scene, which eventually made it to the Supreme Court. The court sided with Garner, holding in a 6–3 majority opinion that Tennessee's statute, and similar laws in twenty-one other states, was unconstitutional. "When a non-violent felon is ordered to stop and submit to police, ignoring that order does not give rise to a reasonable good-faith belief that the use of deadly force is necessary, unless it has been threatened," the court found.

To catch fleeing suspects, officers would now need either new ideas or new tools—tools that could bring people to the ground without killing them. Tasers were an obvious candidate. But a major case would soon cast suspicion on Cover's invention.

WHEN THE UNEDITED video begins, only the date can be seen clearly, written in white block lettering—*MAR. 3 1991*—in the bottom right corner of the shot. Everything else is a shaking blur—grainy gray splotches, red and blue flashes, white spots tinted orange-yellow. The only sound is a droning hum in the background. After about eighteen seconds, the image steadies and begins to focus. The hum, it becomes clear, is the sound of a helicopter hovering overhead, shining a spotlight down on the scene. In the spotlight: a white Hyundai Excel hatchback. It's parked in the middle of a four-lane road, all its doors open save the hatch and the rear driver's-side door. In front of the Hyundai stands a group of uniformed police officers looking down. A figure—twenty-five-year-old Rodney King—lies writhing on the ground in front of them, on his side, in a fetal position. Twenty-five seconds into the video, the camera shakes again, out of focus, and then refocuses. At thirty seconds, as King slowly attempts to crawl away on his hands and knees, the camera zooms in. Thin wires snake from King's back.[56]

These are the electrified copper wires of a Taser.

Repeated Taser shocks fail to subdue King, so officers instead beat him nearly to death with metal batons. When pictures emerge three days later of a badly beaten King—his lips and face severely swollen, his right eye red with broken blood vessels—his plight becomes a rallying call, yet another representation of Los Angeles cops brutalizing a black man. And it was captured on video for the world to see.

Shot hastily on a camcorder by thirty-one-year-old George Holliday from the balcony of his second-floor apartment in the Lake View Terrace community of Los Angeles,[57] the video of King's beating had an immense and lasting effect. The four police officers principally involved in the beating would eventually be tried in both California state and federal courts for violating King's civil rights. When the state jury declined to convict the officers on April 29, 1992, intense protests erupted in South Central Los Angeles that eventually grew into some of the most destructive riots in United States history. The 1992 South Central uprisings both mirrored and dwarfed the Watts riots of twenty-seven years earlier: sixty-three people were killed, nearly twenty-four hundred were injured, and costs to repair damage after six days and nights of rioting in late April and early May 1992 were estimated at more than $1 billion.[58] King would receive millions in a settlement from the city, and a group of cops would face a career-long backlash. To many, they represented a system of law enforcement in Los Angeles that had, for years, discriminated against minorities and brutalized African Americans in the name of public safety.

Before Holliday's camera started to roll, police cornered King's Hyundai at the intersection of Foothill Boulevard and Osborne Street in Lake View Terrace. King and two others then emerged from the Hyundai with hands raised. King's two acquaintances went into police custody without incident, but King—who was intoxicated and afraid that a charge of driving under the influence would violate his parole for a 1989 convenience-store robbery[59]—wouldn't go quietly. Four officers approached him, pushed him over, held him facedown on the ground, and tried to handcuff him. But he was drenched in sweat, making the otherwise routine handcuffing maneuver difficult. King threw the officers off him and stood up, looking around to see a swarm of blue encircling him. That's when Stacey C. Koon, a sergeant with the Los Angeles Police Department, pulled out a Taser, aiming it at King, and commanded him to lie facedown on the ground. When King didn't comply, Koon pulled the trigger. He later claimed that he shocked King three times before resorting to his baton.

In short, he said, the technology had failed. But had it failed or had King been too strong, too hopped up on PCP? Did the technology fail or did it meet a man it could not subdue? Years later, in a memoir about the infamous encounter, Koon insisted that the Taser wasn't faulty; King was simply too strong—as a result of using PCP, Koon assumed—to be affected by the weapon's electric shock. And this, Koon claimed, was why he beat King into submission, striking him at least twenty times with his heavy steel baton while another LAPD officer joined in.

Toxicology results would later show that there was no PCP in King's system. He wasn't high on angel dust at all; he was simply drunk, having just come from a friend's home where a group had been drinking and watching a Lakers game. Koon, however, dismissed the toxicology report, writing in his book, "even if Rodney King hadn't popped some PCP that night, he still could have had a flashback if he'd ever taken the drug in his adult life."[60] Koon also defended the Taser as "a formidable, nonlethal tool."[61]

For decades after King's beating, Koon and a number of other LAPD cops, including Greg Meyer and Dan Watson, would maintain that King was high on PCP, no matter what the toxicology results said. It simply didn't matter to them. PCP was a problem that Tasers solved, and one prominent incident was not going to change that.

WHEN GREG MEYER began investigating the Taser's failure in the King incident for LAPD's internal affairs department, he discovered that a number of LAPD Tasers—it wasn't clear how many—including the one Koon used, had somehow had their power levels decreased from eleven watts to seven.

"I'll say this very clearly," he said. "If Rodney King had been hit with an 11-watt Taser, you would have never heard the words Rodney King."[62]

In other words, the problem with the Taser wasn't the Taser itself. By that time, Cover had sold patent rights to a Newport Beach–based lawyer, Barry Resnick, and a handful of investors. The company they founded, Electronic Medical Research Laboratories, Inc., did business as Tasertron, and had a monopoly on Cover's patent; Tasertron—and only Tasertron—manufactured Taser weapons in 1991. In Meyer's estimation, the only plausible explanation for the lowered power levels was a manufacturing defect. So this was really Tasertron's problem. When LAPD brass asked why the Taser had failed on King, the com-

pany—which by that time had a small staff in charge of calibrating
and manufacturing the weapons—couldn't do much more than apol-
ogize and attempt to fix the weapon.

But Tasertron's problems went beyond wattage. Police claimed that
Tasertron's Tasers often jammed, and that the weapons' somewhat
flimsy plastic housing sometimes "leaked" current, shocking officers'
hands when they pulled the trigger.[63]

The limited data on Taser use weren't terribly compelling either.

The month of Rodney King's beating, Greg Meyer submitted his
thesis toward a master's degree in public administration from California State University, Los Angeles. Using official LAPD use-of-force
data, he compared the effectiveness of newer nonlethal weapons, such
as Tasers and chemical spray, to that of more conventional nonlethal
weapons, like batons. Meyer's thesis, unsurprisingly, argued for
"expanded use of nonlethal weapons." But his research, as it turned
out, did not back up that claim; instead, it showed that Tasers were
not any more effective than batons. The same statistics showed Tasers
as being less effective than chemical spray.[64]

The LAPD had been using Tasers for more than a decade, but the
technology remained, at best, a work in progress. In April 1991, an
oversight group was convened by Los Angeles mayor Tom Bradley to
assess how the LAPD's structure and practices had contributed to an
environment in which officers could act with such impunity as they
had during the incident with Rodney King. It was dubbed the Christopher Commission in honor of its chairman, lawyer and future secre-
tary of state Warren Christopher. Its report, published in July 1991,
stressed the Taser's failure during the King encounter. It also stressed
officers' misgivings about the weapon in general.

> While other options are available at the baton force level—specifically,
> chemical mace and Taser—they are less frequently used than the
> baton and are believed by many officers to be less effective . . . A

large number of officers interviewed urged reinstatement of the carotid chokehold, which restricts the flow of blood, as a "mid-level" use of force option.[65]

In other words, officers had grown distrustful of the Taser—and they wanted their chokehold back. Even worse, the total number of Taser-related police killings in 1991 stood, at the very least, at twenty-four.[66] It seemed inevitable that someone would challenge Tasertron's monopoly.

CHAPTER 3

CHARTS OF THE FUTURE

The use of computer statistics in making crime-fighting decisions is now ubiquitous and widely regarded as common sense, but the practice took decades to develop and bring into the mainstream. Ultimately, it would be just as consequential to modern law enforcement as Cover's Taser—if not more. But unlike the Taser, this idea didn't spring from the mind of a creative outsider; rather, it came from within the policing community, from some of its most prominent members. To understand how this happened, it's necessary to understand New York City, and the unbelievable crime wave that the city experienced during the 1970s and 1980s. It's necessary to understand, in other words, why Bernhard Goetz decided to kill.

A little before 2:00 p.m. on an unseasonably warm Saturday, December 22, 1984, thirty-seven-year-old Goetz descended into the New York City subway beneath Seventh Avenue and Fourteenth Street in Manhattan.[1] On his way to get drinks with friends, the white electrical engineer paid his fare, walked through the turnstile, stepped aboard the train, and sat on the long bench facing the closing doors. Across the aisle from him sat Troy Canty, a nineteen-year-old black man from the Bronx. Three of Canty's friends sat scattered nearby.

No surveillance footage exists to show what happened next, and accounts differ slightly, but according to Goetz's telling, Canty said hello to him, and then stood and motioned for his friends to approach. Goetz was rail-thin, a man who weighed less than one hundred pounds at the time, but he was armed with an unlicensed, five-shot Smith & Wesson .38 Special revolver—a weapon he had purchased a few years earlier after being mugged. In his spare time, he participated in a community group that urged the city to assign more police to patrol the streets of his neighborhood, the West Village, which was dangerous and crime-ridden.

"Give me five dollars," Canty said, as he and his friends surrounded Goetz. Taking that as a threat, Goetz stood slowly and asked Canty to repeat himself. The teenager obliged. Goetz then pulled his silver revolver out from underneath his jacket and began shooting each of the young men, one by one, as they cowered and attempted to flee. After shooting the fourth one, Darrell Cabey, eyewitnesses said Goetz told him, "You don't look too bad, here's another," and then fired the revolver's final round into Cabey's torso. That shot severed Cabey's spinal cord, paralyzing him from the waist down.[2] As the teenagers bled helplessly on the floor, the conductor brought the train to an emergency stop and asked Goetz if he was a cop. Goetz said he wasn't. "They tried to rob me," he said.[3] Then he pried the doors open and fled into the subway tunnel. No one gave chase as he escaped into the darkness.

The incident itself was extreme in every way, playing out like some kind of National Rifle Association fever dream. The aftermath was even more outrageous. After the incident's details appeared in the daily papers and evening news programs on television, police reported receiving hundreds of calls voicing not anger or disapproval, but support for the still-unnamed gunman. The story became a national sensation, covered in media outlets across the country. Dubbed the "Subway Avenger" and the "Death Wish Vigilante," Goetz received strong encouragement, seemingly from every direction. POWER TO THE VIGILANTE. NEW YORK LOVES YA! was spray-painted on New York's East River Drive.[4] "Give Him a Medal" read one headline from the *New York Daily News*.

None of this is surprising considering how bad the national crime problem had become. According to the FBI's statistics, the country's crime rate had reached an all-time high in 1980, four years prior to Goetz's subway attack, and had essentially plateaued after that.[5] By the time Bernhard Goetz shot those four young men on the subway in December 1984, New York City had become a symbol of the crime wave. Like the nation as a whole, its crime problem showed no signs of improving,[6] and meanwhile the city's population remained stagnant after having dropped precipitously between 1970 and 1980. At best, media coverage of the problem was understandably bleak: "1980 Called Worst Year of Crime in City History" screamed a headline from the *New York Times*.[7] At worst, the coverage was gratuitous, exacerbating the perception that the city was hopelessly mired in crime: David "Son of Sam" Berkowitz's thirteen-month murder spree in 1976 and 1977, for example, received wall-to-wall coverage as six people were killed. That number, of course, represented a minuscule portion of the more than three thousand New York City homicides in those years. But the media's focus on sensational murders led many of the city's residents to feel as if they were living in a kind of urban penitentiary, a feeling that was famously literalized in John Carpenter's 1981 film *Escape from New York*, set in a future in which the entire island of Manhattan has been converted into a maximum security prison. It "may be set in the future but the film is essentially . . . about the way New York is today," one reviewer wrote. "It's the hallucination of someone riding the subway at 3 A.M."[8]

News outlets and movie directors weren't the only ones fueling the fear and anxiety. Nearly a decade before Goetz's violent outburst, a coalition of unions representing such municipal employees as firefighters and police officers aggravated the situation further when, during a tense contract negotiation, it attempted to release a pamphlet headlined "Welcome to Fear City: A Survival Guide for Visitors to the City of New York." The pamphlet, which was illustrated with a skull, included instructions such as "If you must leave your hotel . . . summon a taxi by telephone," and, "You should never ride the subway for any reason whatsoever." Intended as both a genuine warning and a scare tactic to dissuade politicians from cutting public safety jobs, the pamphlet was blocked by a court order and went unpublished.[9] But the message was clear: the city's crisis was worsening.

Not much had changed by 1984, when Bernhard Goetz fled into a subway tunnel and vanished. Nine days later, after initially fleeing to New Hampshire, Goetz turned himself in to police there and was returned to the NYPD. When questioned, he was unapologetic. "I wanted to kill those guys," he told investigators. "I wanted to make them suffer in every way I could. If I had more bullets, I would have shot them all again and again," he went on. "My problem was I ran out of bullets."[10]

Soon, Goetz's story was a national phenomenon. After his name first appeared in news reports, supporters began sending him contributions that added up to thousands of dollars to help pay his legal fees. Representatives of the Guardian Angels, an international coalition of volunteer crime fighters, began walking car to car in the subway system to solicit donations for him. The chairman of the New York State Republican party, George Clark, whose wife had been mugged on a subway train years earlier, offered Goetz $6,000, though Goetz turned down the offer, according to reports. A regular subway rider was quoted in one report, saying: "He just did what everybody else in this city would love to do. So just leave him alone—that's the feeling around town . . . He's a hero."[11]

When Goetz was finally brought to trial more than two years after the shootings, he nearly walked free. The only charge that stuck was criminal possession of a weapon. He was convicted of that crime, but rather than receiving a decades-long sentence—which certainly would have been a possibility had he been convicted of attempted murder—he was sentenced to six months behind bars, which was later extended to a full year after appeal. He ended up serving only eight months in a New York state prison, and he was lauded for years to come. He would eventually run for public office in New York City and become the subject of praise in documentaries, television dramas, and books.

But there was a problem. Despite the spectacle of Goetz's killings, they inspired no real change. Goetz may have tapped into the public's deep sense of frustration and anxiety about crime in the big city, but for years afterward New Yorkers would have to continue to live with the same conditions.

THE REASONS FOR New York City's astronomically high crime rate in the 1980s have been the subject of wide-ranging speculation and intense research. Academics, journalists, politicians, activists, and everyday people have all gone to great lengths to explain it, to understand what it meant and how it got so bad. Did a decline in capital punishment send a message to criminals that they could avoid facing severe consequences for their actions?[12] Had lead-based paints and leaded gasolines damaged young people's minds and made them more impulsive?[13] Was the crime wave tied to demographic shifts? Was it simply a matter of declining morals? Or inadequate policing?

Policing was certainly part of it. After a corruption scandal plagued the New York Police Department in the early 1970s,[14] a recession took hold of the city, and politicians struggled to get the municipal budget in order. That led to the NYPD cutting nearly seven thousand jobs between 1975 and 1982[15]—a time period when crime was already rising, and just as crack cocaine began surging onto the streets of New York City. The city's problems became disastrous.

NYPD transit detective Jack Maple's most urgent concern was finding a way to stop crime as fast as possible. The way he saw it, there was a simple solution: cops needed to be more aggressive, and they needed to arrest more of the people who were committing violent crimes in the subways. In a way, he was like the uniformed counterpart to Bernhard Goetz. He was also about as close to a natural cop as anyone in the department. Born and raised in the diverse, middle-class neighborhood of Richmond Hill, Queens, in a family of civil servants, Maple hadn't even graduated from Brooklyn Technical High School when he signed up to wear an NYPD badge in 1970. Throughout his late teenage years and most of his twenties, Maple worked as a beat cop in the subway system—the very setting of Bernhard Goetz's notorious confrontation. At the age of twenty-seven, Maple was promoted to subway detective—the youngest in the NYPD.[16]

Much of Maple's time was occupied by the same kind of snatch-and-grab subway robberies that so incensed and scared Goetz. As a New York City transit police officer, his job was to roam the subways and the areas near its entry points in search of all kinds of petty and sometimes violent crimes. After working for years in such an environment, he began to feel that society is composed of innocent victims and "predatory criminals"—a phrase he used repeatedly in his memoir, *The Crime Fighter*, to describe people who learned to pick pockets and jump subway turnstiles from an early age. In Maple's opinion, few people, if anyone, fell in between. His job was to find the latter and send them to jail.[17]

Maple became known as an aggressive cop who made a lot of arrests, sometimes so many that his bosses became irritated about the overtime this necessitated when Maple was required to testify in court—not to mention the paperwork his arrests generated. But as the crime problem worsened during the 1970s, Maple's aggressive approach caught on. He ascended the ranks through the 1970s, and soon became known for something else: an ability to devise new crime-fighting strategies that were unlike anything police leaders had tried. Appointed a transit sergeant in 1982, Maple would come up with ideas for experimental task forces and then test them on the street to see if his proposals put more people in handcuffs.

A year after Goetz's attack, for example, police were desperate for a new strategy to combat the subway stickups and muggings that had sent Goetz into a homicidal rage. So Maple established and led a team that would dress up as ordinary commuters, sometimes wearing conspicuous accessories as bait, and wait to attract the kind of predatory criminals whom Maple wanted to toss behind bars.

One Associated Press story about this team highlighted the case of two teenagers who tried to snatch a gold chain from a well-dressed officer who was wearing a yarmulke and pretending to have fallen asleep on a subway car. To Maple, these kids were crooks, plain and simple. "They're out for money to buy Guccis or Izod, or Ralph Lauren or $150 sunglasses," he told the AP. "This is not someone who's trying to buy clothes to wear. This is completely different. This is a motive to live in the highest style and dress in the latest fashion rather than just put clothes on one's back."

A flashy dresser himself—often seen on the town looking like a shorter version of Al Capone—complete with a black fedora, trench coat, bow tie, and spats—Maple felt that police had to pursue petty infractions aggressively if there was to be any hope of getting the city's crime problem under control. The decoy patrol would soon come under attack amid accusations of dubious arrests—defendants claimed that undercover cops goaded them into taking valuables[18]— and the transit system's crime rate would continue to increase in the late 1980s. Still, Maple maintained the validity of his approach: the only way forward was to carry out as many arrests as possible. "What we want to put in the predatory criminals' mind," he said, "is that they are no longer the hunters in the subway, but they are now the hunted."[19]

MAPLE CAME UP with the idea that would define his legacy while having dinner and drinks at his favorite bar, Elaine's, on Manhattan's Upper East Side. Elaine's was known as an establishment where celebrities and public officials mingled, and where Jack Maple and other well-known cops of his era sometimes ended up in tabloid photographs alongside boozy authors such as Joseph Heller and Norman Mailer, and celebrities such as Woody Allen, Mia Farrow, and Mick Jagger. On this particular night, Maple was alone, watching as the bar's proprietor, Elaine Kaufman, attended to one of her managers who was signing checks and tallying receipt totals for the night. It struck Maple in that moment that Kaufman "knew at all times, from checking [the manager's] tape, exactly how well the night was going." If the receipts showed a decline in revenue for the night, she'd check in on her waiters to see if they were slacking. Were they paying sufficient attention to customers and doing everything they could to make the evening a success? And if they were, was there something else going on? The numbers were the best way of finding out.[20]

The NYPD simply didn't work in that way, Maple observed. "We didn't check our crime numbers hourly, daily, or even weekly," he later wrote. "Headquarters gathered the numbers every six months, and then only because the department was required to report them to the FBI for inclusion in the national Uniform Crime Reports." Maple could see now what a missed opportunity this was. "I couldn't imagine that many of our precinct commanders checked the tape on their crime numbers every day. If the numbers were going the wrong way, would any of them be out on field inspections to determine what was going wrong?"[21]

Maple came up with a plan based on what he'd noticed at Elaine's and pitched an idea to his commanding officers; by late 1989, he was in charge of a pilot program called the Repeat Offender Robbery Strike Force. He appointed Vertel Martin—a young beat cop whom he'd worked with and learned to trust—to be his executive officer on the project.

"Our job, twenty-four hours a day, was to collect crime statistics from dot matrix printers," she said, recalling Maple's task force.

> We [would] . . . put them on these big sheets of paper, tape them on the walls, then use color-coded pencils and symbols to designate crimes that were reported . . . We began to see what [are] today known as "hotspots"—they were clusters, constellations of crimes where we could see that the same types of crimes were being committed.[22]

After the data were collected and mapped over the course of a week or two, Martin recalled, "Jack would come in and sit down with a cigar, feet on his desk, and say, 'Okay, what do we have here?'" He'd identify where robberies and purse snatchings and shootings occurred, and which crimes were committed near which stations, mapping "the solved versus the unsolved," as he would put it years later. Then he and his task force would look for patterns in *when* certain crimes would occur. Based on all this, they would make conclusions about what was driving the crime—and finally Maple would come up with a strategy for stopping it. "He called it 'perpology,'" Martin said—the study of perpetrators.[23] It may have been "perpology" to fellow cops such as Martin. But Maple used a more grandiose and self-congratulatory name for his system when he presented it to his higher-ups: he called it "Charts of the Future."[24]

Not long after Maple began his new system, in April 1990, the New York City transit police chief, Vincent Del Castillo, resigned. In public statements, he claimed the choice to leave was his own, that he was simply moving on to other things.[25] But the transit police were clearly in turmoil and widely seen as ineffective. The number of felonies committed in the subways reached a record high in 1988. Above ground, the city's crime problem wasn't looking much better, with homicide rates increasing every year. By 1989, more than five people were being killed in the city every day, many of them in or near the transit system.

The resignation was good news for Maple. While he'd been given latitude to experiment with Charts of the Future, it wasn't system-wide; it was still a pilot program. Now he would have an opportunity to put his charts in front of a new chief, one who might have more of an open mind.

That chief was William J. Bratton.

Pulled from his job as superintendent of Boston's Metropolitan District Commission—a four-star position, two levels below the commissioner—Bratton was highly respected in the law enforcement community. Raised in a working-class home in Dorchester, Massachusetts, he enlisted in the U.S. Army at nineteen and served as a military policeman in Vietnam before returning home to war protests. "I believed in order and conformity and the need for everyone to abide by social norms," he later wrote in his autobiography.[26] He signed on as an officer in Boston in October 1970 and rose quickly in the ranks, while becoming a noted strategist and thinker among those who studied policing and crime control. By the 1980s, he began working closely with the Police Foundation, a nonprofit organization that funded scientific research into policing theories and strategies, and started seeing himself as a kind of business executive overseeing law enforcement—a CEO cop. He took classes at the John F. Kennedy School of Government at Harvard and went through professional training with the Police Executive Research Forum—one of the foremost nonprofit policing think tanks in the United States—and the Secret Service.[27] By the time he left Boston as a superintendent, he was widely credited with improving the department's morale and public image.

In New York, Bratton found himself under remarkable pressure to introduce some kind of magical solution to make the crime problem in the city's transit system go away. So he was eager to hear about fresh, unconventional ideas.

In Bratton's first weeks on the job in April 1990, he attended large meetings where he heard from his new lieutenants about what exactly they did, whom they policed, and what strategies they employed. Maple's full-time job—aside from the "perpology" pilot program—was to oversee the transit police's decoy unit, the group of cops who would go undercover on the subway to catch robbers in the act. And in the open session with Bratton, he focused his presentation on that unit's more conventional work. But to tell his new boss about his pet project, his Charts of the Future, he asked for a one-on-one meeting.[28]

They met at the River Café in Brooklyn, a four-star restaurant near transit police headquarters, with views of the East River and lower Manhattan. If Maple had any jitters about pitching an ambitious idea to his new boss, he didn't need to. Bratton was way ahead of him—in fact, he was about a decade and a half ahead.

When Bratton was still climbing the ranks of the Boston Police Department as a sergeant in 1976, the BPD had only recently begun implementing the relatively new technological advancement known as the 9-1-1 call system—the now ubiquitous tool for alerting authorities of an emergency over the phone. At the time, every 9-1-1 call was treated exactly the same. "Robbery in progress, cat in a tree, didn't matter," Bratton would later write. "If there was a car free, whether around the corner or three miles away, you sent him over."[29] Bratton and a few of his colleagues were intrigued by the potential of 9-1-1, but at the same time they felt that the arbitrary nature of the process was self-defeating. To tackle this problem, they devised a system to rank calls so that emergencies would be addressed first. Under their plan, 9-1-1 dispatchers would input calls into a computer that was programmed to dispassionately prioritize robberies over distressed felines, fires over fender benders, shots fired over shouting matches. But Bratton and his colleagues were hoping to do more than just improve the efficiency of emergency response. What they really wanted was to use this computer system to aggregate the entries and plot them geographically, showing police which kinds of crimes were happening where and helping them to discern patterns.

Just as Maple would later do in New York City, Bratton lined the walls of his Boston office with maps of his district, and used information from the new 9-1-1 computer system to chart patterns in crime. "I covered the maps with acetate and assigned a young civilian employee . . . to put up dots: red dots for burglaries, blue dots for robberies," Bratton would later recall. "Each got a date inside to note when the crime took place. We updated the wall every night. Once we got our information organized, you could see exactly where District 4 crime was clustered." Like Maple's, Bratton's maps were given a name by his colleagues—the "Wailing Wall." He even got a nickname for his efforts—"Lord Dots."[30]

So he didn't need much convincing when Maple presented basically the same concept for the NYPD's transit bureau at the River Café in 1990. Plus, Bratton liked Maple. He described him as "a character out of *Guys and Dolls*, with a brilliant police mind."[31] He gave Maple the opportunity to expand the Charts of the Future—to put them to use system-wide in the fight to lower the transit system's unbelievable crime rate.

BRIAN WATKINS HAD been a standout tennis player in high school and college, but like so many others, he gave up competitive play upon finishing school. Even so, at twenty-two years old, he remained an avid fan of the game, following the pro circuit closely and teaching tennis lessons in his hometown of Provo, Utah, while working a day job with a company that organized motivational seminars. That year, a player from Provo was competing in the 1990 U.S. Open Tennis Championships in New York City. Some of Watkins's peers in the Provo tennis community had arranged to go see the local athlete play and Watkins decided to come along, bringing his family with him. Thus, Watkins, his parents, and his brother and sister-in-law set out for New York City in late August 1990 to sightsee and watch the tournament.

The specter of New York City's high crime rate did not escape the fans from Provo. New York City was on its way to a record-setting year of murder and mayhem, and concerns about safety had apparently arisen among the tennis group as the trip was being planned. "I was pretty nervous before going," one of the Watkinses' companions, Debbe Jaspering, would later tell the *New York Times*. "A lot of people said, 'Are you excited?' and I said I was nervous. I wondered if I should take out a life insurance policy. That's not a joke."[32]

It was a little after 10:00 p.m. on Sunday, September 2, when Watkins and his family entered a Midtown subway station on their way to a late dinner at the ritzy Tavern on the Green restaurant in Central Park. As they descended the stairs toward the platform, a group of rowdy older teenagers entered the subway platform in front of them, laughing and yelling.

Loud teenagers weren't unusual at the Fifty-Third Street and Seventh Avenue station where the Watkins family waited: it was late on a weekend night, and this subway stop was one of the last on the way to the Roseland nightclub on West Fifty-Second Street. That night, a popular deejay was playing there, and witnesses later said that several of the teenagers walking on the subway platform that night had forgotten money with which to pay the $15 cover charge. So they concocted a scheme to "grab a wallet." Witnesses on the scene would later say that a few of them approached the Watkins family. One held a four-inch folding knife and threatened harm if they didn't hand over cash.

Unlike Bernhard Goetz, nobody in the Watkins family was an

aggrieved New Yorker carrying an unregistered firearm. But when one of the kids grabbed Brian's mother by the hair and kicked her, and another slashed his father's pants pocket and cut him deeply on the leg, the former athlete tried to intervene. He was stabbed in the chest. Brian's father had been carrying a wad of bills containing $200. One of the perpetrators grabbed it and yelled, "We got it!" before fleeing up the subway stairs toward the surface. Brian gave chase, not aware of how severe his injuries were. He collapsed on the stairs. Police brought him to street level and called an ambulance, but it was too late. Watkins died on the way to the hospital.[33]

AS THE WATKINS family grieved in the following days, they were surprised to find that a media swarm had begun to converge on the heartbreaking tale of their son's death. "Tennis Buff, in Town for U.S. Open, Killed in Subway as He Defends Parents" read one Associated Press headline. The story was an ideal representation of the city's—and especially the transit system's—worsening crime problem. It also reinforced the "Welcome to Fear City" narrative that had warned tourists to "never ride the subway for any reason whatsoever." Many New Yorkers were despondent at the news. As syndicated columnist Bob Greene wrote:

> When the murderers roam your streets and then go dancing; when people who grew up loving the city are afraid to return the glances of strangers; when lifetime residents look around them and don't recognize what they see, then it's over . . . What sign is there that the spiral is not destined to worsen and worsen?[34]

Calls for something to be done came from every direction. A *New York Post* headline in the wake of Watkins's killing read simply: "Dave, Do Something!"—a plea for the city's first African American mayor, David Dinkins, to step up policing efforts.

Crime had been rising for decades in New York City, but by the time of Watkins's killing, the city was truly in the midst of a crisis. In the subway alone, a record number of robberies had taken place in 1988; that number increased by 29 percent in 1989 and was on track to rise yet again by the time of the U.S. Open in the late summer of 1990. Citywide, 1990 turned out to be a record year for murders—2,245 in a single year, more than six per day.

Tasked with "doing something," Mayor Dinkins and the NYPD decided to aggressively pursue arrests. Within a week of Watkins's killing, a total of eight people had been arrested in connection with his death. This approach became a model for how policing would be carried out in general from then on in New York City.

To those who knew him, it was obvious that Bill Bratton would relish the opportunity to implement this aggressive policing strategy from his perch atop the transit police department.

In the years when he was ascending the ranks of the Boston Police Department, Bratton was a close follower of academic studies of policing, and he increasingly began to align himself with a relatively new idea called the "broken windows" theory of policing. First brought to the public's attention in a March 1982 article in the *Atlantic Monthly*, the concept was conceived by policing researchers George L. Kelling and James Q. Wilson, who had studied the Newark Police Department for the Police Foundation. Their main judgment was straightforward: "if a window in a building is broken and is left unrepaired, all the rest of the windows will soon be broken," Kelling and Wilson wrote for the *Atlantic*. To these researchers, broken windows were a stand-in for all petty crimes. In their estimation, one petty crime left unpunished would eventually lead to a vast number of petty crimes going unpunished, and eventually to a kind of chaos.

"Untended property becomes fair game for people out for fun or plunder and even for people who ordinarily would not dream of doing such things and who probably consider themselves law-abiding," they wrote. Soon, a "piece of property is abandoned, weeds grow up, a window is smashed," and lawlessness takes hold.

> Adults stop scolding rowdy children; the children, emboldened, become more rowdy. Families move out, unattached adults move in. Teenagers gather in front of the corner store. The merchant asks them to move; they refuse. Fights occur. Litter accumulates. People start drinking in front of the grocery; in time, an inebriate slumps to the sidewalk and is allowed to sleep it off. Pedestrians are approached by panhandlers.[35]

The broken windows philosophy was, in essence, a refutation of "The Challenge of Crime in a Free Society," the all-encompassing 1967 report from President Lyndon Johnson's administration. That report had emphasized the underlying conditions that helped to fuel crime increases, such as poverty and institutionalized racism, and made extremely ambitious, wide-ranging recommendations—from rethinking how civic organizations and employment agencies work, to calling for the invention of an effective nonlethal weapon. Kelling and Wilson all but dismissed the entire report. The solution to crime was much simpler, they argued, and it didn't require transforming civic institutions or digging deep into the root causes of crime. Instead, police just needed to make more arrests, even if it meant putting people in handcuffs for petty crimes.

In Bratton's estimation, Kelling and Wilson had identified a huge problem in law enforcement: many police simply didn't consider low-level crimes to be worthy of expending effort to combat. In the midst of a colossal crime wave, there were more important offenses to prioritize. And this, Bratton reasoned, was exactly what had allowed New York City's subway system to become so dangerous. Officers were, by and large, accustomed to being reactionary—responding only when emergencies arose and not bothering to prosecute minor offenses, such as spray-painting train cars or breaking car windows. And because Bratton's predecessors had supported this hands-off, wait-and-see approach, many New Yorkers had come to see cops as being uninterested in public safety. In such an environment, Bratton figured, petty crimes would become more and more common, and before long they would escalate into serious felonies—like the murder of a young white tourist from Provo, Utah. To stem the tide, Bratton decided a crackdown on petty crimes was needed. Whether it was hopping over turnstiles to ride trains for free or so-called quality-of-life offenses like public urination, defacing public property, or aggressively panhandling under the guise of squeegee-cleaning drivers' windshields, officers would have to make arrests or issue some other form of penalty.

BY THE TIME Brian Watkins was killed in September 1990, Bratton and Maple had become closer. They were seen together at bars—often Elaine's, though just as often elsewhere—commiserating about the difficulty of their work and formulating new strategies. Though they agreed on most subjects, Maple took a more skeptical view of broken windows policing than Bratton—to him, the whole notion represented a false promise. "The implication is, if the police would take care of the little things, the big things would take care of themselves," he would later write.[36] "That's not how it works."

Maple certainly didn't have any problem with aggressive, quality-of-life policing, but to him, its purpose wasn't to eliminate petty offenses; it was to find and punish those who were committing more serious crimes.[37] He wasn't suggesting that graffiti artists and so-called squeegee men should be ignored; he wanted them to be detained and fiercely questioned. He called this approach, which he had pioneered prior to Bratton's tenure with the transit police, "Quality-Of-Life Plus." As soon as officers arrested someone for one of these minor offenses, they would call the NYPD's central office to check for warrants or other outstanding issues. Next, they would interrogate the suspect, hoping to force a confession of the crime in question. All that was relatively standard. But they would also, during the interrogation, try to badger the suspect into making "statements about any other crimes the suspect might admit" or giving "information about the prisoner's accomplices" or "information about crimes committed by other people."

Since June 13, 1966, the Miranda warning has been mandatory when police carry out an arrest.[38] "You have the right to remain silent," it begins, words familiar to anyone who's watched a television crime drama in the last fifty years. But Maple's approach basically ignored the principles behind this warning—most important, that police should be forthcoming with arrestees about their rights. For Maple, the goal was to coerce confessions on the spot, plain and simple—before the defendant had access to an attorney. What's more, his rationale for choosing whom to arrest and interrogate in this aggressive way wasn't exactly scientific. Though Maple and his staff talked enthusiastically about his commitment to "perpology," his approach to arrests and interrogations was arbitrary and "instinctual."

"A bunch of young Wall Street analysts doing Jell-O shots during a pub crawl along Madison Avenue may be just as likely to piss in the street as a crew of robbers drinking malt liquor on a corner in East New York," he wrote. "But only one of those groups is likely to include somebody who's relaxing after a long day of robbing or who's building up the courage to go out and rob."[39]

In the end, despite their differing views on broken windows, Bratton and Maple worked to roll out a strategy that targeted *the right kind* of quality-of-life offenses, and to then interrogate the hell out of whomever they ended up arresting. Maple identified seven types of crimes that would allow cops to "catch bad guys on relatively minor violations": "beer and piss" (public drinking and urination); gambling (illegal dice games on corners, three-card monte shell games); noise (boom boxes, car stereos, loud clubs); truancy (kids out late or during school hours); prostitution; graffiti; and traffic violations, including driving under the influence.[40]

BY THE FINAL months of 1990, the public outcry over crime and mayhem in the New York City subway—as well as throughout the city at large—began to get serious attention in City Hall. Bratton's appointment was itself part of City Hall's efforts to reduce crime, a way to shake up at least one of the city's police operations.

Bratton, with Maple at his side, began by flattening the transit police's command structure—getting rid of as many middle managers as possible—and assigning more cops to ride and inspect trains. Even commanders were forced to mingle with civilians in the tunnels. They were also required to attend meetings. It wasn't enough for Bratton and Maple to follow the day-to-day crime statistics and come up with plans for counteracting spikes in robberies or assaults. Their lieutenants needed to keep up with the numbers as well and to have their own ideas. So every morning, the various heads of departments in NYPD's transit bureau would meet with Bratton and Maple to go over numbers and strategies before beginning their shifts. It was a way to weed out uncreative or ineffectual managers, and to get everyone else acting and thinking in lockstep.[41]

To show their commitment to the new regime, many captains planned and conducted train car sweeps and instituted strict crackdowns on petty crime. Naturally, this was a welcome change for many ordinary transit cops, who, like Jack Maple, felt that aggressive arrests would lead to reduced crime. The president of the city's Citizens Crime Commission—an advocacy group of business leaders pushing for stricter crime enforcement[42]—would later say that Bratton "revitalized them so they were like the Marines, the few, the proud."[43]

A media push went along with these changes. Bratton brought in a television journalist and a corporate communications executive to help the department present its new tactics to the public and convince New Yorkers that they were waging a war against the despicable crooks who had made the city's transit system unbearable. Train car sweeps to dispatch the homeless were accompanied by messages of "Thank you for your patience" on the intercom. Posters were splayed throughout the city with promises that "We're taking the subway back—for you."[44]

Arrests skyrocketed. Whatever minor differences there may have been between Maple's Quality-Of-Life Plus policing philosophy and Bratton's traditional broken windows view—they worked together with a singular purpose of putting more people in handcuffs. It started with basic infractions. "Fare evasion was the biggest broken window in the transit system," Bratton later wrote. "We were going to fix that window and see to it that it didn't get broken again."[45] In February 1991, when the *New York Times* ran a story about protests against the transit police's brutal treatment of the homeless, Bratton penned a response boasting that he'd carried out one of the most aggressive, prolonged sweeps in recent memory, and that it was a necessary good.

"We are now engaged in the most concerted and most successful effort ever undertaken to enforce subway rules," he bragged. Under his and Maple's leadership, transit cops had kicked thirteen times the number of people off the subway for rules violations as they had in December 1989. "Transit police enforcement activity of all kinds is at an all-time high," he went on. Summonses doubled. Misdemeanor arrests more than tripled. Felony arrests rose almost 13 percent. And the results, for the most part, were positive: between December 1989 and January 1991, felony crime decreased by 11 percent and robberies by 14 percent. "We have not and will not abandon our obligation to enforce the rules of civility in our subway system," Bratton wrote.[46]

In the end, his stint with the transit police lasted only twenty-one months. But when he left the role in January 1992 to move back to Boston to take up a post as BPD's superintendent in chief, its second-in-command, he was seen as a hero among New York City's power brokers, including by groups like the Citizens Crime Commission. Yes, there was dissent in some communities about how people of color and the homeless were being indiscriminately thrown in jail as part of Bratton's push. Yes, the sweeps may have violated civil rights. But the city's leaders, on a whole, did not seem to care. If the alternative to Bernhard Goetz shooting people on the subway was a police state underground; if avoiding an *Escape from New York*–esque future involved thousands more cops on the streets; if the alternative to tourists such as Brian Watkins being killed was a militarized force arresting people for minor offenses every hour of the day, then that's what the city needed.

It was this mind-set that, in 1993, swept Rudolph Giuliani in as New York City's mayor on a platform of getting squeegee men off the street and busting crime. When newly elected Mayor Giuliani began looking for a police chief—a new leader to take charge of the nation's largest police force—there was only one man to fill the role: William J. Bratton. He accepted. Jack Maple, who for the intervening two years had remained a lieutenant in the transit department, came along for the ride, joining Bratton at NYPD headquarters as deputy commissioner.

MAPLE'S ASCENT FROM his role in the transit division to deputy commissioner was remarkable. Thomas A. Repetto, a onetime president of the Citizens Crime Commission, would later remark that Maple's promotion was "like making a Coast Guard lieutenant a three-star admiral in the Navy."[47] But Maple and Bratton were intertwined in their crime philosophies and no one else could fit the role, in Bratton's estimation. It's rumored that Maple sketched out the core of

Giuliani's crime strategy on a napkin at Elaine's. It was by no means to be a shoestring operation: Bratton and Maple essentially had a blank check from the city to do what they thought needed to be done. Their plan, naturally, was to bring the transit department's aggressive crime-fighting approach—and its strict adherence to maps and statistics—to the entire city. The culmination of Bratton and Maple's efforts was Compstat—a program that would eventually transform the practice of policing in the United States.

"Compstat" was a neologism meant to abbreviate either "computer-generated statistics,"[48] "computer statistics," or "comparative statics,"[49] depending on whom you asked. Whatever the name's origins, Compstat was a simple idea that expanded upon the map-based concepts that Bratton and Maple had tested out years earlier. By 1994, technology had progressed such that the gigantic maps on Bratton's office wall could be replaced by a computerized map that could easily be shared with every police commander.

At the time, this effort represented the most sophisticated application of computers in police work nationwide—no one else had done anything like it. Maple and Bratton saw it as a corporate-inspired adaptation—a natural extension of Bratton's "CEO cop" self-image.[50] Bratton even brought in a management consultant, John Linder, to advise him on administrative matters and to market the NYPD's accomplishments to the public.[51] Under Bratton's direction and Linder's advice—and informed by this new corporate policing mentality—Maple took great pride in making the department's command structure more efficient by eliminating large numbers of middle managers whose roles were loosely defined, just as he had done in the transit division.

Twice weekly, Bratton and Maple would gather all seventy-seven of their precinct commanders in one large room to review the data—precinct by precinct—and discuss why crime was rising or falling in each one. Bratton relished the idea that each one of his precinct commanders was communicating directly with the chief and deputy commissioner rather than through some go-between. These meetings became legendary, not only because twice a week two hundred members of the NYPD brass would have to squeeze into a room made for about half that many people on the eighth floor of police headquarters in lower Manhattan, but because even these senior officers would face intense criticism in front of everyone if their numbers weren't satisfactory. Maple, along with his bulldog chief of department, Louis Anemone, would question the commanders' work, the strategies they deployed, even the decisions their detectives made about which specific cases to pursue. Maple would heckle them when they said things he didn't believe. Once, he even displayed a computer image of Pinocchio on a projection screen behind a commander reporting his precinct's numbers—which Maple clearly thought were bogus.[52]

The new system appeared to work. As the months ticked by, the citywide stats began to speak for themselves. Homicides dropped from 1,946 in 1993, the year before Bratton took over, to 1,177 in 1995—a drop of nearly 40 percent. Rape, aggravated assault, burglary, and theft all dropped, as well. Robberies—Maple's specialty years ago in the transit department—dropped nearly 31 percent. Across the board, crime rates finally seemed to be moving in the right direction. And when it came time to give credit for the huge declines, it wasn't Rudy Giuliani who was chosen for the cover of *Time* magazine—it was Bratton. "Finally, We're Winning the War Against Crime" read the cover headline on the January 15, 1996, edition of the magazine, set over a photo of Bratton looking confidently into the camera's lens. "Here's Why."

Bratton may have had the answers for *Time*, but his boss, the notoriously spotlight-hungry Giuliani, didn't appreciate the competition for publicity. There were even rumors that Bratton was weighing a mayoral bid of his own.[53] Then the unthinkable happened—having swept into power and completely transformed the NYPD's approach to crime, Bratton announced he was quitting. He was under scrutiny by the city's Law Department over a $350,000 book deal he'd signed while in office, and he resigned amid growing tension between him and Giuliani. The CEO cop was no longer commissioner by the end of March 1996. Maple's resignation soon followed.

Even with Maple and Bratton gone from their high-profile NYPD jobs, accolades for their accomplishments continued to roll in from all over the country. In addition to fawning media coverage, the John F. Kennedy School of Government at Harvard University awarded the NYPD the 1996 Innovations in American Government Award—not for its zero-tolerance approach to crime or its broken windows philosophy, but for Compstat. In its press materials, the Kennedy School praised the NYPD's "high-tech 'pin-mapping' approach," which, it said, allowed officers to "quickly identify trouble spots as well as causal relationships and then target resources to fight crime strategically."[54]

In reality, Bratton's and Maple's success couldn't be attributed to a single innovation. The strategy that was so effective in lowering New York City's crime rate in the mid-1990s was, in fact, multipronged: a combination of putting thousands more officers on the streets, policing more aggressively, weeding out corruption within the ranks,[55] and, yes, deploying officers more efficiently to high-crime areas using computer data. But it was simpler—and frankly sexier—to say that a new era of technological policing was upon the nation. It was easier to see Compstat technology as the silver bullet that solved the city's crime problem. And many did.

Around the country, a technological narrative began to take shape as other cities aspired to replicate New York's miracle turnaround. Police departments in Philadelphia, New Orleans, Birmingham, and elsewhere began contacting the NYPD, asking about the technology it deployed. Around the country, police leaders discussed Compstat in conferences and meetings and on calls. They were wondering how they could have a Compstat of their own and what sorts of other technology might be at the forefront of policing.

Before long, Bratton and Maple began to take lucrative consulting gigs with cities and companies, offering their insights as to how police departments might better use technology—and what kinds of products companies might produce to help them get there. The CEO cop worked to help others think of themselves as CEO cops, too.

BUT WOULD COMPSTAT live up to its renown—or was it overhyped? There's no question that New York City's crime rate dropped. But there are questions about why it happened and how big of a role Compstat played.

Simply looking at the numbers is enough to understand the uncertainty. Year-over-year crime data show that the total number of violent infractions recorded by police in New York City climbed consistently over a period of two decades before it reached an all-time high in 1990, when there were 174,542 violent crimes on the books, including homicide, rape, robbery, and aggravated assault. Bratton began his tenure as NYPD commissioner on January 1, 1994. In the three years leading up to that, during the Dinkins administration, those numbers had already dropped by 12 percent, to 153,543.[56] The decline would accelerate under Bratton and Maple, but violent crime was already trending down when they began their shake-up. Property offenses showed a similar downward trend prior to Bratton's taking office.[57]

What's more, New York was far from the only city that experienced a precipitous drop in crime starting around 1990; the phenomenon occurred nationwide. Throughout the country, each of the seven index crimes (homicide, rape, robbery, aggravated assault, burglary, larceny, and motor vehicle theft) fell over the course of the 1990s by an average of about 40 percent. This was the largest crime decrease of the twentieth century.[58] San Diego, San Antonio, and Boston each saw a particularly significant reduction in murders, enough to rival New York's numbers. Murder rate decreases in Los Angeles, Houston, and

Dallas were slightly less dramatic, but still incredible considering that the numbers had been moving in the opposite direction for decades.[59]

Criminologists who have studied the 1990s crime decline in New York City agree that Bratton's and Maple's innovations, especially Compstat, contributed significantly to the reduction. But they also agree that economic and sociological factors played a huge role in both starting the decline and keeping it going.

"Demographic trends played an important role in building favorable conditions that enabled crime rates to crash during the 1990s," wrote Andrew Karmen, a sociology professor at the John Jay College of Criminal Justice in Manhattan. For example, the city's population of young men in their late teens and early twenties—the demographic most at risk of becoming criminals—shrank significantly during this time. "Many active criminals fled the City," Karmen continued. "Others disappeared from the scene due to homicides by fellow offenders, drug overdoses, AIDS contracted from injecting drugs, and deportations by the [Immigration and Naturalization Service]."

Regardless of the degree to which Compstat was responsible for New York City's turnaround, it was widely seen as the key to ensuring that it continued, so NYPD leaders built it into an elaborate system and spent heavily on it. By 1997, its budget had reached $15 million and cops were logging everything—criminal complaints, shootings, summonses, arrests, and even locations of schools, subway entrances, pawnshops, and addresses of parolees. The idea was to develop a more comprehensive understanding of how crimes came together—where a suspect might have purchased a gun before holding up a store, for example, or which school a kid might have left before snatching someone's wallet. As the volume of information collected grew, police were able to decipher more and more.[60]

Soon, arrestees were fingerprinted with a computer scanner rather than ink. Mug shots were taken with digital cameras. Lineups were generated on computer screens.

A data-based policing revolution was about to take hold. But it wouldn't happen organically—and Maple and Bratton would play a big role.

IT WAS SEEN as almost comical when Bratton left the NYPD to take a role as president of the security consulting firm First Security Services. "From the cover of *Time* magazine to 'a night-watchman company from Boston,'" read a line in the *Boston Globe*.[61] New York's CEO cop had left for "a company known not for stocks and bonds but for 'old men with flashlights and nightsticks, checking to see that the plant gate is closed.'" Maple's initial post-NYPD pursuit didn't seem quite right either. He left the NYPD to start his own consulting company with the administration's managerial consultant John Linder. Wouldn't a cop's cop like Maple look for a role at another major city police department?

But they knew exactly what they were doing.

First Security Services was a billion-dollar company with tens of thousands of employees known for providing security to major companies. Bratton pushed it in the direction of consulting with police departments. "Everyone is very interested in what's working in reducing crime in New York," Bratton said within a month of leaving the NYPD.[62] "I think there's a phenomenal market. I'll bring a lot of attention to it." Soon enough, he was spearheading reports in cities such as Birmingham, Alabama, pushing for the police department there to adopt Compstat.[63] By the end of 1996, First Security under Bratton had landed consulting gigs in New Bedford, Massachusetts, and in Washington, D.C., where it partnered with the mega management consulting firm Booz Allen Hamilton to do a top-down review of the Metropolitan Police Department. In its recommendations to each of these departments, First Security again pushed for Compstat adoption. Birmingham, Philadelphia, New Orleans, and others would soon follow. And in many of the places where First Security didn't land contracts, Bratton gave paid speeches about Compstat and his approach to policing, charging $20,000 per appearance. He also landed a book contract with a considerable six-figure advance, which would help to push his ideas to the nation at large.[64] Before long, he was making appearances as a police expert on *Good Morning America* and various evening news programs.

Maple was making rounds himself with the Philadelphia and New Orleans police departments, working—sometimes with Bratton, sometimes on his own as an independent consultant—with commanders to implement computer statistics and related technologies.

Bratton was a national brand by that point—a name that represented crime reduction and the promise of reducing malfeasance all over the country. Maple was less well known, but still familiar to many police chiefs, and he continued to help promote Compstat to everyone who would listen.

All the while, the U.S. economy was steadily improving each year. In fact, according to the National Bureau of Economic Research, the period between March 1991 and March 2001 was the longest economic expansion that the organization had ever recorded since it began keeping track in 1854.[65] People were spending, and tax dollars were rolling in. Money was therefore readily available by the end of the 1990s to many police departments to make the kinds of investments that Bratton and Maple were encouraging. Between 1981 and 2001, the amount spent on "police protection" nationwide, according to the U.S. Bureau of Justice Statistics, increased from a little more than $16.8 billion[66] to more than $72.4 billion.[67] Adjusted for inflation, that's an increase of about 121 percent over the course of twenty years. And though Bratton had apparently left the NYPD under a cloud of conflict with Mayor Giuliani, New York City's mayor continued making speeches all over the country praising the transformative potential of Compstat.

These were boom times for police consultants like Bratton and Maple. These men had found a niche in that nationwide growth; they were, with each department they consulted, establishing a fundamental and permanent shift in the way policing is carried out in the United States. Compstat was considered state-of-the-art by cops everywhere, and any department without a robust data-gathering program was lagging behind. Bratton and Maple were more than happy to help bring these departments up to speed—and they were well compensated for it.

CHAPTER 4

THE TASER REVOLUTION

One of the most memorable concepts from the television series *Star Trek* is the phaser, a kind of ray gun carried by Captain Kirk and the other crew members of the starship *Enterprise* as they explored the galaxy. But unlike laser beams and ray guns from other science fiction shows and films, the phaser could be adjusted as desired to either stun or kill. It was an idealized version of what Jack Cover hoped his Taser would be: a weapon that could effortlessly incapacitate a person without any danger of *accidentally* killing them. One *Star Trek* fan in particular wondered if he might make the phaser a reality.

Born in 1970, Patrick "Rick" W. Smith had dark, piercing eyes, and kept his dark brown hair slicked back and to the side. A self-described sci-fi geek and an aspiring entrepreneur, he went on to study biology at Harvard. He knew that someone had invented a Taser, which, like the phaser, could stun a person from a distance. But Rick also knew that this invention was unreliable, and he believed cops wouldn't trust a Taser if it had any chance of failing the way it allegedly had during the LAPD's 1991 encounter with Rodney King. "I was thinking, 'This is something that really needs to kick ass, otherwise it's basically useless,'" Rick said. "You're telling me a cop is going to use one of these Tasers instead of a gun, when this thing isn't guaranteed to work?"[1]

As the Rodney King episode dominated the news, Rick thought to himself that surely someone must be able to build a better Taser, one that would be more powerful, more reliable, and safer than Tasertron's offering. But, for the time being at least, he wouldn't be the one to pursue that idea; he was headed to the University of Chicago in pursuit of a Master of Business Administration degree.

But then, on December 7, 1991, two people whom Rick knew from high school were shot and killed in a hotel parking lot in his hometown, the upscale Phoenix suburb of Scottsdale, Arizona. In Belgium on a study abroad program associated with the University of Chicago, Rick heard about the shooting during a phone call with his mother, Patty. With little public information to go on, Patty worried there was an armed killer on the loose. She was almost always home alone: Rick's older brother, Tom, had also left home to start a career as an accountant, and their father, Phillips, spent his weekdays in Silicon Valley as CEO of a tech company. She told Rick she was thinking about buying a gun.

Until he went abroad, Rick was only vaguely aware of the ubiquity and danger of guns in the United States. So he was surprised to hear some of his Belgian classmates declare that they never wanted to visit America, where everyone totes a gun and riots run rampant. "And I'm telling people, 'Come on, it's not like that at all,'" he recalled. "There were several instances where people asked, bluntly, 'Do you know anybody who's been shot and killed?' And I had to say, 'Well, yes, I do.' . . . And that made me look at the issue differently."[2]

Rick remembered reading a *Wall Street Journal* article about the rise in gun-related deaths in the United States: according to the Centers for Disease Control and Prevention, there were more than thirty-eight thousand in 1991. "I thought, 'This has to be a typo,'" Rick said.

"'There's no way thirty-eight thousand people are getting shot and killed every year. We wouldn't let that happen; we would do something about that.'"[3]

Two of those deaths touched him directly, and now his mother was looking to buy a gun. If she just wanted to protect herself, Rick thought, there must be an alternative. Why not buy a Taser instead, he suggested. But after a week Patty called Rick back and told him the gun store wouldn't sell her one. Rick was baffled. "I said to her, 'Wait a minute. You're in a gun store—which means you're standing in a place that sells AK-47s—and they won't sell you a Taser?'"[4]

Whether the gun store owner Patty approached had erroneously assumed that Tasers were illegal for civilians in Arizona or simply didn't have any in stock, Rick thought it was strange that his mother couldn't buy a Taser. He saw an untapped market. And he had an idea how to reach it. Tasertron devices used gunpowder to propel electrified darts, legally making them handguns; Nova stun guns, still available in some markets, had replaced the darts with barbs, but that meant they would be useful only at close range. Rick returned to his idea of improving the Taser. Someone had to do it, so why not him?

He had confidence and ambition. And he had the support of his professors at the University of Chicago, one of the world's most prestigious business schools. During his final semester, he enrolled in an intensive entrepreneurship class. "For my class project, all I'm doing is researching the Taser industry and . . . nonlethal weapons," he recalled. "I had my mind made up. This is what I was going to do."[5]

In becoming an entrepreneur, Rick was following in his father's footsteps. Phillips W. Smith was a West Point graduate with an M.B.A. from Michigan State University and a Ph.D. from St. Louis University, who spent most of his career building companies.

"My dad was in the military before I was born," Rick explained. "And then, [when I was] growing up, he was always either working in marketing for high-tech firms or doing start-ups." Phillips cycled through possibilities and suffered numerous failures, but Rick could see that his father always pressed ahead to the next thing. "He started a restaurant at one point. That failed. He bought a medical distribution business. That failed. And in between these, he would go back and get a safe job. So we bounced around a lot. We were moving every two or three years." Finally, in the early 1980s, Phillips helped found an early computer-aided engineering company called CAE Systems, which was then acquired for $75 million. "One day dad was struggling and then the next, he was buying a Ferrari," Rick said. "So I saw the benefits of his success." Phillips was energized and happy; he wasn't frustrated the way he'd been while working for someone else. Rick saw his father doing work that mattered to him and recognized he wanted the same for himself. "So I already had the bug," he said. In Tasers, he saw his opportunity.[6]

Then came the patent, a turn of events that Rick later described as though it were an accident—a spate of luck. In a library at the University of Chicago, Rick read up on Cover and his companies. He studied the original 1974 Taser patent, with its flawed flashlight shape and gunpowder-propellent design. Then he found a second patent from Cover, just issued in 1991. "And it was like we were communicating with each other without having ever met," he said. "[Cover's] new patent was for a compressed air system for launching darts." The brilliance of this design, Rick could see, was that it didn't use gunpowder. In his research, he'd learned all about the restrictive classification that the Bureau of Alcohol, Tobacco, and Firearms had placed on Cover's original design because it used gunpowder.

Rick called the ATF: Would a Taser using compressed air instead of gunpowder still be classified as a firearm? Would it be legal? It seemed Cover's new design was sound: it would *not* be a firearm and it *would* be legal. But for Rick, this was a dead end: Jack Cover was already ahead—it seemed unlikely that Rick would be able to forge ahead, improve on Cover's design, and secure his own patent. On the other hand, he thought, why not track down Cover himself and propose a partnership?

Soon, he'd looked up Cover's address, which as it turned out was just two hours away from Rick's parents' home in Scottsdale. Rick knew he'd found a product that could make his career. And maybe he'd found an inventor who could help.

BY 1993, JACK Cover was seventy-three years old, retired, and had long ago moved away from the Los Angeles area to live in Tucson in a modest home, among people his age. His role in Tasertron was minimal and edging toward nonexistent—so when a promising young man with an impressive résumé (including a biology degree from Harvard and multiple M.B.A.s) called him on the phone hoping to learn everything he could about the Taser, Cover was happy to talk. Cover's third wife, Ginny, recalled that he was pleased to have invented a product that police found helpful, but he had always been disappointed at his failure to build the Taser into an international phenomenon— or even a flourishing business. Rick Smith, the bright young man on the phone, seemed to be his last shot at changing the world with his invention. And Rick was serious about learning everything he could from Cover; in the summer of 1993, he moved the Smith family camper onto Cover's Tucson property. On September 7 of that year, Rick Smith co-founded the Incapacitating Electronic Restraints Corporation—ICER Corp.—with his older brother, Tom, who also had an M.B.A. Their father, Phillips Smith, who was flush with cash after selling his own company, supplied the capital to get it off the ground.

Jack Cover was hired as a contract consultant, and agreed to share everything he'd learned while developing and marketing his invention. For this, he received a monthly stipend, but no equity in the company. The company's first board meeting occurred at the Smiths' dining room table.

Though the Smiths achieved an early victory when ATF sent them a letter certifying that their compressed-air-powered Taser would not be regulated as a firearm, they soon found themselves in the corporate line of fire. Barry Resnick, Tasertron's CEO, initiated a lawsuit alleging patent infringement against the Smiths. Rather than spend their dad's money fighting Resnick in court, the Smiths settled, conceding to Tasertron the exclusive right to sell Tasers to North American law enforcement and military agencies until Cover's 1974 patent expired in 1998.[7] (Cover secured his 1991 patent for the compressed air system after he parted ways with Resnick, so it wasn't a part of the settlement.)

Initially, the Smiths found this to be a completely reasonable compromise: 1998 would come soon enough, and in the meantime, they could still sell to civilians. But the Air Taser 34000—the first model that the Smiths manufactured for civilians—carried a price tag of $249, which made it a tough sell for average consumers. To bolster those sales—and to hone their police department pitch for 1998— the Smiths began targeting law enforcement agencies outside North America. To reflect this strategic change, they renamed their company Taser International.

One of the Smiths' first prospects was a commander with the Czech Republic's national law enforcement agency, who expressed interest in the Air Taser 34000 and asked Rick to give a live demonstration in Prague. Rick and Tom thought this would be easy and predictable: they themselves had been the Air Taser 34000's first test subjects, and they knew what it felt like to take a hit. In their parents' backyard, they had staged a promotional video: Rick, in sunglasses and a turtleneck, stood still while Tom shocked him with the device. Likely exaggerating the effects of the weapon, Rick immediately dropped to the ground, writhing on the grass. The Smiths also tested their weapon on dozens of volunteer test subjects, who responded in the same way: quick incapacitation, falling directly to the ground.[8]

They had every reason to believe they would get the same result in Prague. But this time, the demonstration did not go according to script. In front of an audience of officers, a Czech police trainer selected a cadet to serve as the test subject. Before Rick could proceed, the trainer screamed at the cadet, laying into him in Czech. Rick had no idea what the trainer was saying, but whatever it was, it had the effect of getting the cadet more revved up than any volunteer Rick had ever seen.

Rick fired the Air Taser and, as usual, the cadet clenched up—but instead of collapsing, he staggered, and stayed on his feet, fighting off the electric current. Rick later wrote that he was "amazed to see this happen." He held the trigger as the cadet staggered several more feet and then grabbed him by the arm. The cops sitting in the crowd erupted in laughter.[9]

Thinking it must've been a fluke, Rick asked for another volunteer. The trainer repeated his motivational speech, and the second cadet, too, stayed on his feet. The crowd's laughter grew louder. The devices were not as effective as they needed to be. "It was the most embarrassing and humiliating day of my life. If those guys had a fruit-and-vegetable cart, I would have been pelted with tomatoes."[10]

For Taser International, the alarming lesson of the Prague demonstration was that a motivated, aggressive attacker could fight through a Taser's shock. This would be a huge problem whether they were selling to police officers or civilians.

INSTEAD OF A solution, the Smiths settled for another shot at redemption: the 1998 gathering of the International Association of Chiefs of Police, or IACP. Founded in 1893, the IACP is the largest, oldest, and most important policing organization in the world. In addition to publishing a trade magazine, *The Police Chief*, it hosts an influential annual conference, where hundreds of entrepreneurs hoping to sell products and services into the policing market purchase exhibition space. For police contractors, the conference is a particularly valuable opportunity, because the IACP's membership is restricted to police *leaders*—chiefs, superintendents, or command-level officers. In other words, the conference is entirely populated by those who wield influence over purchasing decisions. It's where big ideas are shared and major business deals get made. These exhibition halls are something to behold—a gathering of every company in the world with any interest in selling to police departments.

It was here that the Smiths again put their Air Taser 34000 to the test.

This was a big deal. It was now 1998, and the crippling settlement with Tasertron was a thing of the past; this would be the Smiths' first presentation to a large gathering of U.S. police departments, all in one place. The stakes were high. If their weapon succeeded, they were bound to have orders. If it didn't, it would be a huge embarrassment that would be difficult to overcome.

Of course, by this point, they knew that it was possible for someone to fight through the Air Taser's shocks, as the Czech cadets had. But there seemed to be no other choice; the Air Taser was the only model they had. And maybe the Czech demonstration had been a fluke after all. In any case, the Smiths decided to take a gamble.

Again, they had one very eager volunteer.

This time, it was a hand-to-hand combat trainer with the U.S. Marine Corps—a shorter man, about five feet, seven inches tall, with a solid figure. His name was Hans Marrero.

In front of a roomful of cops, Marrero took a fighting stance, facing Rick.

Rick aimed and pulled the trigger—*click*.

Marrero grunted but barely budged. The Taser didn't even have the effect of a besting on the marine. After he removed the Taser's wires from the skin on his chest and from his shirt, he shook Rick's hand. "It *did* hurt," he said encouragingly.[11]

It was another disastrous embarrassment for the struggling company—and it came at exactly the wrong time. It reinforced what many cops already believed—that Tasers were unable to incapacitate a determined attacker.

———

WITHOUT A STAMP of approval from cops, the Taser was a worthless jumble of plastic and wires—and Taser International's position was becoming ever more precarious. Sales were barely bringing in enough revenue to justify production costs, and the introduction of a new product—the ill-fated Auto Taser, an anti-theft device that shocked would-be car thieves—failed spectacularly. The company was $2.7 million in debt, with just $50,000 in cash, and on the verge of bankrupting the family. Patty Smith stopped talking to her sons.[12]

Facing such a bleak outlook, the Smiths decided to go back to the drawing board and rethink the Taser's technical specifications with an initiative they called "Project Stealth." The electrical potency of a Taser's shock was simply too weak. So Rick settled on what seemed like an obvious solution: making the Taser even stronger. "At that point, we knew we had it," Rick would later say. "It was a matter of cranking up the power."[13] For help with the reconfiguration, Rick contracted Dr. Robert Stratbucker, who had done some testing on previous models. This time, he performed tests on anesthetized pigs at his farm in Omaha, Nebraska, incrementally increasing the Taser's wattage. His goal was to find the level at which the electrical current forced muscles to involuntarily contract; if the Taser was going to incapacitate a determined attacker like Marrero, it needed to do more than just cause pain.

Stratbucker worked very much in the freewheeling inventor tradition of Jack Cover. He'd shock the pigs, observe how their muscles contracted, then use his best judgment about how the same wattage would affect humans. Then he would ramp up the power, shock more pigs, and make calculations to determine how much of a difference the increase had made. At twenty-six watts—nearly four times the power of the initial Taser tested by the LAPD nearly two decades prior—he had his breakthrough: the Taser caused not just pain but complete incapacitation.

Stratbucker's work in this case led to the development of a higher-wattage model of Taser that became known as the M26 Advanced Taser. Rick set up a rematch with Hans Marrero, only this time the marine hand-to-hand combat instructor would face the newer model with its twenty-six watts of power. It was another gamble. If Marrero went down, the Taser would be almost instantly redeemed. If he remained standing, well, there wouldn't be much left of Taser International.

The face-off took place in April 1999 and produced one of Taser International's most famous pieces of marketing. The video begins with an all-caps declaration in white text on a black background: "NON-LETHAL WEAPONS CANNOT STOP A FOCUSED, AGGRESSIVE ATTACKER."[14] The text zooms forward to reveal Marrero, clad only in workout shorts, standing on a blue mat, the top-down lighting casting shadows over his muscular physique. Text then zooms dramatically back onto the screen: "UNTIL NOW."

A montage of macho theatrics follows: a muscular man in a POLICE T-shirt punches and chokes Marrero, who promptly disarms him; Marrero flashes his grappling skills as he flips a helpless volunteer into a WWE-style leg-lock. Then slow-motion shots of Marrero cut to whooshing sound effects; text appears on the screen listing his accomplishments in the Marine Corps, finally concluding, "HANS IS CON-SIDERED TO BE ONE OF THE TOUGHEST MEN ALIVE."

Then Hans meets the new-and-improved Taser. With two M26 Taser wires clipped to his chest, he is challenged to grab a gun five feet away. Before he can move, the device utters its distinctive series of staccato clicks. Marrero collapses to the floor. After recovering, he spends the rest of the video explaining how the Taser had done what no human could.

Rick sent the video to police departments around the country, like a hype trailer for a summer blockbuster. Finally, the company seemed to be on its way to mending its reputation.

But increasing the Taser's power had unexpected consequences.

From the moment of its invention, the Taser's status as a nonlethal weapon had provoked controversy. By the end of 1999, the weapon had been involved in at least forty-seven publicly reported fatalities.[15] Even when Jack Cover was marketing his original three-watt Taser—a device with only a small fraction of the M26's electrical intensity— he refused to say it couldn't kill.[16] As early as 1991—eight years prior to the M26 tests—forensic scientists established that a Taser shock may have contributed to a death.[17] Meanwhile, around the world, Tasers and stun guns—both real ones and knock-offs—were becoming "the torturer's high-tech tool of choice," according to a report from the civil rights organization Amnesty International. "We even have reports of school teachers wanting to have stun weapons," said an Amnesty representative. "We think the whole thing is going completely out of control."[18]

For Rick, concerns about the higher power levels were inconsequential compared to the company's financial troubles. For years, Taser International had been battling for its life, saddled with a reputation among cops that its products were simply too weak. The M26 model represented a chance to finally shake off that reputation. But the question of safety couldn't be completely ignored. Because Tasers, an electrical weapon, often make contact near the heart, one of the most serious potential medical issues is ventricular fibrillation, a potentially fatal disturbance of the heart's natural rhythm that causes its lower chambers to shudder and inhibits its routine function of pumping blood.

With a working production model in hand, Rick called Stratbucker to investigate whether the twenty-six-watt M26 Advanced Taser could cause ventricular fibrillation. Stratbucker enlisted the help of Dr. Wayne McDaniel, an electrical engineer and professor at the University of Missouri specializing in defibrillation research.

"We did a ridiculously cheap study," McDaniel would recall years later. "They didn't have any money."[19]

Still, he wanted to help. Rick gave Stratbucker stock options in

Taser International and promised McDaniel that if the company made it big he'd be rewarded. "When the tide comes in, all the boats will rise," McDaniel remembered being told.

Over the course of two days, Stratbucker and McDaniel tested the twenty-six-watt Taser on five different dogs a total of 192 times.[20] They gave some of the dogs epinephrine and ketamine—drugs that can jump-start mammalian hearts—in an attempt to simulate drug use in humans, which can make the cardiovascular system more sensitive to electric shocks. Using an experimental setup, they hooked Taser wires up to electrodes and moved them in as many positions as they could around the dogs' chests.

Even though, as McDaniel put it, he and Stratbucker "did everything we could to make them fibrillate," the dogs showed no signs of irregular heart rhythms. This was far from a conclusive finding—in fact, considering the small sample size and other limitations of the test, it is difficult to see the exercise as anything more than a perfunctory attempt to limit liability. The Smiths just didn't have the capital to enlist a full team of university researchers to conduct a serious scientific study. Since their Taser used compressed gas and not gunpowder, it wasn't regulated by the ATF. It therefore faced significantly fewer hurdles, as though it were comparable to a kitchen appliance, rather than a dangerous weapon. It's unclear whether a serious study would have been possible anyway: Would researchers agree to expose humans, in a randomized study, to shocks from an experimental weapon that might cause ventricular fibrillation or death? Unlikely.

McDaniel made sure to emphasize that the test wouldn't have passed muster in any peer-reviewed journal. It was simply too limited—almost absurdly so. He certainly did not conclude from this test that Tasers were incapable of causing death.

"I have a statistician I've worked with," he said. "He has a kind of motto: 'All studies are wrong, but some have utility.'"[21]

Rick didn't share McDaniel's reservations.

"At the end of two or three days of studies, Rick was convinced it was safe," McDaniel said. "I remember he was on the phone with somebody, and he said, 'Let's go ahead and ship it.'"

TASER INTERNATIONAL'S RIVAL company Tasertron had had the exclusive right to sell Tasers to North American law enforcement for most of the 1990s, but during that time it had done little to take advantage of that opportunity. It spent almost nothing on marketing, did little to advance its technology, and never significantly expanded its reach beyond the relatively small number of police agencies it already did business with. Tasertron's CEO, Barry Resnick, was a managing partner at a busy law firm in Newport Beach, California, and led a hectic life, including being involved in several other secondary business ventures. He also participated in volunteer work and even managed a stable of racehorses. In other words, Tasertron was only one of Resnick's many competing priorities, and in practice the company did little beyond maintaining its existing accounts—such as with the LAPD.[22]

Unsurprisingly, the problem of aggressive policing and police brutality was as pressing as ever in 1999. When two police shootings in New York City began drawing attention once again to the potential utility of a nonlethal weapon, it was not Resnick who sprang into action, but Tasertron's desperate and nimble competitor Taser International.

Amadou Diallo was a twenty-three-year-old Liberian immigrant living in the Soundview section of the Bronx who made a living peddling goods like videotapes, gloves, and socks on the street.[23] Just after midnight on February 4, 1999, Diallo was standing outside his apartment complex after finishing a late-night meal when four NYPD officers in street clothes rolled by in an unmarked cruiser. Believing Diallo matched the description of a serial rapist last seen in the neighborhood, they parked the cruiser and approached him. The officers would later testify that they had identified themselves as NYPD, but an eyewitness said they didn't. In any case, Diallo ran toward the front door of his apartment complex. When he got there, perhaps thinking that the men were trying to rob him, Diallo reached into his pants pocket to retrieve a black wallet and held it up. One of the officers mistook it for a gun. They fired a total of forty-one shots at the young man, nineteen of which struck him. Diallo died at the scene.[24] (The serial rapist the cops were looking for was later found and convicted.)[25]

The case sparked protests throughout the city and drew the attention of national news outlets, but even under such heightened scrutiny, the NYPD did little to immediately enact change. However, when a similar killing occurred just months later, NYPD brass knew they wouldn't be able to get away with another passive response.

Gidone Busch, a thirty-one-year-old medical school dropout and spiritual explorer with a history of mental illness, had recently moved to a primarily Orthodox Jewish community, the Borough Park section of Brooklyn. On the evening of August 30, 1999, Busch was playing loud music in his basement apartment and allegedly threatening people outside with a hammer. After his neighbors complained, police arrived, and he emerged outside nearly nude, carrying the hammer above his head. After unsuccessfully attempting to subdue him with chemical spray, NYPD cops encircled him, guns drawn, on the street outside his apartment. It was unclear what caused the officers on scene to begin shooting, but media reports indicated there was a single shot fired, followed by a dozen more. Busch fell to the pavement, dead.[26]

The leaders of the NYPD knew they needed to respond in a way that would show their seriousness about reform, and there were many options for such a response—they could have fired the officers, for example, or held them personally responsible for legal damages. But union protections and a rule known as qualified immunity—which protects officers from being held civilly responsible for "reasonable actions" performed while on duty—made most of those options either inconvenient or impossible.

Pursuing a technological solution seemed far more attainable. The Busch case in particular demonstrated the potential utility for some kind of alternative weapon. The lesson was, in essence, the same as it had been for the LAPD after the Eula Love incident in 1979: an effective nonlethal tool might have ended the standoff without bloodshed or death.

At the time, in the late 1990s, a limited number of NYPD officers were already equipped with Tasertron Tasers, but New York cops generally had the same misgivings as police around the country: electrical weapons were just too weak to trust with one's personal safety. Sensing a massive business opportunity, Rick Smith swooped in, presenting his new M26 as a kind of technological imperative: it was, he argued, the only weapon that could reliably prevent deadly encounters with civilians. And with nearly three times the power of Tasertron's weapons, Rick's new model was dependable. It would revolutionize policing, he told the NYPD brass. Deadly shooting incidents like the Diallo and Busch cases would be a thing of the past.

In December 1999, the department, under its then-commissioner, Howard Safir, who had taken over after Bill Bratton's departure in 1996, became one of the first law enforcement agencies in America to begin field testing the M26 Advanced Taser. Within months, it would sign with Taser International.

AS TASER INTERNATIONAL began to expand into such large new markets as the NYPD, as well as police agencies in Orange County, Sacramento, and elsewhere, its sales strategy stayed simple: seeing is believing. After the embarrassing botched demonstrations both in Prague and at the 1998 IACP convention, some police had understandably come to believe that Tasers were not a serious weapon. Now the Smiths planned to show them they were wrong. The video they had shot pitting marine combat trainer Hans Marrero against the new high-powered M26 model became a blueprint for overcoming this skepticism. Rick, along with his vice president of communications, Steve Tuttle, and a few other employees—including, at times, Marrero himself, who became a Taser employee—hit the road on something of an M26 Taser tour, bringing it to officers around the country who were eager to witness its power in person.

Like a carnival game, Rick would challenge the toughest officers at each stop—the "studs," as Tuttle called them—to step right up and test their resilience against the latest in police weaponry. Of course, like most carnival games, it was rigged. Rick knew exactly what would happen before he pulled the trigger.

"Agh! Okay! Okay!" one of the volunteers yelled, when shocked. "Fuck! Fuck! Fuck!" another screamed, as the other officers in the room exploded in laughter. Rick captured dozens of demonstrations on film. The videos—and subsequent testimonials—were marketing gold.

"Couldn't do a thing. Helpless. Absolutely helpless."

"If I meet the guy who can stand up to that, I'll turn in my badge and gun and become a florist."

"Do you think there's any way you could fight through that?" Rick asked in one video.

"Oh, hell no," a defeated volunteer replied.[27]

The M26 roadshow gave previously incredulous officers a front-row seat to the future of policing.

"These guys would leave just absolutely evangelical about the product—because we would just drop them all," Rick said.[28]

With the arrival of the M26, Rick hoped, there would be no more fights and no more batons for police. In his mind, perhaps even shootings could be eliminated. "If we could get a Taser on every officer's belt," he said, "it would save hundreds of lives or thousands of lives a year."[29] Rick finally had a weapon he could sell, and the company was generating some revenue. In 1999, when the M26 hit the market, the company was in debt and losing money, but just a couple years later, in 2001, it was raking in millions in net sales.

With a steady revenue stream and a more dependable signature product, the Smiths felt comfortable enough to take the company public—and in February 2001, they filed papers to support an initial public offering on the NASDAQ stock exchange.[30] This would allow them to raise cash from investors, which would help significantly with the debt problem. But going public would bring other challenges—the company would now have to regularly make a case for the value and effectiveness of its products, not only to potential customers, but to shareholders, in quarterly calls and public filings. If Taser International was ever motivated by noble aspirations to reduce police brutality by outfitting cops with sophisticated, safer weapons, that mission would now be tempered by the less noble objectives of stock speculators.

The Smiths' plan to raise money didn't work out as expected. Despite the company's growing popularity with law enforcement, investors remained skeptical that Taser International would be able to maintain and build upon its gains—for several reasons. Crime rates were falling fast, and the widespread anxiety that had gripped Americans during the crime wave of the early 1990s was beginning to dissipate. While this may have been good news for police leaders, it also meant that they would be less desperate to find new technologies to help solve their problems—and less amenable to marketing pitches from companies like Taser International. Furthermore, Taser International had decided to pitch itself as a so-called concept company, a category of business popular during the dot-com bubble of the late 1990s. Rather than relying on fundamental business indicators such as revenue and profit to attract investors, concept companies would use the promise of an unproven yet transformative technology with huge sales potential to convince the public of their worth. When the dot-com bubble burst in 2001, Wall Street became understandably cautious about concept stocks. Finally, potential investors were troubled by the company's spotty history and its seeming inability to break into the civilian market. As a result of all these factors, Taser raised only $8.4 million when it went public in May 2001, a disappointing result.

"We were meeting with people just as NASDAQ fell," Rick would later say, referring to the dot-com collapse of 2001. "We had to pull brokers from under desks to talk to us."[31]

FOUR MONTHS LATER, the terror attacks of September 11 shook the nation. Many of the fears that had dissipated with declining crime rates were jolted back to the surface, but the attacks particularly brought into focus concerns about airline safety. The U.S. Air Marshals had considered switching to Tasers rather than firearms in the 1970s, back when the invention was still brand new and Jack Cover was touting it to any agency he could get on the phone, but the idea never went anywhere. Now the possibility seemed alive again.

There would of course be many other opportunities for a company like Taser International in the post-9/11 world. For state and local leaders, making strident commitments to fighting terrorism and backing them up with plenty of cash became a political necessity. The newly formed U.S. Department of Homeland Security—a massive federal body encompassing twenty-four agencies and ostensibly designed to further protect America's borders—handed out hundreds of millions of dollars in grants for first responders and police departments, on top of existing state and federal programs, under the guise of fighting terrorism. With the sudden influx of money, city councils and other governmental bodies now had the resources to buy Tasers. The Smiths responded with a marketing blitz to aggressively push their products, sending out a fresh wave of salespeople to police departments nationwide.

They also began exploring ways of partnering with certain police leaders whom they determined to be particularly influential—one was Bernard Kerik, the NYPD commissioner who led the department during 9/11. Kerik had enjoyed a nontraditional ascent to power. During the 1993 mayoral election, he had served as personal driver and body-guard to Rudolph Giuliani, who soon after winning appointed Kerik to lead the investigative division of the city's Department of Correction and later promoted him into the prison system's top post. When Howard Safir resigned as the NYPD's leader in August 2000, Giuliani was still in power, and he tapped his former bodyguard to be the new commissioner.[32] Kerik would hold the job for only a little more than a year, but he was the one who happened to be in office on the morning of September 11, 2001. So despite his unconventional career path and his relatively short time in office, Kerik became a commodity of sorts—a police leader who'd overseen a huge police department's response to the most significant terrorist attack ever on U.S. soil. Kerik was eager to capitalize.

The Smiths had been doing business with police long enough to know that relationships mattered at least as much as the product itself. The police market was limited, and leaders with access to their departments' cash were even more limited. But the Smiths weren't just focused on establishing relationships inside individual departments; they also wanted to associate their company with people whose names would be familiar to police nationwide. When they showed up at the International Association of Chiefs of Police conference every year, they wanted to have friends who commanded respect.

In June 2002, Taser International named Kerik to its board of directors. He began making himself useful right away, flying around the country to tout the M26 at events and conferences—including the IACP convention, where he served as a keynote speaker. After thanking the gathered police leaders "for their tremendous support during the recovery from last year's terrorist attacks," he went directly into a sales pitch, explaining the importance of "effective less-lethal force like the Advanced Taser . . . in dealing with the myriad threats [that police] face on the street."[33]

Kerik wasn't making this pitch for free—as part of his appointment to the board, Taser International paid him approximately $6.2

million in stocks.[34] Nor was he the only police leader being paid to shill for Taser International. All over the country, the company was deploying a strategy to accumulate influence and build a law enforcement superpower.

"They brought in the celebrity cops," Dr. Wayne McDaniel explained. "That was a stroke of genius."

When they weren't using celebrity cops, they were paying insiders—officers who, unlike Kerik,[35] were still on the payroll of police departments around the country—to train other officers and champion the weapon.

The Smiths called these salesman cops "master instructors."

"IT'S SO BACKWARD, the way this happened," said Mike Leonesio, who spent years as a certified Taser master instructor and worked alongside both Rick and Tom Smith to develop training material. "It's really not training. It's marketing that they mask as training. It's really kind of a farce."[36]

Taser International's Master Instructor Program started out of necessity. After all, for most officers, Tasers were completely unfamiliar—more like something from science fiction than anything they'd encountered in the real world. "We [cops] never had weapons that dealt with electricity," Leonesio recalled. As a result, he explained, "we looked to [the company] for some initial guidance. The problem is, they dug their claws in, and have held on ever since."[37]

To address this need, Rick created a training program with which they could show cops exactly how to use Tasers. The company would fly them out to its headquarters in Scottsdale, pay for their hotels and meals, and then put them through a multiday training—under the tutelage of certified master instructors. On its face, this was a dubious proposition. Jack Cover had designed the Taser to be simple and easily operated. The Smiths had tinkered with the design, increasing the power and making other superficial changes, but in terms of basic operation, Tasers in 2002 worked exactly as they had for decades: point and pull the trigger. The M26 even had a laser sight. The only complication was that the weapons didn't fire more than about fifteen feet.

Just as Jim Scroggins and Dan Dowell had seen with the Nova stun gun, the Smiths realized that putting cops through a multiday master instructor training in Scottsdale—though not really necessary—could serve as a form of indoctrination. Maybe there wasn't much to teach, but the cops would hear from other cops who were using the device; they'd share their experiences, talk about the strength of the weapon, make friends with other police officers from around the country who were also interested in Tasers. And then, having completed the master instructor training program in Scottsdale, they could go home and conduct their own Taser training sessions, for which they would be paid by Taser $600 per session, plus expenses. Master instructors were all either active-duty or retired law enforcement personnel—and most were genuinely committed to the company's vague mission of saving lives. The Smiths learned quickly that officers trusted one another implicitly—which made the training sessions particularly effective.

"It worked because those people speak the language," Leonesio said. "The Smiths said, 'Hey, wait a minute, we can use these guys. These guys can be our disciples.'"

Matt Masters, a SWAT team officer with the Kansas City Police Department whose son was nearly killed after being shocked with a Taser,[38] recalled his first training session with the weapon. "They'd show you videos," he said, of Tasers being demonstrated in a variety of different settings. "And we'd laugh about it. Nobody really thinks, 'Man, that probably hurts like hell.' . . . Taser was just masterful in how they marketed their product. Cops believed everything, *everything* Taser told them."[39]

Leonesio claims that as a master instructor, he was encouraged to paint a rosy picture of Tasers, downplaying the risks and teaching officers to think of the weapons as something of a panacea. "One of

Taser's early mantras—they actually said this to us, I heard this on many occasions—[was] 'Taser early and often.' . . . The way they sold it to law enforcement was, 'They're completely safe.'" In other words, if the devices can do no lasting harm, there should be no problem in using them liberally and indiscriminately.

The company warned about hazards, Leonesio says, such as Tasering people on high ledges who might fall to their death while immobilized. But as far as the weapon's electricity was concerned, the language in Taser International's training material was unequivocal: in early manuals, under the heading "What Advanced TASER won't do," a bullet point reads, "No effect on cardiac rhythm or pumping."[40] Another section, called "Myths and Urban Legends," stated, "Will not cause heart or pacemaker failure." Elsewhere, the manual claimed, "The output of the M26 is 1/100th of the dangerous level."

"It wasn't even subtle in the early days," said Leonesio. "They'd go through example after example after example of why this weapon is so safe." To back up their safety claims, Taser International cited studies done on older generations of Tasers—weapons that were far less powerful—such as a January 1987 *Annals of Emergency Medicine* study showing that "similar Taser technology leaves no long term injuries."[41]

For Matt Masters, the evidence seemed overwhelming. "As a cop, you're like, 'that sounds pretty good—good enough for me,'" he said. "Most cops sitting there in that training don't question what they're being told." In fact, he went on, most of his colleagues at the Kansas City Police Department simply assumed that their bosses were independently verifying the company's material. They didn't understand the scope of Taser International's influence. "Who is a master instructor? Is that a Taser employee?" he asked rhetorically. "Well, no, he's a cop . . . What blows my mind is that when we got the Taser, nobody did any other studies or research. They believed everything Taser told you and took it at face value."

In a letter to officers in training, Rick justified the company's less-than-meticulous research methods by claiming that he had simply chosen "to follow the same approach . . . as is used in the pharmaceutical and medical device industry."

"It's exactly the same mechanism of product development that I had learned when working for a pharmaceutical company," he later said. "Exploratory research, computer modeling, animal safety studies, human [studies]."

Of course, unlike pharmaceutical companies, Taser International was not subject to an independent regulatory agency, such as the Food and Drug Administration, that could verify its claims. Without such oversight, the company could get away with astoundingly shoddy research standards. Its animal testing, for example, consisted of Robert Stratbucker's initial test on a single pig and Wayne McDaniel's follow-up test on five dogs. Neither test studied potential risks other than immediate fibrillation—and only a handful of the shocks were administered for longer than five seconds.

Referring to the possibility of adverse cardiac reactions to Taser shocks, McDaniel protested: "We never said it can't happen."

TASER INTERNATIONAL'S HUMAN testing, however, was even less rigorous than the animal testing—it was entirely anecdotal, consisting exclusively of promotional volunteer demonstrations. The Smiths pointed to these volunteers as proof that Tasers were safe, but as it turns out, every one of them was zapped for no more than a second, while facing away from the shooter—meaning they were never shot near the chest. None of the early volunteers was measured for any physiological or biomedical changes before, during, or after being Tasered.

Perhaps most misleading, however, was the company's method of calculating the intensity of the M26's electrical current. The Smiths opted to define the weapon's overall power as the "average" current discharged each time it was fired, which was about 3.6 milliamps, according to Taser. In reality, the current fluctuated dramatically, reaching a peak of 15 to 17 amperes—much more than the "average." Using the average current, Taser International routinely suggested in charts and literature that the M26's electrical power was well below the threshold of internationally accepted safety standards.

"This chart is totally indefensible," said McDaniel, referring to one of the company's slides. "Average current just doesn't mean anything. It's like if you had an electrocution shock that was over in thirty seconds, but you timed it over a day, then the average current over a day would be really low."[42]

"This is just BS," he added. "You may be able to sell more guns with it, but it's not scientifically defensible."

DURING THIS TIME, competition between Taser International and its once-mighty rival Tasertron began to cool off, as the Smiths gained the upper hand, pushing their product to cops around the nation with no restrictions and building an enthusiastic shareholder base. In 2001, Taser International conducted research showing that its rival had contracts with about four hundred police departments, while it barely had any itself. But by 2003, roughly forty-three hundred departments were using Taser International's Tasers—and Tasertron was still stuck at around four hundred departments. The Smiths were coming out on top in part because of the wildly successful master instructor program and in part thanks to their shrewd marketing. More than any other factor, Taser International's emerging advantage could be traced back to their decision to increase their weapon's power. Despite the seemingly positive results the Smiths were having with a higher current, however, Tasertron didn't show any intention of following their lead. Tasertron's patent attorney and lead technological advisor, James F. McNulty Jr., had a background in electrical engineering and thus a fuller understanding of the risks Tasers might pose at a higher power level. The risks, as he saw it, weren't worth the potential advantage of a more effective weapon.

During the original patent infringement lawsuit that restricted the Smiths' operations until 1998, McNulty had explained—in an open court hearing—that after designing Tasers for the better part of two decades, he'd determined that a safe output level for the devices was five watts. Taser International's signature product used more than five times that amount.

"[The] defendants now put a high-power product out," McNulty said at the hearing. "It gets the police officers excited . . . they have more power. That's what they want . . . [but] that type of power can be lethal."[43]

As McNulty explained, cardiac fibrillation was not the only potentially lethal consequence of being struck with one of the Smiths' Tasers.

> The trouble is, it's going to affect whether they can breathe or not if you leave it on long enough . . . There are muscles involved, intercostal muscles involved in the mechanics of breathing. This affects twenty skeletal muscles. If you leave it on long enough, at [Taser International's twenty-six-watt] power levels, someone is going to asphyxiate.

By the early 2000s, it still remained unclear how many people police had killed with electroshock weapons. There were several reasons for this. On a most basic level, the U.S. Department of Justice wasn't even attempting to count the *total* number of people killed by police—and wouldn't begin doing so until years later.[44] Another reason was that in cases involving a Taser, the cause of death was often difficult to establish—the types of situations where police would typically need them tended to be messy and involve a number of other factors, including mental illness, drug use, and other types of force. Many police had a strong financial incentive for not keeping track of

Taser deaths, because more and more officers were on Taser International's payroll, being fed information from Taser about how the weapons simply could not kill.

The company hired former officers not only to run its master instructor trainings, but also to manage its sales teams and perform other duties—all were compensated, either with stock options or with outright employment. Taser International never disclosed how many former police officers were hired as employees and paid salaries. These cop consultants all had a direct financial stake in the company, which created an incestuous business environment. Beat cops wanted Tasers; other beat cops were making money as master instructors by effectively selling them. For cops—or chiefs nearing retirement—Taser International offered easy consulting work or a cushy full-time sales job in addition to their pension. Everybody won. There was simply no incentive for police leaders to question the nonlethality of Taser weapons.

IN 2003, TASER International introduced the X26 Taser—a smaller and supposedly more reliable weapon that quickly replaced the M26 as the company's flagship product. In June that year, the Smiths announced another triumph—they had arranged to buy out their longtime rival Barry Resnick's Tasertron for just $1 million, establishing a virtual monopoly on the Taser market. The success that the Smiths had sought for so long was finally within reach. Dramatic videos of officers using the weapons started hitting the nightly news in segments highlighting the company's success and the safety and effectiveness of its weapons. Such headlines as "Brothers Stunned by Their New Success in Taser Trade"[45] and "Brothers' Stunning Invention Electrifies America"[46] were on the front pages of major newspapers.

Taser's sales exploded. In the fourth quarter of 2003 alone, soon after its acquisition of Tasertron, the company added eight hundred new departments to its list of customers. Its revenue jumped from a record $25 million in 2003 to $67.8 million in 2004. By the end of

2004, more than seven thousand law enforcement agencies equipped at least some of their officers with Tasers, most of them choosing the newer X26, which, priced at $799, brought in nearly twice as much profit as the previous model.

One of the few lingering difficulties for Taser International was the perception of its product as an unnecessary extravagance. In most areas, officers didn't encounter dangerous situations regularly enough to justify the cost of equipping the whole police force—or even a majority—with Tasers. "These things were like eight hundred bucks," said Matt Masters. "How many departments you think would buy a bunch of Tasers if the officers could hardly ever use them?"

To counter these attitudes, Taser International made a concerted effort to integrate Tasers more comprehensively into the everyday experiences of cops. Master instructors taught officers, for example, that "early" and "aggressive" use of Tasers—even when dealing with non-violent or nonthreatening people—could prevent encounters from escalating into situations requiring deadly force. They emphasized again and again that Tasering a suspect multiple times carried no risks. "The teaching in the early days, and then all the way through the mid-2000s, was, basically: 'Use it for anything. If you tell a guy [to] sit on the curb, and he doesn't sit on the curb, Tase him,'" Mike Leonesio said. "And the way they got away with that, the way they sold that to law enforcement was, 'They're completely safe.' . . . Of course, nobody questioned anybody."

With no competitors and complete control over the training program, Taser International played an essential role in shaping how officers used Tasers in the field. The company marketed the devices to the public as a lifesaving alternative to deadly force. But, increasingly, officers came to think of them as a means of eliciting obedience. "We're so bad, as officers, at controlling ourselves," said Matt Masters. "You give them an opportunity to use something, and they're going to use it."

By 2004, reports of outrageous cases of abuse were popping up across the country—a nine-year-old girl Tasered while in handcuffs;[47]

a seventy-five-year-old woman Tasered in a nursing home;[48] a sixty-six-year-old woman Tasered for honking at a parked police car blocking her driveway.[49] A six-year-old boy and a twelve-year-old girl were both Tasered in separate incidents within weeks of each other in Miami, prompting the Dade County School Board to officially request that officers "refrain from deploying or discharging Tasers against elementary school students."[50] According to the company's own survey examining several thousand instances in which police shocked someone with a Taser, the most common reason that officers gave to justify the use of force—in 37 percent of the cases—was "verbal non-compliance."

The *Arizona Republic* found that the Phoenix Police Department's overall use of force increased by 22 percent after it began using Tasers, despite a sharp reduction in officers' use of batons and pepper spray. Another study, conducted by the *Orlando Sentinel,* showed that Florida's Orange County Sheriff's Department's overall use of force shot up by 37 percent the year after Tasers were introduced there, despite a similar reduction in other forms of force. Taser International gave no indication that it was concerned about whether its products were encouraging police to be more violent. To the contrary, Taser appeared focused on making sure the products were moving. More cops were using Tasers and they were using them more frequently than ever. But when Taser-involved fatalities started to increase, that was harder for the company to ignore.

It is generally understood that the first case of a Taser-related death was Vincent Alvarez, in 1983—LAPD officers shocked the twenty-seven-year-old man after finding him shaking and acting strangely on the streets of Los Angeles's Lincoln Heights neighborhood.[51] Between then and 2001, there were occasional incidents in which suspects died after police shocked them with Tasers, but never more than five per year. In 2002, as officers were encouraged to use Tasers earlier and more aggressively, that shot up to fourteen deaths. The following year it was twenty-two.[52]

On April 5 and 6, 2004, *CBS Evening News* ran a two-part investigation into more than forty Taser-related deaths, which included interviews with Rick Smith and other representatives from Taser International. Rather than concede that perhaps his company's claims about safety were overzealous, Rick Smith adamantly refused to allow even for the possibility that Tasers had played a role in the deaths. Correspondent Wyatt Andrews was incredulous. "You're saying this is a coincidence, that these people would have died anyway?" he asked.

"In every single case, these people would have died anyway," Rick answered.[53]

"The fact of the matter is our Taser technology has not been the cause of a single death. Period," Steve Tuttle, the company's loyal spokesman, wrote in an op-ed for the *Atlanta Journal-Constitution*.[54]

DESPITE THE CLOUD of controversy surrounding Taser-related deaths, Taser International's stock price enjoyed a meteoric ascent. Taser started its run among the small caps—companies with a total shareholder value under $2 billion—in late 2003.

Retail investors—those who buy and sell stocks for their personal accounts, not necessarily professional traders—drove the action, trying to outsmart a market that had largely looked down on the company during its first couple years on the NASDAQ. They took notice as the company kept smashing its own financial records each quarter, turning Taser's stock into a gold rush.

Taser's stock went from less than $6 per share in April 2003 to $146 by April 2004—a 2,333 percent increase. "It's insane," one trader who bought Taser early told *Barron's*.[55]

In May 2001, just after its initial public offering, Taser International was worth $8.4 million. In April 2004, the week after *CBS Evening News* aired its two-part investigation into Taser-related deaths, Rick and Tom Smith's company had a total shareholder value of $1.9 billion. They were *the* story on Wall Street.

But as Taser International drew a rapturous following, skeptics, with fresh wounds from the dot-com crash, smelled blood. In early 2004, a significant number of the company's investors sold short, or bet against, Taser's stock. It was a concept stock, and many observers felt that there were too many lingering safety questions about Taser's only viable product. In all, roughly one-third of Taser's freely tradable stock was shorted—meaning that it was borrowed from a broker and sold at one price under the assumption that it could later be purchased back at a lower price after it declined in value. The short selling made the stock extremely volatile; any hint of bad news could send its value plummeting. On the other hand, good news could trigger what's known as a short squeeze.

That's exactly what happened. Taser's next round of quarterly earnings far exceeded analysts' projections. The investors who had shorted—which is to say, those who had borrowed in anticipation of the stock price declining—began to panic as the good news pushed Taser's stock price up. If they bought at a higher price than they'd shorted, they would lose money—so scores of them jumped into the market all at once and bought back their shares of Taser stock in an effort to curb their losses. The volume of short sellers buying stock simultaneously amplified the value of each share, driving it from $135 to $149 in just a few days.

Insiders at Taser took advantage. Between February 4 and 18, 2004, Taser International executives allegedly sold 883,117 shares for a combined $38.5 million, including sales of a massive number of shares by Rick, Tom, and their father, Phillips Smith, with each reportedly receiving more than $10 million.[56]

However, the possibility still remained that bad news might push the stock down again, just as dramatically, by causing a panic among investors and convincing them that the short sellers had been right all along.

In the week leading up to Taser's 2004 first-quarter earnings report, the stock rose about 35 percent based exclusively on investors' anticipation of another profitable quarter.

Though Taser again announced record sales, it barely beat projected earnings, and its largest institutional investor sold its entire 10 percent stake. Even Taser's true believers grew paranoid, and those short sellers who had hung on and resisted the urge to buy back their shares early made a fortune as the stock plunged 29 percent, wiping out nearly half a billion dollars in shareholder value in one trading session. Taser's value became a guessing game that played out among traders. The Smith family, meanwhile, even after the recent sell-offs, had the vast majority of its wealth tied up in shares of a company whose value sometimes changed by hundreds of millions of dollars in a day.

By the summer of 2004, Taser's stock rebounded, though not quite to its previous April peak. No matter how investors felt, there was no denying that Rick and Tom Smith's flagship product was in high demand—officers wanted Tasers, and Taser International's sales kept climbing. Unfortunately for the Smiths, the more success they had, the more attention Taser-related deaths and abuses received.

All the drama in Taser stock brought Taser International to the attention of journalists Robert Anglen and Alex Berenson. Anglen was an investigative reporter at the *Arizona Republic* in Phoenix, right in Taser International's backyard; Berenson was a business reporter at the *New York Times.* Though they never collaborated, Anglen and Berenson did some of the most consequential reporting on the company.

"It seemed to me that they were true believers," Berenson said. "[The Smiths] were young, they were brash, they were very confident. They were a couple of bros. They thought cops were cool, and cops thought they were cool. Once I started looking, I realized this was a good story."[57]

"Their stock price was soaring. This was a Cinderella story," Anglen offered. "What surprised me was, when you started looking at the claims, they didn't hold up." One of the most frequent claims made by Taser executives was that no medical examiner had ever cited a Taser as a cause, or even as a contributing factor, in a death. Responding to the *CBS Evening News* investigation in April 2004, Rick Smith said, "It is not Taser International that says the Taser is not to blame. It is the medical examiner's opinion in every single case across the country."

Anglen encountered this same response when he visited Taser headquarters in 2004 to write a profile of the company. His assignment was to compose a feel-good feature about a local company making it big.

"They insisted that no medical examiner had ever cited the device as a cause of death," he recalled. "I said, 'That's great. Can I see the autopsy reports?'"

He meant it almost as a throwaway question, Anglen said, but "they froze up." That was when he knew something about their answers didn't add up. "That question right there changed the course of my next two years," he said.

Anglen eventually discovered that Taser had never collected the autopsy reports it was citing as proof, and that in five out of the twenty-two autopsies he was able to collect, medical examiners found the Taser was either a cause, a contributing factor, or could not be ruled out in the death. "They not only didn't have the autopsy reports, they were misinforming their shareholders, the media, and most important, police departments about what those autopsies showed."

When Anglen took his findings back to the Smiths and Steve Tuttle, he was baffled by their reaction. "Their response was: 'The medical examiners got it wrong.' Their scientific rebuttal was paper thin. They didn't have one."

While Anglen was collecting autopsies, Alex Berenson took a hard look at the company's position that its weapons had gone through rigorous testing and had been scientifically proven safe. "I just couldn't believe that the core of their safety claims came down to one pig and five dogs," he said, referring to Stratbucker's 1996 test used to develop the M26 and McDaniel's 1999 study on five dogs. "I think [the Smiths] didn't understand the science that well."

Though he was shocked to learn how little evidence existed to back up the company's broad claims, what he found more surprising was that Taser International seemed to be getting away with it.

"You think that all products are regulated. We have a big government," Berenson said. "There was literally no federal government agency with oversight. I mean they could have said the thing made you ten feet tall." Berenson laughed at the brazen assurance displayed by Taser's executives. "They said whatever they wanted."

On July 18, 2004, both the *Arizona Republic* and the *New York Times* published front-page investigations highlighting Robert Anglen's and Alex Berenson's findings. Despite offering little counterevidence to dispute the allegations, Rick Smith didn't budge. "I know in my heart what the truth is," he said. "Taser hasn't killed any of these people."[58]

Berenson spoke to several scientists and doctors who doubted the validity of Taser International's claims and suggested that additional research was needed. "I would urge the U.S. government to conduct those studies," said one researcher who had studied earlier, less powerful iterations of the weapon. "Shocking a couple of pigs and dogs doesn't prove anything."[59]

Again, Rick had only his conviction to offer as a defense. "We tell people that this has never caused a death, and in my heart and soul I believe that's true," he said firmly.

By July 19, 2004, Taser's stock had dropped 10 percent from the high it reached earlier that summer.

ANGLEN'S AND BERENSON'S stories turned up the heat on Taser International. By the fall, not only the press, but such civil rights groups as Amnesty International and the American Civil Liberties Union were aggressively pursuing the company. Rick Smith went on offense, sending out press releases calling negative news stories "unfounded" and "sensational." He accused Amnesty International of conducting an "ongoing smear campaign" and a "techno-phobic rant against non-lethal weapons."[60]

Taser International was behind a technological imperative in policing; anyone speaking out against it was simply behind the times.

Taser had no qualms about attacking Robert Anglen and Alex Berenson personally, either. After Anglen wrote a story in August critical of how Taser's training may have led to officers misusing Tasers in the field, executives accused Anglen of waging a "crusade" against the company.

Taser's relationship with Alex Berenson was even more contentious. The day after his first story ran, Rick Smith sent out a multipage press release attacking Berenson. "The fact that the reporter failed to mention even a single life-saving incident tells you all you need to know about his intentions," Smith wrote. "To go through line by line and correct all the misleading information would require a manuscript longer than the article itself."

After several critical stories ran throughout the fall of 2004, Taser even sent a letter to the president of the *New York Times* suggesting that Berenson's coverage was compromised because he owed poker money to the hedge fund managers shorting the company's stock.

Berenson didn't take it personally. "I've always been a clean reporter, in part because I know this stuff always comes out," he said. "I knew it was going to get ugly. The bigger the story, the bigger the blowback."

Taser's leadership soon grew bitter as the controversy swelled.

In 2004, one of the biggest scandals yet emerged when officers with the Miami-Dade Police Department, in two separate incidents, ended up shocking two children—a twelve-year-old girl who was allegedly skipping school and a six-year-old boy who, according to authorities, threatened to cut his leg with broken glass. When the *Miami Herald* e-mailed Taser's press team to get a comment about the company's protocols for shocking children with Tasers, one executive wrote in an internal e-mail, "Is she serious that we are supposed to do studies to see how these crack babies are supposed to deal with Post Taser Stress? Give me a break!" When discussing potential issues with pacemakers, another executive wrote, "Pacemaker patients (median age 67) are typically not the ones overdosing on crack. So, I would not worry about it for our policy."[61]

In other messages, Taser officials called one critical scientist an "asshole" and accused another of being "a professional whiner and limousine liberal who lives in a guarded and gated community and is full of crap."[62]

Those internal e-mails were from redacted communications collected by the U.S. Securities and Exchange Commission, so the executives weren't named. Taser executives told the *Herald* that studies conducted by Dr. Wayne McDaniel on early Tasers showed the weapons to be safe for use on kids as young as two. When the *Herald* followed up with McDaniel, he refuted the claim. "I don't know that I had ever envisioned the use of this thing on small children," McDaniel said. "I don't think anyone has ever tried to draw any inferences as far as use in children . . . The design of this device is for bad guys."[63]

BY THE END of 2004, Taser and its critics were at an impasse. Reporters and activists continued to question the company's claims, and Taser International refused to soften them.

On October 18, Taser International announced that a U.S. Department of Defense study had found Tasers to be safe. It was a timely validation, and the Smiths hoped it would finally put to rest the endless doubting and debating and criticism of its product.

"The . . . study is the latest chapter in a series of comprehensive medical and scientific studies which conclude that Taser technology is safe and effective," Rick Smith said. "This study re-affirms the life-saving value of Taser technology and is consistent with the recent independent findings of researchers in the United Kingdom and Canada."[64]

Taser released only an abstract of the study, but on its face it was a full-throated endorsement. "Taser was acting like this military study was the definitive evidence that put to rest all arguments about the stun gun's safety," said Robert Anglen, reporter with the *Arizona Republic*.

But as both Anglen and his counterpart at the *New York Times* Alex Berenson would later report, Taser had significantly exaggerated the Department of Defense's findings. "The government study never looked at safety, and it was far from independent," Anglen said. "Taser was involved in every aspect of that . . . test."

The Department of Defense study, as it turned out, was a basic literature review, not a "comprehensive medical and scientific" study. Its purpose was not to test the Taser's safety effects or to determine its suitability for military use, but rather to summarize the existing research that had already been done on it. The vast majority of the data the DOD reviewed came straight from Taser International.

Larry Farlow, who oversaw the study for the DOD, told Anglen that his team didn't make any conclusions about the Taser's safety, and when asked about Taser International's brash characterization of the study he said, "The simple answer is consider the source . . . The press and public relations folks are doing their jobs."

Anglen received e-mails that showed DOD researchers actually contacted Taser representatives and asked them to tone down their rhetoric—even telling the company that if it wanted a safety test, it should commission its own. "There's a reason I was able to obtain these documents," Anglen said. "It's because people were outraged. The very people involved in the studies were outraged."

It would be months before Berenson and Anglen were able to put all the pieces together and publish the truth about the DOD study—and by then Taser's insiders had made millions more by touting the credibility they claimed the study brought.

In the month after Taser's initial announcement of the study, Rick aggressively pushed out press releases announcing several new developments, to hype Taser's stock. On October 19, 2004, for example, Taser announced that it was revising its projected yearly revenue—which it now anticipated would be up 175 percent, compared to 2003 (the projection had previously been for a 150 percent increase). In the weeks that followed, the company's stock climbed almost 6 percent in response. On November 3, Taser's leadership announced its largest order yet, a $4.7 million deal to provide X26s to every Houston Police Department patrol officer. The stock shot up another 10 percent in two days, adding $135 million to the company's total value. On November 8, Taser International announced the Transportation Safety Administration had approved a major international airline's application to carry Tasers on flights within the United States. Again, the stock climbed immediately in response, by 16.5 percent this time, adding about $221 million in value.

All in all, the company's stock grew 38.5 percent between October 15, the last trading day before Taser International announced the DOD study, and November 15, a week after the TSA announcement—from $37.46 to $60.84, adding around $678 million to Taser International's total shareholder value. It has also been alleged that over the course of that month, the Smith family again cashed out a significant portion of their stock in the company, selling a total of 1,356,440 shares for a combined $67,835,908.

Throughout 2004, other company executives and insiders allegedly made a combined $120 million selling shares. Among them were Bernard Kerik, the former New York City police commissioner and Taser's most visible salesman, and Bruce Culver, the Smiths' only other original investor other than their father.[65]

At the end of 1998, Phil Smith's investment in his boys' vision had him teetering on the edge of bankruptcy. Six years later, in 2004, the family business that had held its first board meeting at his dining room table reportedly earned him almost $50 million in stock sales. He announced his retirement that fall.

Jack Cover, who first envisioned all the riches an electric weapon might bring, never got a taste of Taser International's success. Despite sharing decades of research and working with Rick Smith for more than a year to develop the company's landmark product, Cover never got anything more than a licensing agreement and some consultant's fees from the company that eventually made tens of millions selling his invention. "He died a very poor man," his widow, Ginny, later said.[66]

Dr. Wayne McDaniel, whose initial study became the catalyst for Taser International's ardent safety claims, was also left with a light wallet. "I e-mailed Rick, and I said, 'Hey, you said all the ships were gonna rise,'" McDaniel recalled, referring to his handshake agreement with the Smiths that he would be amply compensated for his discount research work once the company became successful. "And he said, 'You know, there's been a couple people that kind of got missed.'"

"Ultimately, they offered me like $25,000," McDaniel estimated. "And they said, 'We're really sorry, but this is all we can do.'" McDaniel claimed he was gradually elbowed out by the company's official medical director, Dr. Mark Kroll, who made about $2.8 million in stock in 2004.

Despite the complaints of those who had been "missed," the company was thriving. The *Wall Street Journal* selected Taser International as its top-performing stock of 2004, and by the end of that year the company had climbed back to its previous peak shareholder value of $1.9 billion. It appeared the Smiths' best days were still to come.

CHAPTER 5

A DIFFERENT WORLD

The beginning of the twenty-first century was a time of swift change in the way everyone—including law enforcement—related to computers and technology. Commerce on the Internet was booming and Silicon Valley's wave of dot-com companies increasingly played a role in ordinary people's everyday lives, as a generation of entrepreneurs set about devising technological solutions to problems large and small.

Expanding the role of technology in the law enforcement market, however, would be far more difficult than in the consumer market. Even though plenty of cops were intrigued by the potential applications for technology in their work, the layers of bureaucracy within police departments made it time consuming and labor intensive to adopt new tools on any significant level. Some police chiefs undertook experiments, but generally speaking, if they wanted to try out new tools, they would have to either arrange for trial runs in which the companies would provide the technology for free, or obtain federal grants, which involved an arduous process. Smaller and midsize regional departments were hesitant to invest their cities' money in new technology on any consequential scale unless the tech had already been endorsed by the country's most prominent police leaders—the ones overseeing big budgets and big departments.

The development of technology in police work, therefore, would be largely determined by a partnership of business leaders and prominent police officials in large, influential jurisdictions. Ultimately, despite the best efforts of companies including Tasertron and Taser International to market their products in innovative new ways to law enforcement, it would be the decisions of two men in two of the country's biggest departments that would blaze the path for the era of high-tech policing.

IN 1999, THE Los Angeles Police Department was again in trouble. Less than a decade after George Holliday filmed LAPD officers beating Rodney King nearly to death, the department was again ensnared in scandal. The trouble didn't stem from a specific tragedy as had Marquette Frye's or Eula Love's deaths. This time, the problem was a widespread culture of corruption.

The first hints of the scandal to come were revealed in September 1999 when a thirty-two-year-old LAPD officer named Rafael Perez signed a plea bargain in which he agreed to spill secrets about widespread misconduct within the department. Perez had been working as part of a special gang-focused investigative unit in Los Angeles's Rampart district when he was caught stealing $1 million worth of cocaine from evidence-storage facilities. When questioned, he told investigators that he was just a small part of a much larger system of corruption, one that involved some of the highest-ranking officials in the department. Dishonesty and criminality were endemic, he said: cops often falsely arrested civilians, giving made-up testimony to support baseless charges. Perez's theft from the evidence room was not anomalous but part of a culture of impunity and lawlessness that was well known among the LAPD's ranks.[1]

Perez's allegations made it into the press and into court, where judges overturned more than one hundred convictions connected to bogus arrests. Perez implicated about seventy officers in the scandal, and the city attorney's office estimated that the overall costs resulting from related lawsuits would be in excess of $125 million. The *Los Angeles Times* called the ensuing debacle—known as the Rampart scandal—"the worst corruption scandal in LAPD history."[2]

The federal government soon got involved.

Five years earlier, in 1994, Congress had passed the Violent Crime Control and Law Enforcement Act—written by then Delaware senator Joe Biden—which was one of the most substantial criminal justice reform bills ever. Part of that law was United States Code 14141, the Law Enforcement Misconduct Statute, which gave the U.S. attorney general authority to investigate and bring legal cases against law enforcement agencies that engage in "a pattern or practice of conduct" that violates civil rights.[3] Thus, the Justice Department's Civil Rights Division began carrying out investigations and lawsuits directed at major police departments. Once the Justice Department determined whether the department's wrongdoing amounted to a "pattern and practice" of misconduct, it would negotiate an agreement—known as a consent decree—with the department outlining how to fix the problem.

After the Rampart scandal came to light, Attorney General Janet Reno directed the Civil Rights Division to conduct an investigation of the LAPD, which confirmed Perez's allegations: the department's officers had indeed engaged in a pattern of civil rights abuses dating back years. The DOJ came to a consent decree with the city in November 2000 in which police leaders agreed to hire an "independent monitor" to make recommendations and oversee reform efforts in the department. Under the Law Enforcement Misconduct Statute, the monitor can be either an individual or a company, and is tasked with assessing the effectiveness of the department's reforms as well as mediating any disputes between the DOJ and the department.[4]

To the DOJ and LAPD leaders alike, Bill Bratton seemed an ideal choice for the position of independent monitor. In order to perform the job well, an independent monitor needs to have experience overseeing law enforcement agencies, dealing with cops and their higher-ups, and implementing institutional change. Bratton had done all of that during his time with the NYPD, and in the years since he'd worked with numerous police departments to implement Compstat programs. By November 2000, when the LAPD sought an independent monitor, Bratton was ideally positioned to step into the role.

After leaving the company he had joined immediately after his departure from the NYPD, Bratton took a job with Kroll Associates, Inc., a corporate security and investigations firm perhaps best known for providing protection for James P. Hoffa during his election as Teamsters president. Bratton's association with Kroll made it a competitive candidate to serve as the independent monitor that would oversee the LAPD's court-ordered reform process. Both the DOJ's Civil Rights Division and the LAPD respected Kroll's work and agreed that the company, with Bratton's guidance, would make a fair and impartial monitor. Kroll would soon be awarded the $11 million contract[5] with the City of Los Angeles. Bratton, who until that time had remained in New York City, headed west.[6]

Bratton's official task was to root out corruption in the LAPD, but for him that job could not be distinguished from the work of implementing a program of data-focused, intelligence-led policing, just as he'd done in New York City, Birmingham, Philadelphia, New Orleans, Washington, D.C., and elsewhere. Though the department had already implemented a Compstat-like program called FASTRAC, he encouraged the city to gather even more intelligence, and to do more with what it collected. As he spent more time in Los Angeles, its police department would begin to trust his judgment about which new technologies it needed to adopt, and how fast.

WHILE BRATTON DUG into the LAPD's practices—and considered which technologies might be appropriate for the department's twelve thousand–plus officers[7]—tech companies tried to attract police leaders' attention by testing new security equipment in high-profile ways.

In December 2000, legislation sponsored by a Republican congressman from Florida helped steer a $3.5 million federal grant to the Pinellas County Sheriff's Office, in his district near Tampa, to test out a new facial recognition software. This tool, it was hoped, would allow sheriff's deputies to more easily identify crime suspects by using computers to check photographs or composite sketches against existing mug shot databases. "It will give us some direction," a Pinellas County spokeswoman said in a newspaper story about the grant. "Detectives will still have to go out and put cases together, but the information developed by this technology will advance their case by narrowing the field of the investigation."[8] To many observers, the technology sounded intriguing, but it wasn't quite clear how it would be used, and in what circumstances.

A little more than a month later, in late January 2001, Floridians got some answers. On January 28, more than one hundred thousand football fans descended upon the Raymond James Stadium in Tampa for Super Bowl XXXV between the Baltimore Ravens and the New York Giants. It wasn't until the morning after the game ended that Graphco Technologies, Inc.—a biometric authentication systems developer based in Newtown, Pennsylvania—put out a surprising press release. According to the release, Graphco and a group of other companies had been working with the Tampa Sports Authority, the Tampa Police Department, and other law enforcement agencies to conduct a trial of a facial recognition system during the week leading up to the Super Bowl and at the Super Bowl itself. The companies working on the trial included Graphco, which had developed a technology called FaceTrac, a tool that could scan photographs against criminal mug shot databases; Viisage Technology, a publicly traded company based in Massachusetts that had developed the code on which FaceTrac was built; and VelTek International, which supplied cameras for the project.

This package of technologies, which were deployed at the Super Bowl, helped to ensure that "Criminals [Were] No Longer Another Face in the Tampa Stadium Crowd," Graphco's press release read. But that was far from the whole story. Without first notifying the public, this group of companies and law enforcement agencies had photographed, scanned, and analyzed the faces of literally every one of the game's more than one hundred thousand attendees, as well as an untold number of additional faces in the surrounding area, during the week leading up to the game. The press release was unapologetic in tone. "Not everyone comes to sporting events with good intentions," said David Watkins, Graphco's managing director, in the release. "The multiple distractions at the nation's premier athletic events provide criminals with opportunities to engage in a variety of illegal activities."[9]

While Graphco claimed the stunt served to "deter crime," there's no evidence it did anything of the sort. Tampa's police chief told reporters the facial recognition tech hadn't matched any criminals to Super Bowl attendees, and no arrests resulted from the stunt.[10] It mainly served to garner publicity—to advertise to law enforcement agencies all over the world that this sort of technology was ready for the mainstream and available from companies such as Graphco, Viisage, and VelTek. It also served to gauge the degree to which the general public would tolerate such an intrusion.

Press coverage suggested that it made many people uncomfortable. "I find it disturbing," said one privacy expert when asked about the stunt. "It smacks of Big Brother societies that keep watch over people."[11] Another security expert called it "yet another nail in the coffin of personal liberty . . . another manifestation of a surveillance society, which says 'we're going to watch you all the time just in case you might do something wrong.'"[12]

Nevertheless, the police department still seemed intrigued by the potential of the technology and defended the failed trial. "It's just another high-tech tool that is available," said Tampa's police spokesman afterward. "We used it for a week to test it, evaluate it and see if we liked it. And yes, we did like it." Local police decided to team up with the companies for a more extensive, two-year test in Tampa's Ybor City neighborhood.

Police leaders around the country were watching. Months later, the terrorist attacks of September 11 would give them an urgent reason to consider using facial recognition everywhere—whether or not the early trials had been successful.

IT'S DIFFICULT—BOTH morally and emotionally—to think of the September 11 attacks in financial terms, but the fact of the matter is this: for companies that sold technology to police departments, the attacks represented a significant windfall as law enforcement agencies received an unheard-of influx of new funding. Understandably, the attacks fueled an urgent call to action, and both Congress and President George W. Bush were eager to meet that call with ample financial support for protective measures. Huge sums were allocated to the Department of Defense, the National Security Agency, and, soon, the newly established Department of Homeland Security. The Bush administration began to call this response the Global War on Terror—a conflict that would stretch for more than a decade and cost trillions of dollars. This frenzy to aggressively fund the nation's security trickled all the way down to local police departments, which received surplus military gear such as guns, body armor, and tactical vehicles. These agencies also found themselves much better positioned to ask for federal funding for crime-fighting tools and technology.

Through the Department of Homeland Security, legislators made federal block grants available, state by state—hundreds of millions of dollars per state, for whatever public safety initiative a police department's leaders could think up.

Compstat programs also got a huge boost from this influx of money. As covered in earlier chapters, the nationwide attention that the program received in the late 1990s began a trend within the policing community toward using data to make decisions about how to approach crime. That trend depended a lot on the influence of Bill Bratton and Jack Maple. When Maple died of colon cancer at age forty-eight on August 4, 2001, Bratton was left as the lone Compstat evangelist who could claim to have been there at its conception.

When 9/11 happened, the data trend in policing received just the boost it needed. Suddenly, every police department in the country wanted to amass as much data as possible about the civilians within its jurisdiction. Federal and state officials established a national intelligence strategy for collecting and sharing criminal justice data.[13] In such states as California, New Hampshire, and Florida, police and schools began partnering to track and share information about unruly students and those with criminal histories.[14] So-called fusion centers—data hubs where information was shared between federal, state, and local agencies—were created all over the country to facilitate this work and track terror threats by sharing criminal incident reports and suspects' personal data.[15]

Setting up the mechanisms to share data was only one part of these efforts toward a national intelligence network. Just as the NYPD had spent millions on new computers, cameras, and scanners in order to bolster the Compstat program by transitioning its records from paper to digital in the late 1990s, now the rest of the country's police departments were looking to do the same, as urgently as possible.

This change represented a fundamental shift in the business of policing. And it opened up a new market that few could have predicted even a decade earlier.

RAY KELLY FELT snubbed.

It always bothered him that Bill Bratton had been widely credited with the accomplishment of getting New York City's squeegee men off the streets and kickstarting the city's incredible 1990s-era reduction in crime. Kelly had in fact made significant contributions to the department's successful crime strategy during his short year-and-a-half stint as NYPD commissioner under Mayor David Dinkins just prior to Bratton's tenure—and he believed he deserved some credit, too. When the *New York Post* published its now-famous "Dave, Do Something!" headline, it was Kelly, not Bratton, who led the response. In 1993, when the World Trade Center was attacked for the first time by terrorists, Dinkins was in Japan, so it was Kelly who addressed the city on television and made the decisions about how to proceed in the immediate aftermath. Once Dinkins was voted out of office and Bratton was sworn in as the new police chief, Kelly's legacy would be largely overlooked.[16] He would, however, have another chance.

Only two short months after 9/11, New York City residents voted to elect a new mayor to replace Rudy Giuliani, who was barred from running again due to term limits (though, with 9/11 in the rearview mirror, he lobbied briefly, and unsuccessfully, for special approval to extend his tenure under the emergency circumstances[17]).

In the Sunday edition of *Newsday*, two days prior to the November 6, 2001, election, Kelly wrote an op-ed backing Republican billionaire entrepreneur Michael Bloomberg for mayor over Democrat Mark J. Green. Though polling showed Green leading the race in the days before 9/11, the attacks pushed many voters toward the security-minded Republican. Ray Kelly was no different. His op-ed in support of Bloomberg doubled as a pitch for his own candidacy to serve once again as police commissioner and included an outline of the vision he hoped would carry the department into the post-9/11 era. Part of this pitch involved continuing Bratton's focus on quality-of-life policing and keeping crime low with an aggressive approach to petty offenders. But the main push would be technological: "an emphasis on giving police officers the technology they need to patrol their beats."

The NYPD had been at the forefront of developing and implementing Compstat and had been a pioneer of the data-policing movement of the mid-1990s—and yet at the same time, Kelly wrote, the department was "so behind the technological times that UPS delivery people have more information at their fingertips than officers do." After 9/11, he argued, New York City existed in a new and profoundly different world, one in which local police were on the front lines in the fight against terror. If the NYPD was going to succeed in that world, it would need to be connected. It would need the most sophisticated technology available. Officers, Kelly continued, "need to have remote database capability in their squad cars and handheld devices to access information on suspects or those stopped for traffic offenses . . . Scanners that read the bar codes on driver's licenses would put a wealth of information in the hands of police officers."[18]

Of course, Ray Kelly wasn't the only one with such ideas. Dozens of other officials and security experts weighed in during the months following the attacks, proposing a wide range of technological options. Proposals included placing cameras equipped "with biometric facial imaging software" in prominent public places,[19] installing shatter-resistant film on the windows in St. Patrick's Cathedral, and requiring people to pass through metal detectors in additional locations around the city. Where there weren't already surveillance cameras, more could be installed. X-ray equipment could be rolled out to screen tourists at the Statue of Liberty.

Indeed, a little more than a week prior to Kelly's *Newsday* op-ed, the Bush administration signed the USA Patriot Act into law (the name was an acronym for "Uniting and Strengthening America by Providing Appropriate Tools Required to Interrupt and Obstruct Terrorism"). It gave police unprecedented latitude to search, surveil, detain, seize, and listen in on conversations in the name of Bush's War

on Terror. Among its provisions was one easing standards for warrants sought from a foreign intelligence surveillance court. Targets of
those warrants would not need to be informed that they were to be
monitored.

After his election, Bloomberg rewarded Kelly for his public endorsement, asking him to serve again as police commissioner. Soon after
being appointed police commissioner, Kelly outlined an aggressive
counterterrorism strategy that included taking the broadest, most
sweeping recommendations from security experts.[20]

ON THE OTHER side of the country, Bill Bratton, too, was getting
another chance.

In 2002, when Los Angeles city officials began looking for a
new police chief, Bratton was working with Kroll Associates on the
independent monitor team overseeing the LAPD's consent decree
with the Justice Department. He made it publicly known that he
was ready to get back into the policing game—not as a well-paid
consultant or an independent monitor but as a leader. He wanted
to take the department's reins. "The LAPD is the most urgent, most
challenging and—most importantly—doable turnaround policing
opportunity in America today," Bratton said in a statement. "I look for
organizations in crisis and in need of cultural change. I'm a professional turnaround man. That's what I do."[21]

Bratton also seemed to be motivated by a desire to secure his legacy. He wasn't oblivious to the changing views on broken windows
policing, driven in large part by scholars such as Andrew Karmen at
the John Jay College of Criminal Justice, who argued that demographic and economic shifts were the most significant factors in the
dramatic drop in crime in New York City during the 1990s. During
a speech Bratton gave in 1999 in New York City, he decried these
interpretations. "There's a revolution going on in American policing,"
he said. Yet some people were attributing the lower crime rates to

"demographic or social changes that mystically caused this decrease in crime. Let me tell you that nothing infuriates me more. In fact . . . it drives me crazy!"[22]

Bratton saw the job with the LAPD as an opportunity to prove that his ideas were legitimate—that he really could turn around a major department, that it wasn't mere happenstance that had driven his success with the NYPD.[23]

Bratton hadn't been part of the Kroll independent monitor team in Los Angeles all that long—about fourteen months—when he left Kroll and put his name in the running for LAPD's chief of police, but he'd shown himself to be valuable. While some in the LAPD leadership had reservations about the consent decree in general and about cooperating with the independent monitor, Bratton had gone on ride-alongs in squad cars with officers and encouraged an atmosphere in which they could approach him and the independent monitor team to discuss departmental problems. City leaders appreciated his seemingly sensible suggestions, presented to the city council and the public in quarterly reports. One was to implement a data-driven "early warning" system that used the underlying principles of Compstat to identify specific cops who were at risk for misconduct. However, Bratton cautioned against adopting the program too quickly, urging "careful implementation" of the computerized system.[24] He maintained his role as a proponent of new tech, but he did so pragmatically. "He's an A-list candidate," said Los Angeles councilman Eric Garcetti when asked about Bratton's candidacy for chief. "Much of what he did in New York was pioneer work in policing. A world-class city like Los Angeles would definitely welcome his candidacy."[25]

In 2002, the LAPD was in a position similar to the NYPD's when Bratton took over that department in 1994: slowly emerging from a protracted and damaging scandal. After the Rodney King riots in 1992, longtime LAPD chief Daryl Gates—who had spearheaded the department's search for a nonlethal weapon and approved its initial purchase of Tasers in 1980—resigned under pressure from Los Angeles's mayor, Tom Bradley, and the Christopher Commission. His successor, Willie L. Williams, was the LAPD's first African American chief and brought with him a mandate to reform, but he found only modest success. Under Williams's watch, arrests increased and murder rates decreased—and, perhaps most significant, police relations with minority communities improved significantly. But he ran into political opposition and low approval ratings within the department. When Williams requested to be rehired for a second five-year term, the Los Angeles Police Commission cited his inability to push reforms within the department and denied his request.[26]

Though five years had passed since the Rodney King riots, little had changed within the department. Williams's successor didn't fare much better. Bernard C. Parks had similar problems winning over the LAPD brass, and, less than two years into his tenure, he faced the Rampart scandal—a clear indication that there had been no real attempt toward reform despite the swarm of controversies. Parks was forced out before the end of his term.

Meanwhile, crime rates were on their way up again. After years of declining crime rates through the 1990s, Los Angeles experienced three years of increases, and by 2002 had the highest number of killings of any U.S. city.[27] Between this and the widely publicized Rampart scandal, the LAPD was an ideal mark for the kind of "turnaround" rhetoric Bratton was using to promote himself—a strategy that combined increased data collection, accountability for commanders who didn't perform, and aggressive enforcement of petty crimes. There was a short list of contenders for the chief of police job—a few current and former high-ranking LAPD officials, as well as sitting chiefs in San Diego, Santa Ana, and Oxnard.[28] But Bratton began a lobbying campaign in July 2002, speaking publicly about his plans for the LAPD and his eagerness to take over. The committee in charge of selecting the LAPD's new chief was easily swayed in Bratton's direction—largely because he was a household name at that point. "Not many people can name police chiefs in America," said Los Angeles mayor James K. Hahn. "His is a name that people know."[29]

Bratton took over the LAPD in October 2002, bringing with him some key deputies from New York: Louis Anemone, who had been Jack Maple's second-in-command on the transit department's Compstat team; John Linder, the management professional who started a consulting business with Maple after Bratton's departure in the '90s; and John Miller, a close ally of Bratton's who had since joined the television news program *20/20* to cover international terrorism.[30]

RAY KELLY WASN'T just an NYPD veteran.

After fighting in the Vietnam War, he joined the NYPD in 1966 and served in various roles before ascending to lead the department as commissioner in 1992. After he was passed over to remain in that job when Giuliani became mayor, Kelly worked with the International Police Monitors of the Multinational Force in Haiti, then as undersecretary of the Treasury for Enforcement at the U.S. Department of the Treasury, and finally as commissioner of customs for the U.S. Customs Service, where he worked until 2001.

With those years of experience managing thousands of employees in the federal government, along with a deep understanding of how major federal agencies gathered information—and his decades of experience with the NYPD—Ray Kelly knew that he could bring a new perspective to the NYPD, forming a close partnership with the feds. In the early 2000s, with 9/11 still a fresh memory, the Bush administration was eager to aid local law enforcement throughout the country, but especially in New York City. Through the newly formed Department of Homeland Security, the feds began offering everything from soldiers to planes, antiaircraft weapons, and shared intelligence. Kelly, as the NYPD's new commissioner, was happy to accept the assistance, but he also emphasized that the city would have to take responsibility and act proactively on its own to combat terrorism. Kelly had a mandate and essentially a blank check from DHS to design his ideal counterterrorism program under the NYPD umbrella.

So in Kelly's first year on the job, he set about building this antiterrorism infrastructure within the NYPD. This new division, the Bureau of Counterterrorism, would move far beyond the typical mandates of a local police force.

"Look, it's a different world," Kelly explained to a *New York* magazine reporter. "We've redeployed. We've got 1,000 people on this . . . It's taken constant attention."

Perhaps the best representation of how Kelly used his mandate and his DHS funding was in the Bureau of Counterterrorism's Global Terrorism Room—a high-tech monitoring hub in an undisclosed location in one of New York City's outer boroughs. NYPD brass showed it to reporters and photographers to illustrate what the new high-tech terror war looked like. High-end audio and visual reconnaissance equipment—utilizing facial recognition and other biometric technologies—sat alongside intel on global terrorist organizations and a team of language specialists hired to monitor international news broadcasts for hints of potential threats. It took a total of one hundred twenty-five employees to staff this room, which operated twenty-four hours a day, seven days a week under Kelly's direction. From this central hub, the Bureau of Counterterrorism's reach would soon extend not just throughout the city but around the world. Kelly stationed officers with New Scotland Yard in London, at Interpol's headquarters in Lyons, and in other outposts in Toronto, Tel Aviv, Hamburg, and Washington, D.C. Officers were even sent as far afield as Afghanistan, Egypt, Yemen, and Pakistan on fact-finding missions. In New York City itself, intelligence reports from these far-flung missions were sent to police commanders who would then send teams of cops in black Chevy Suburbans to high-risk potential terror targets around the city—the Empire State Building, the New York Stock Exchange, or the Brooklyn Bridge. In short, Kelly was expanding the

NYPD's surveillance efforts to a level never before seen in the United States.[31]

ALL ACROSS THE country, attitudes on surveillance and privacy began to shift dramatically in the wake of 9/11. Calls seemed to come from every direction for developing new technologies and continuing to expand the reach of the cameras. Polemics against privacy appeared in newspapers and other media, many arguing that the potential benefits of constant surveillance outweighed the harms, since ordinary civilians were already under constant watch. Less than a year after the 9/11 attacks, for instance, the conservative *Boston Herald* columnist Beverly Beckham wrote a column praising the recent developments in security technology.

> The civil liberties people are furious. It's Big Brother snooping, they say, the government tromping on our ever-shrinking right to privacy. But is it? Isn't it a fact that we're being watched all the time anyway? We're watched in stores, in banks, in lobbies, in dressing rooms, in clubs, even at stoplights. We're monitored every time we use our Fast Lane pass or a Metro pass or our Visa cards or our bank cards. If we have a Global Positioning System in our car, there's a record of our every move. Our lives are an open book.[32]

With both law enforcement and many influential civilians voicing enthusiastic support for surveillance, businesses scurried to profit by developing new products and pushing old ones more aggressively. In the years that followed 9/11, Homeland Security agents began scouring emergent Silicon Valley companies for "computer programs that can constantly monitor video surveillance cameras and notify guards when something seems amiss," as one federal official told the *San Francisco Chronicle*.[33]

Viisage Technology and Graphco Technologies continued to

expand, selling the same facial recognition products they'd unveiled after the Super Bowl trial in Tampa.

One facial recognition competitor, a company called Identix Inc., loaned its cameras and facial recognition software to the NYPD to surveil the Statue of Liberty and Ellis Island. Some airports began to adopt biometric identification systems—including iris scanners and fingerprint readers—to perform security clearances.[34]

Despite a complete lack of any indication that the underlying technology worked, these biometric companies seemed impervious to failure so long as law enforcement leaders remained intrigued by their products' potential to increase safety even the slightest bit. Meanwhile, the two-year facial recognition trial in Tampa's Ybor City neighborhood was coming to an end. The goal had been to determine whether the facial recognition cameras were at all effective in deterring crime, but in the end they produced not a single match or arrest. "It's just proven not to have any benefit to us," a Tampa police spokesman said in 2003.[35] Tampa police suspended the program.

Critics were confused and alarmed at the apparent willingness to sacrifice privacy for even a mediocre improvement in security. It was as if the failure of the Ybor City trial didn't matter.

In a column for the *St. Petersburg Times*, Robyn E. Blumner, a lawyer and former executive director of American Civil Liberties Union affiliates in Florida and Utah, conceded that deploying facial recognition at airports might seem futile and unobtrusive—comparable to security agents confiscating tweezers out of carry-on luggage. But she warned that accepting the technology now might have unforeseen consequences in the future. "While face recognition products might not be advanced enough yet to peruse a crowd and successfully identify every person who corresponds to the database, one day they might be," she wrote. "At that point the government would have the tools to track us wherever we are and wherever we go."[36]

WHEN BILL BRATTON took over the LAPD in 2002, he started by directing his team to conduct a "cultural diagnostic"—a survey in which officers could say what they thought the department's problems were and what changes might help. Even though Bratton had already been working with the department for more than a year as part of the court-appointed independent monitor team, he still felt he lacked a comprehensive understanding of the department's problems. Bratton would later say that the survey responses showed "how dysfunctional" the LAPD was.[37]

Changing the culture from the ground up would be a tall order. Perhaps taking a cue from the usefulness of the survey, Bratton decided to begin by expanding the department's collection of data.[38] A top priority, he said, would be tracking gang activity with a program that used information collected directly from community and church leaders. Police commanders would meet with these leaders and share information they had gathered about local gang activities and the community leaders would do the same.

In these meetings, however, there were hints that this data-gathering effort was worrisome to some. At least one activist during an April 2003 community meeting referred to the new gang-focused Compstat effort as an "oversized snitch program" built to "cover up strong-arm tactics" with the tacit approval of the church leaders.[39] But the program seemed to work. After an initial uptick in gang killings during Bratton's first months in office, gang activity soon declined, and before long he had won the support of a majority of Angelenos and city leaders.[40]

The focus on data didn't end with the community. Bratton began to see the LAPD as a kind of policing laboratory that could experiment with collecting different kinds of information and then determine what its potential applications might be. His longtime collaborator the former *20/20* journalist John Miller soon took charge of the LAPD's Counter-Terrorism and Criminal Intelligence Bureau, a project developed in Bratton's first year as LAPD chief, which would serve as a

kind of fusion center within the LAPD, facilitating intelligence sharing with federal, state, and local agencies.[41]

LAW ENFORCEMENT AGENCIES around the country used local and
federal funds to install more cameras and tap into a growing federal
surveillance infrastructure designed to surveil pretty much everyone,
all the time. One federal program took this to a point of either omi-
nousness or self-parody, depending on one's point of view.

In 2003, the Defense Advanced Research Projects Agency, or
DARPA, launched a program that it called Total Information Awareness, or TIA. Its goal was to amass the video from every one of the
country's three million surveillance cameras and statistical data from
all eighteen thousand law enforcement agencies in one central database. The program's announcement immediately drew intense criticism.

"The growing piles of data being collected on Americans represent
an enormous invasion of privacy, but our privacy has actually been
protected by the fact that all this information still remains scattered
across many different databases," wrote ACLU representatives Jay
Stanley and Barry Steinhardt in a report on the program. "As a result,
there exists a pent-up capacity for surveillance in American life
today—a capacity that will be fully realized if the government, land-
lords, employers, or other powerful forces gain the ability to draw
together all this information."[42]

TIA could do that, Stanley and Steinhardt warned.

"A particular piece of data about you—such as the fact that you
entered your office at 10:29 AM on July 5, 2001—is normally innocuous," they continued. "But when enough pieces of that kind of data
are assembled together, they add up to an extremely detailed and intru-
sive picture of an individual's life and habits."[43]

Concerns like these received a significant amount of attention in the
media. They were met almost immediately with arguments from those

who, like the *Boston Herald* columnist Beverly Beckham, argued that our information was already out there—so why shouldn't the federal government use it to keep us safe?

New Yorkers would soon find out why.

WHEN RAY KELLY was building the NYPD's Bureau of Counterterrorism on the other side of the country, he tapped CIA official David Cohen in 2002 to be his deputy commissioner for intelligence. Cohen had been in charge of clandestine services for the U.S. Central Intelligence Agency and had once served as its deputy director for operations. To Kelly, the decision to bring in someone from the nation's most prominent surveillance operation made sense. "Our intention is to work more closely with the federal government," he said at the time. "To do that, we had to put in place a structure to train our officers and find people from outside the police culture to do it."[44]

But a crucial difference between the CIA and the NYPD was the former agency's mandate to gather intelligence internationally, while the latter's was to serve and protect American citizens. CIA leaders and agents therefore, unlike the police, were not accustomed to working within the constraints of constitutional rules. CIA agents didn't need to obtain a warrant before gathering intelligence on specific individuals, for example, nor did they need to read anyone their Miranda rights under any circumstances. But if bringing a CIA-style influence into the NYPD led to some civil rights being curtailed, Kelly reasoned, it was worth the trouble. "Our whole world has changed as a result of Sept. 11," he said shortly after announcing Cohen's appointment.

The full consequences of that appointment would not be felt until two years later, in the wake of the 2004 Republican National Convention, held in New York City's Madison Square Garden from August 30 through September 2. Inside the event, thousands of RNC leaders and members, along with reporters, lobbyists, and other interested parties from around the world, gathered to laud President

George W. Bush and his vice president, Dick Cheney, for their robust response to 9/11, which grew larger and more expensive by the day. Outside, tens of thousands of demonstrators railed against the amorphous War on Terror.

Protests at political conventions aren't just common; they're expected—by civilians and law enforcement alike. But the policing of the RNC protests was more aggressive than anyone predicted. The funding for such an extreme response, which ran into the tens of millions of dollars, was made possible because the Department of Homeland Security declared the convention a "National Special Security Event," automatically opening up the federal government's massive wallet. For its part in that response, the NYPD deployed at least ten thousand cops, carrying submachine guns and rifles, to patrol the streets of New York City. Cops from around the nation volunteered to help them. They were all uniformed in body armor and riot gear; bomb-sniffing dogs were stationed on commuter trains, and everyone within a block of the Garden went through a security check.

Even considering the great expense and effort invested in securing the convention, the number of arrests police carried out that week was still astounding. In all, more than eighteen hundred people found themselves in handcuffs for either protesting or merely being in the vicinity of protests at the RNC. By comparison, the DHS gave the same "National Special Security Event" designation to the Democratic party's national convention in Boston earlier that summer—and the federal government provided approximately the same amount of funding to the Boston Police Department, which in turn deployed an equivalent force to patrol and protect the event. But fewer than ten people were arrested in Boston for protest activities.

What was happening in New York City during the RNC?

One factor, of course, may have been that there was an angrier, more robust opposition to the RNC that year than to the DNC. The Republicans were in power, they were setting the agenda, and their policies, which took a narrow view of civil liberties, offended a large coalition of libertarians and those on the left. So it made sense that arrests might be higher at the RNC than at the DNC. But there was more going on. In the end, the city dropped a vast majority of the charges against the RNC protesters. When reporters began to look into the police's tactics and when lawsuits forced the release of NYPD documents, a troubling story began to emerge.

For more than a year prior to the Republican convention, officers with NYPD's intelligence division had, under the leadership of David Cohen, conducted surveillance missions in which officers infiltrated community meetings and political action groups across the country. The operations represented an unprecedented expansion of the NYPD's mandate and authority as the department took on functions that seemed more characteristic of law enforcement under oppressive dictatorships: surveilling groups of people based on their political affiliations and then throwing them behind bars for voicing dissent.[45]

It took about three years for this information to come to light; the details came only when the city was forced through a court order to disclose hundreds of pages of documents outlining surveillance activities. What those documents showed was that the NYPD had gone after anyone who expressed any interest in dissent at the RNC event. Groups with names as innocuous as September 11 Families for Peaceful Tomorrows were tracked alongside groups such as the Ku Klux Klan and the Westboro Baptist Church. Satirical situationist groups such as the Surveillance Camera Players were surveilled alongside major national groups such as the American Civil Liberties Union, the DNC, the Sierra Club, the National Lawyers Guild, and the National Council of Arab Americans. In all, some three hundred groups had been tracked.[46]

Commissioner Kelly was unapologetic.

"I think a close examination of the documents is going to show that the New York City Police Department did an outstanding job in protecting the City during the Republican National Convention," he said. "People wanted to come here and shut down the City, to replicate what happened in Seattle, Montreal and Genoa. We simply didn't let that happen, and I think it'll just underscore the outstanding work of the men and women of the Department."

Kelly went on to describe the way NYPD had gathered info. "The vast majority of information that was gathered was open-source information," he said. "It was gathered from the Internet; these groups that were coming here were advertising what they were going to do— bragging about what they were going to do. It wasn't particularly difficult to get the vast majority of this information."[47]

Civilians had done it to themselves, in other words.

WHILE RAY KELLY worked to deepen ties between the NYPD and federal agencies, Bill Bratton focused on encouraging his department to collaborate with private companies. The LAPD soon formed alliances with Cingular Wireless and BlackBerry to provide handheld devices to officers[48] and purchased, from a company called Vytex, Inc., twelve hundred Portable Officer Data Devices, or PODDs, handheld devices that allowed officers to scan identification cards at pedestrian and vehicular stops without returning to their vehicles.[49] Because the department remained under federal oversight owing to court-ordered reforms following the Rampart scandal, Bratton bought a $35 million computer system from Sierra Systems Group Inc. and Bearing-Point Inc. designed to track complaints and other officer-related data, as a way to identify bad cops.[50]

Around the country, more and more police departments, both large and small, were spending taxpayer cash on data-based programs similar to Compstat and other high-tech tools. These included departments from Dallas to Hartford, Boca Raton to Baltimore, Kansas City to Omaha and Chicago.

CHAPTER 6

THE WARNING LABEL

With the support of the federal government and endorsements from such big-name police chiefs as Ray Kelly and Bill Bratton, new technologies were quickly spreading to police departments all over the country. Taser International—the company at the center of it all—was making millions upon millions of dollars for its founders and investors. As 2004 drew to a close, those earnings showed no outward signs of slowing down. Taser International's stock value shot to an all-time high in early November 2004, and with good reason: net sales of its products had nearly quadrupled in comparison to the year before. Its products were being used by police officers all the time, all over the country. The company that had successfully branded itself as the face of the early twenty-first century's high-tech police revolution was a rousing success. So, too, was the promise that technology could revolutionize policing.

Taser shareholders would soon get an indication that something was amiss—and that the high-tech police revolution was perhaps built more on hype than on substance. On Christmas Eve 2004, an investigator for the U.S. Securities and Exchange Commission faxed Taser International a notification that the SEC was initiating an informal investigation into the company. At first, company leaders kept their shareholders in the dark. It was only after *Arizona Sun* reporter Robert Anglen learned of the investigation and sought a comment from the company's PR department that Taser International sent a letter to shareholders disclosing the SEC inquiry. On January 7, 2005, Alex Berenson at the *New York Times* and Anglen broke the story wide open, explaining that regulators were specifically investigating two things: whether Taser fraudulently inflated its sales figures to meet revenue targets and whether the Smiths misled shareholders about the safety of their company's weapons. On the matter of inflating sales figures, the SEC was specifically interested in two suspect fourth-quarter transactions that helped Taser International meet its revenue targets. On December 20, with the end of the quarter looming, Taser International had announced a $1.5 million sale of the consumer model Taser to one of its coziest distributors. The deal looked suspicious given the consumer model's previous record of tepid sales. On December 30, the last business day of the year, Taser booked a $700,000 sale with another distributor who wrote in the purchase order, "Hope this will help out!!!!"[1]

Over the four days following Anglen's and Berenson's reports, the company's stock cratered. On January 6, 2005, about 7.5 million Taser shares were traded on the open market; the next day, that number climbed to 35.7 million shares, and by January 13 nearly 70 million shares were traded in a single day. Short sellers made a fortune as bullish investors desperately tried to dump their Taser stock. Taser's price was cut nearly in half, from $27.62 on January 6 to $14.10 on January 11.

"The business we had built with the mission of making bullets obsolete was at risk of complete ruin if we handled this wrong," Rick Smith would later say.[2]

The way Rick spun it, he boldly went against the advice of his own attorneys to save his company: he marched into the SEC's San Francisco office and "simply gave them everything they were asking for—a transparency judo kick."

Whatever documents he turned over to the SEC, they didn't do much to help the company's overall position, which was deteriorating by the day. On January 10, 2005, mere days after the *Times* story broke, shareholders filed a class-action lawsuit against the company in Arizona's federal district court alleging fraud and insider trading. According to the lawsuit, the company's executives made deliberately false statements about the safety of Taser's weapons, exaggerated sales figures to mislead shareholders about the strength of the company, and acted on insider information to enrich themselves.[3]

Later, attorneys for the shareholders submitted a massive 149-page complaint, complete with testimony from Taser employees and insiders that painted a devastating portrait of the company's misdeeds and subsequent deceptions.[4] The most straightforward charge was Taser's misrepresentation of the safety of its product. The plaintiffs pointed to medical examiners' reports and a handful of studies—including research from Amnesty International—showing that Tasers were capable of causing fatal injuries and that company executives either actively misrepresented or ignored such information to make the weapons seem safer than they were. The complaint also alleged that Taser suffered from massive quality control and manufacturing failures that management purposefully hid in order to meet the company's aggressive sales and production targets.

The ever-increasing expectations of both shareholders and customers had put immense pressure on Taser's management to keep pace. In 1999, when Rick sold the first M26 Tasers to the NYPD, the company's operation was still quite small—a bit of office space and a modest warehouse in a nondescript industrial park in Scottsdale. At the time, the Smiths were personally helping to fill orders—spinning copper wire around coils in the back of their warehouse alongside workers. By 2004, the Smiths were successful enough that they could work in the front office only; they were selling tens of thousands of Tasers a quarter, all of them still assembled by hand. The company, the shareholders alleged, simply wasn't able to effectively control quality given the size and scale at which it was operating.

Six former employees familiar with the company's manufacturing process and a master instructor who also worked as a distributor for Taser spoke confidentially to the shareholders' lawyers in the class-action lawsuit. They claimed that both the M26 and X26 were "plagued by design flaws and manufacturing process problems that caused massive product returns and weapon malfunctions"—most of which were not reported to shareholders.[5] The alleged defects varied. Some Tasers purportedly failed to fire. Some failed to *stop* firing electricity when users released the trigger, due to an "unstable" circuit board design. Some supposedly had badly soldered joints, which caused them to break easily. As many as 70 percent of the M26 and X26 devices tested in-house were defective, according to one witness. "There was absolutely no standard manufacturing process," said another, who added that factory workers didn't even have assembly manuals.

There was little chance that any of this had escaped the Smiths' attention. The shareholders alleged that the high failure rates and lack of quality control were frequent topics of conversation at production meetings that they attended. Though the company's official policy was to set aside defective Tasers, one warehouse manager was allegedly fired for repeatedly complaining about the company's lack of quality control. After confronting Rick about the malfunctioning Tasers, one witness claimed that Rick delivered a clear directive in response: "Just get them out." That is, send them out to police departments, despite whatever flaws may exist. "As long as they sparked, we would ship them out," the witness said. According to another, "the quota went up every quarter. They wanted to keep ramping it up to meet the expectations [of the shareholders]."

The testimony piled up. Another witness claimed that Taser's manufacturing workers "were forced to build 7,000 to 10,000 a month. It was like they would just ship anything out to meet demand." One said, "They were shipping out guns that were poor quality to make their numbers. We got cash bonuses if we got a certain number of units out the door. There was a lot of shady stuff going on. I quit my job because of it." Still another recalled, "The impression that I had is that Taser wanted to get them done and put them out there as quick as possible because the sooner you get them out the door, the sooner you can show them as actual sales."

While Taser International eagerly advertised the number of weapons that went out the door, few outside the company realized how many were being sent back. "We're talking pallets of returns," said one witness. In the summer of 2003, customers allegedly returned about six thousand M26 Tasers due to malfunctioning circuit boards. Two witnesses said employees were instructed to remove the boards, which were then placed in new casings with new serial numbers and reshipped without fixing the problem. The X26, which debuted in 2003, was supposedly even less stable than the M26. A witness claimed there was a "tidal wave" of X26 returns in early 2004—so many that Taser International had to set up an extra room in a building across the street to hold them and hired three additional employees to process them.[6]

In a motion to dismiss the shareholders' lawsuit, Taser's lawyers argued that the confidential witnesses were unreliable, and that, even if they were telling the truth, "these issues are no more than routine, daily matters facing manufacturing companies like Taser." The shareholders, however, took a different view. They believed the company's management had been willfully negligent in an effort to prop up Taser's stock, and then had cashed in on privileged information by selling shares before the stock price tanked.

The complaint also asserted that the Department of Defense study in late 2004 that seemed to bolster the claim that Tasers were safe was, in fact, fraudulent. Executives and insiders had made a combined $85 million selling shares after the stock boost produced by that report.

Even so, safety questions had continued to weigh the company down, causing sales to slow. To compensate, Taser's executives allegedly fudged sales to meet revenue projections and keep the stock price high. One confidential witness said it was common for distributors to order extra Tasers at the end of quarters when Taser's sales staff was struggling to meet its targets. Then Taser would allow the distributor to return the Tasers at the start of the next quarter. "They had to call it a defect, otherwise they couldn't return it, even if they called it an 'unfounded defect,'" the witness said. This pattern was corroborated by the two late December 2004 sales that the SEC was already investigating, including the one with the message "Hope this will help out!!!!" appended.

WHILE TASER DENIED any wrongdoing, Rick Smith's choices were catching up to him, and his company was headed for a reckoning.

In their letter to shareholders announcing the SEC investigation, the Smiths tried to reassure investors. They admitted, however, that between the SEC investigation and lingering safety concerns, law enforcement agencies may become wary of their product and sales would likely take a hit in the coming months.

Adding to the bad news, reporter Robert Anglen published a story on Sam Powers, a Maricopa County sheriff's deputy who had volunteered for a Taser demonstration and claimed that the weapon caused his muscles to contract so hard that he fractured his T7 vertebra. Powers's claim directly contradicted one of Taser's favorite talking points: that no officer of the tens of thousands who had volunteered to be shocked had ever been seriously injured. Though the company's own doctor agreed Powers's injury was caused by the Taser, in its public financial disclosures, Taser continually said Powers was seeking damages for an alleged shoulder injury. "They're telling their shareholders, 'Well, Powers is just complaining about a shoulder injury.' No, he's complaining about a fractured back!" Anglen said.[7]

The Powers story opened the floodgates. Dozens of other officers claimed to have been seriously hurt after voluntarily getting shocked in training. The injuries included fractured vertebrae, ruptured disks, severe burns, and nerve damage. Some officers alleged that their injuries forced them to quit the police force early. One officer committed suicide several years after he was injured.

Rick and Tom Smith's executive assistant at the time, Pamela Schreiner, would later reportedly testify during a deposition that Taser executives not only had known about the injuries, but had ordered her to bury the evidence. After the Smiths learned of the SEC investigation, she said, she helped the Smiths to shred reports of officer injuries.

Taser International had become a toxic investment. In April 2005, a year after the company had been valued at $1.9 billion, Taser's stock had plummeted to less than $8 a share—a drop of nearly 77 percent. In May, Anglen's report on the Department of Defense study completely undermined Taser's most significant piece of "independent" research, accelerating the freefall. Before long, just as Taser executives feared, enthusiasm among officers began to wane. For the first six months of 2005, the company's net income was a paltry $677,069—a fraction of the more than $8 million it had earned during the first six months of the previous year.[8]

By September, when the SEC upgraded its inquiry to an official investigation,[9] Taser stock bottomed out at $5.42 per share. It seemed quite possible that Taser International was not going to survive.

Still, Rick Smith refused to back down on safety issues. During a call on October 26, 2005, about the company's latest earnings report, Rick told shareholders that "there doesn't necessarily seem to be a correlation or plausible relation" between Taser shocks and death. Instead, he blamed "other factors such as drug use" for any fatalities. The hard times would pass, he told shareholders.

There was no spinning how brutal 2005 was for Taser International, but Rick Smith knew he had to keep up the fight. Despite the company's precarious financial situation, he moved Taser International in the second quarter of 2005 into a new corporate headquarters—a one-hundred-thousand-square-foot[10] fortress that he had built to resemble a battleship, complete with a retina scanner in the front atrium and a secret top-floor research lab. The building was a reflection of Smith's personal commitment to never surrender. This was war, and Rick was determined to write his own history.

AS HE HAD promised in the shareholder earnings call, 2006 was a "very exciting year" for the company, an opportunity for a turnaround. To combat reports about Taser-related deaths, Tom and Rick Smith promoted a range of alternate theories, including the notion that the fatalities were really caused by drug use. But the explanation that resonated most with cops was that civilians were simply lying. Taser decided to capitalize on this by marketing a new solution: the Taser Cam.

Introduced in 2006, the Taser Cam was a simple idea: a camera would be affixed to the bottom of the X26's grip, pointing in the same direction as the barrel. When the Taser's trigger was pulled, the camera would begin recording. In practice, the cameras were more problematic than anticipated: they turned the sleeker and lighter X26 devices into bulky, unwieldy weapons. They were also costly to produce and almost immediately began eating into the company's profits. But the cameras sent a message to shareholders and to the public: Taser was now all about transparency.

One of the Taser Cam's first customers was Joe Arpaio, the controversial sheriff who then oversaw Maricopa County, Arizona. Officers in the county's correctional facilities had already been outfitted with regular Tasers, but upon hearing of the company's new offering in 2006, Arpaio decided to give them an upgrade, buying 623 Taser Cams at a cost of $1,199 each.

"Now we'll have proof of the situation a detention officer is in when he deploys a Taser," Arpaio said in a news conference. "Everything's on camera, and we'll have nothing to hide. It's about the safety of the people."[11]

While imperfect in its design, the Taser Cam represented a shrewd new way of marketing the company. If journalists and pundits on CNBC were going to claim Taser hid information from the public, the Smiths were going to paint the exact opposite picture. If a suspect accused a cop of using a Taser improperly, the Taser Cam would provide a record of the incident in dispute. Quality complaints soon emerged about the Taser Cam itself—about the awkward angle and low resolution of the video—but the Smiths viewed those complaints as less important than creating the impression that Taser International was radically transparent.

Rick was working on a similar strategy to the one he'd begun back in the early weeks of January 2005 when he dropped in to the SEC's San Francisco office with piles of documents to deliver a "transparency judo kick." By early 2006, Smith and Taser's executives had sat for numerous interviews with SEC investigators and offered their attorneys a massive, overwhelming cache of at least seven thousand pages of records, including training manuals, studies, and e-mails—a significant portion of which didn't relate to the focus of the investigation at all. This was the new, open-book Taser International.

WHETHER IT WAS Taser's transparency push, or the fact that the Bush administration had recently slashed the SEC's budget, or some combination of factors, Taser International escaped the SEC's inquiry relatively unscathed. On May 11, 2006, the SEC sent a letter to Taser informing executives that the investigation had been terminated "in its entirety with no recommendation of enforcement action," according to a statement from the company.

One major hurdle crossed, Taser's stock immediately rose.[12]

Though the lawsuit filed by shareholders in January 2005 was still

ongoing, it focused on many of the same allegations as the SEC investigation. It was, ultimately, a creature of the SEC's inquiry: threat of
enforcement action by the federal regulator sank the company's earnings, and shareholder losses could have ended up being incredibly
high if the SEC took serious action. Taser might have even folded
in response.

But the SEC did not take serious action, and with that threat gone,
it appeared the company's path would be much easier. Shareholders
had lost money, yes, but the tide of their losses had been stemmed; it
was now fairly clear how much they had lost.

Lawyers representing the shareholders thus began discussing a settlement agreement that would mitigate the losses. Three months after
the SEC investigation closed, in August 2006, Taser admitted no
wrongdoing and agreed to pay shareholders $20 million to settle the
case. Some protested: at least eighteen shareholders filed official objec-
tions with the court. But the settlement was eventually approved and
the case closed in March 2007.

It was a landmark for the company—the event that would allow
it finally to move beyond the troubles that began in January 2005.

WHICH TASER INSIDERS would be there to help the company move on?

Rick Smith's most trusted advisors were almost all company lifers
who had been there with him through Taser's early wars: his brother,
Tom; their father, Phil; company spokesman Steve Tuttle; and chief
electrical engineer Max Nerheim. "I think loyalty's a big thing with
Rick," said Dr. Wayne McDaniel, a key player himself in the company's history. "If he sees you as not being loyal, then you're gone."[13]

That's why McDaniel took his own banishment from the inner
circle so personally. He believed that he and his partner Dr. Robert
Stratbucker had proven their loyalty during the early safety tests they
conducted on the Smiths' behalf. Their fatal error, he later realized,
had been their caution. McDaniel and Stratbucker were unwilling to

say "never" when it came to the question of whether Tasers could cause a death. According to McDaniel, their eventual replacement was happy to oblige the Smiths on this point. "Kroll, when he got in there, he said, 'It can't happen. No way, on God's green earth, it just can't happen.'"

Dr. Mark Kroll, a biomedical engineer then serving as the chief technology officer of a medical device manufacturer, became Taser International's official medical director in January 2003. He was an outsider, and Rick Smith was initially cautious. But Kroll had impressive credentials, and Phil Smith pushed his son to include Kroll as a way of bolstering Taser's scientific legitimacy—he had advanced degrees in electrical engineering and held hundreds of patents.

Perhaps more important to Taser, he outwardly projected a scientific manner—he looked the part, with a slight resemblance to Bill Nye, from his haircut to his trademark bow tie. After joining Taser International, he quickly earned a reputation for bombastic rhetoric that exceeded even Rick Smith's claims. "You have Tylenol in your home? As far as an electronic control device killing you, this stuff is safer than Tylenol," he said in front of an audience of hundreds of medical examiners, emergency room physicians, and police officers at a conference in 2007.[14]

Both McDaniel and longtime Taser employee Mike Leonesio claimed that Kroll was the driving force behind the company's dubious decision to define the Taser's electrical output in safety tests using average current, a method of calculation that significantly underestimated both the power and the danger of the weapon.[15] "I have no respect for Kroll as a scientist," McDaniel said. "He writes papers with no data. He just does these thought experiments." Still, Dr. Kroll had a first-rate résumé, and—as even McDaniel acknowledged—he was "a very convincing person."

As Taser International's medical director, Kroll downplayed issues with the Taser's safety to everyone concerned—police officers, medical examiners, and government officials—even as the body count continued to climb. To do this, he formed Taser's Science and Medical Advisory Board (SMAB) in 2004, just as the debate over the weapon's safety was reaching a fever pitch. The board's primary objective was to facilitate the publication of studies and articles that reinforced the Smith brothers' safety claims—namely that Tasers, categorically, could not kill—all authored by well-regarded doctors and researchers. The authors of these studies, according to McDaniel, had something else in common as well: they were all "Kroll handpicked devotees . . . his good buds." Kroll's goal, he explained, was total dominance: "Once Kroll came on board, he controlled the dialogue. He didn't want anyone challenging him."[16]

Mike Leonesio began working with Taser's SMAB after becoming a master instructor in 2005. As he explained it,

> they did all their own research, which was just total crap . . . They would not do a study if they knew, or if they had a good idea, that the result was going to be negative. I've been involved in some of the medical studies where things went bad, and animals died, and they never published that. The only thing you ever see them publish is stuff that makes them look good.[17]

According to McDaniel, the company was overt about its desire for studies that fit neatly into its narrative.

> The research hasn't been to try to find out what's happening. The research has been, 'Give me evidence that I can present in court that shows we're not liable.' . . . I think that really became their focus. What they didn't want was any explanation out there that— maybe—they were causing some of these deaths.[18]

Another alternate theory offered up by Taser International's executives and allies was something called "excited delirium."

Excited delirium is a dubious syndrome that supposedly makes people violent, erratic, and uncontrollable—and occurs mostly in long-term drug users and those with mental illness. Some say it can be traced all the way back to the 1840s, but the syndrome first gained widespread recognition during the drug-fueled club scene of the 1980s, when it was used as a kind of shoulder-shrug diagnosis by medical examiners, emergency room physicians, and police officers to explain growing numbers of people who were, according to authorities, acting with wild abandon, injuring themselves and others—and, in too many cases, dying at the hands of law enforcement officers. The symptoms almost always included some combination of paranoia, profuse sweating, irrational behavior, imperviousness to pain, and superhuman strength. Advocates insisted that excited delirium was a medical emergency that required immediate treatment. But while it was interesting to a handful of researchers throughout the 1980s and 1990s, excited delirium wasn't widely accepted as a medical diagnosis.[19] Starting in 2005, however, Taser International began to make it famous in law enforcement circles.

In the instructor notes for Version 12 of Taser International's training material, first released in November 2004, Taser trainers were directed to tell officers that deaths "typically involved suspects undergoing toxic drug use and/or excited delirium." Officers were to be warned to look for "erratic" behavior, including "overheating while still being naked in extremely cold weather, biting a deputy's ear off in a fight, breaking hobble restraints while in custody, nonsensical language, running amok, fighting family members, extreme self-mutilation, etc."[20]

The manual then directed instructors to say something that seemed somewhat tangential: "With over 150 law enforcement agencies purchasing new Taser nonlethal devices per month, the chances of encountering suspects involving toxic drug use and excited delirium will surely increase."

Matt Masters, an officer with the Kansas City Police Department, was sold on the concept of excited delirium when he was trained to use a Taser by a master instructor representing the company. "They have this science that they say proves the Taser doesn't kill, and it looks legit," he said. "Then they have this other excuse: 'It's drugs, it's the physical resisting that made their heart give out, it's excited delirium.'" Because these talking points are coming "from someone [whom trainees] automatically assume knows what they're talking about," he continued, "that's just accepted."[21]

The problem with excited delirium as a diagnosis is that it lacks a clear pathology to link the symptoms directly to death. Excited delirium is not recognized by the American Medical Association, nor can it be found in the *Diagnostic and Statistical Manual of Mental Disorders*. Critics argued (and still argue) that it was a convenient catchall to justify Taser-related deaths.

"Taser made excited delirium the bogeyman," Masters said. "And their weapon was the only way to kill the monster."

Even when Taser-involved deaths couldn't possibly be attributed to excited delirium because they didn't involve people on drugs, with mental problems, or who fought with police, Kroll and Taser International's other representatives were ready with a broader list of potential causes: preexisting heart conditions, diabetes, stress of police interaction, obesity, untreated mental illness—anything except the Taser shock itself.

With Dr. Kroll leading the charge, Taser International began a campaign to, as executives put it, "educate" medical examiners and scientists who might study the Taser. Taser employees contacted both law enforcement agencies and these examiners immediately after a Taser-related death to offer assistance. They sent unsolicited literature about the Taser's purported safety to medical examiners around the country, and representatives like Dr. Kroll attended conferences where medical examiners gathered.

When medical investigations of Taser-related incidents produced results that didn't fit with the company's narrative, both its PR and legal teams kicked into high gear. In one instance, Taser sued two medical examiners to get findings reversed, saying they didn't have the proper background to make the claim that the weapon had contributed to deaths.

"We will hold people accountable and responsible for untrue statements," Steve Tuttle said. "If that includes medical examiners, it includes medical examiners."[22]

Rick Smith insisted that the lawsuits were simply meant to support officers who were facing criminal charges because of the medical examiners' findings. By getting the rulings reversed from "homicide" to "undetermined," he said, Taser International was able to protect the officers involved from criminal liability.

To critics, though, Taser's tactics were terrifying.

"It is dangerously close to intimidation," Jeff Jentzen, president of the National Association of Medical Examiners, told the *Arizona Republic*. "At this point, we adamantly reject the fact that people can be sued for the medical opinions they make."

Rick Smith had doubled down on his scorched-earth strategy, and it was working. Sales jumped from about $67 million in 2006 to just north of $100 million in 2007. Some 12,400 police departments were using Tasers, with more coming on board each month. Smith turned the controversy surrounding his company's weapon into a culture war, and at least among law enforcement officers his side was winning. As Matt Masters, the officer with the Kansas City Police Department, put it, cops "believe the Taser training because we want it to be true. We want Tasers, and we don't want to believe we're responsible when we kill someone with one." The Smiths, Mark Kroll, and everyone at Taser International were able to successfully convince officers that Taser's interests were the same as their own. "They make all the cops feel like they're your best friend," Masters said. "I truly don't understand how we could've been so stupid. I've really struggled with that . . . All we had to do was ask the right questions."[23]

ON JUNE 6, 2008, a federal jury in Salinas, California, awarded more than $6 million in damages to the family of Robert Heston, who had died after being shocked at least twenty-five times in the span of seventy-four seconds by officers of the Salinas Police Department.[24] Though the payout was later significantly reduced on appeal, the decision was remarkable; it was the first time that Taser International was held liable, in a U.S. court, for a "negligent failure to warn" that its weapons could cause cardiac arrest. Heston's case marked the tip of the iceberg for Taser. The company had always been the target of product liability lawsuits. But this set a new precedent for the company's legal exposure. As 2008 wore on, the company would face dozens of similar cases trying to take advantage of the Heston findings.

It was becoming nearly impossible to manage. And then, in June 2009, it became untenable. More than a year and a half earlier, Royal Canadian Mounted Police in the Vancouver International Airport had shocked and killed a Polish immigrant, Robert Dziekański, with a Taser. Subsequently, a group of Canadian public officials known as the Braidwood Commission investigated the incident and the RCMP's use of Tasers—as well as Taser International's sales tactics and training protocols. In June 2009, the commission released the first phase of a groundbreaking report. Its central point was that Tasers could kill—or, to be precise, that the electricity of a Taser shock could overpower the rhythms of a person's heart and ultimately cause cardiac arrest. Furthermore, it asserted that multiple shocks and shocks close to the chest could exacerbate the risk. The report recommended that police completely rethink the way they interact with people who resist arrest as well as those with mental health issues. Much to the Smiths' frustration, the report even directly refuted the company's favored theory for explaining away Taser-related deaths.

"It is not helpful to blame resulting deaths on 'excited delirium,'" the report read, "since this conveniently avoids having to examine the underlying medical condition or conditions that actually caused death, let alone examining whether use of the conducted energy weapon and/

or subsequent measures to physically restrain the subject contributed to those causes of death."[25]

These findings—years in the making—represented the most comprehensive look thus far into the dangers that Tasers posed. The report completely contradicted what the Smiths had been saying for years to regulators, the police, the press, and the public. Even though the report was Canadian, it would be highly influential in the United States, especially coming on the heels of the Heston ruling. For its entire existence, Taser had reiterated again and again that its weapons were nonlethal. And it was because of this basic premise that the company began encouraging officers to use them indiscriminately, even in low-risk situations—in other words, "Taser early and often," as the mantra went.

The Braidwood inquiry shattered the company's "nonlethal" argument and, most important, forced Taser to do something it had never done before: admit fault.

DURING THE LATE 2000s, Taser International would send out training bulletins every few weeks to all the police departments that used its weapons. These were typically single- or double-page documents with new corporate developments or information about online training courses. The bulletin on September 30, 2009, was a stark departure. This bulletin was not one or two but eighteen pages, divided into two sections. Most significant, it included a warning label—a never-before-seen sticker that would be affixed to Tasers—and a callout box that would be printed on Taser training materials. Matchbook-size, it contained a yellow caution-sign illustration of a flailing figure with wires attached to its chest.

The warning read: "Electronic control device . . . Can cause injury."

(Later versions were amended to read: "Can cause death or serious injury.")

While the eighteen-page bulletin went to great lengths to qualify and minimize the possibility of death, it nevertheless acknowledged that a Taser shock to the chest could cause cardiac arrest. Taser salespeople and instructors had been saying for years that shots to the chest were both acceptable and expected. Now, a 180-degree shift, in obfuscatory legalese: "In order to increase the safety margin . . . users should aim for the back or (when practical) toward the mid lower abdomen and avoid intentionally targeting the chest area with probe applications to increase effectiveness and avoid the remote potential risk of cardiac effect."[26]

The warning sent a profoundly confusing message and perplexed cops across the country.

"It hit hard," said Mike Leonesio, then an officer with the police department in Oakland, California, and a certified Taser master instructor. "Agencies are looking at this, saying, 'Wait a minute. You've been telling us for years that these things are supposed to be safe, and now you're telling us not to hit the chest?'"

Many departments were ready to take Tasers off the streets, Leonesio said. "Taser was freaking out."[27]

The company quickly issued a follow-up bulletin in which Taser's vice president of training, Rick Guilbault, claimed that the new warnings and guidelines were meant only as "best practices risk management and to avoid any excessive use-of-force claim or litigation against law enforcement." But this failed to assuage police concerns. "What it did was create a ton of confusion," Leonesio said. "It was a bunch of hogwash. You could see right through it."[28]

Taser was getting calls from police all over the country who were unsure about how to interpret the new directives. Rick Smith decided to confront the situation head on, in two conference calls with officers and police leaders on consecutive days in October 2009, during which he would answer questions about the bulletin and the follow-up letter.

The first call started slightly late; law enforcement professionals from all over the country sat on hold for about five minutes while airy rock music played on a loop. Then Rick picked up the line: "Are chest hits with the Taser dangerous? The answer to that is definitively no." He went on: "As I pointed out in the e-mail announcing this call, the most prominent plaintiff's expert against Taser estimates the risk of VF"—meaning ventricular fibrillation, the potentially life-threatening disturbance of the heart's natural rhythm—"from a Taser shot at 0.0000061 [percent]. That's a probability of one in 163,000." It's unclear where Smith came up with that number, as it seems impossibly low considering the hundreds of people who, by October 2009, had been killed after being shocked with Tasers. But his point was clear: "To put that in perspective, the probability of everybody on this call being killed in a car accident within the next year is one in ten thousand. So we're talking about something with less than 10 percent that probability being killed with a Taser hit."[29]

Dr. Jeffrey D. Ho, a Minneapolis-based doctor who conducted research for Taser International, chimed in: "The chest shot is not prohibited. I think it's a great idea from a litigation risk management standpoint to try and take that argument off the table, but from a medical risk standpoint . . . I don't think there's any issue with applying a Taser to somebody's chest." Ho concluded: "The risk of inducing something harmful from a chest shot is so close to zero that I wouldn't know how to characterize it other than rounding to zero."

The confusion was understandable. There was—both on the call and, previously, in the bulletin and the letter—a sense that Taser was attempting to deliver two contradictory messages simultaneously. Rather than "aiming for center mass"—as every police officer in the country had been trained for generations to do with firearms—police would now need to aim Tasers differently, with new caution. Was the Taser nonlethal or lethal? It was unclear. On the call, an officer from the Chicago Police Department put the question directly to Rick: "What I need to do is clarify target area, and exactly why we're lowering the point of the target . . . to avoid striking the chest," the officer said.

After a pause and some stammering, Rick responded:

Of course, as situations evolve and escalate, and people are moving around, you're going to hit 'em where you can hit 'em. We will stand behind you with that. But if you've got the time and opportunity, on the subject—and particularly if you're real close in where you're firing it at 'em—we're just sayin' go down into the abdomen. It's more effective, and it avoids all this controversy.

The officer dug in. "So," he asked, "there is an acknowledgment that there's a minute possibility that a shot to the chest could result in cardiac arrest?"

Rick paused again. "I think the better way that I would answer that . . . is that we cannot prove it's zero. And that seems to be the standard that many of the public interest groups are hung up on."

He was right that public interest groups were involved—but so were the courts, and they had now ruled against Taser International. Many of the police on the call were concerned about this. Would Taser go to bat for police departments in court if they were the target of a wrongful death lawsuit?

Rick addressed these concerns as well: "The answer is unequivocally, yes. We pride ourselves that we stand up for our technology and for officers here."

Doug Klint, the company's primary staff attorney, backed up this promise.

"We will do everything we can to defend law enforcement," he said.

BUT WHEN IT comes to defending law enforcement in court, Taser has been largely absent since 2009.

On January 20, 2010, less than three months after the company's conference call, a man named Kelly Brinson was admitted as a psychiatric patient to the University Hospital in Cincinnati, Ohio, where he quickly became agitated and combative with hospital staff. Seeing the seriousness of the situation, the staff called the University of Cincinnati police department and, before long, two officers rushed Brinson at the hospital. After a tense interaction between the officers, a doctor, and Brinson in a hallway, Brinson voluntarily walked into a "seclusion room." When the doctors and officers entered the room, Brinson backed himself into one of its corners. Brinson had been given a cocktail of medications—including Haldol, Ativan, and Benadryl—to sedate him. But the drugs hadn't yet taken hold. According to eyewitness accounts (a video of the incident was allegedly destroyed), one of the officers took charge and approached Brinson in the corner, pointing a Taser at his chest, trying to get him to put handcuffs on and sit compliantly. A wrestling match followed as the officers attempted to bring Brinson to the ground.[30]

In the process, they shocked him with a Taser repeatedly, and he quickly went into cardiac arrest. He died three days later.

When Brinson's family filed a lawsuit against the doctors, nurses, and police officers involved, they did not target Taser International.[31] Instead, citing the warning label in Taser's own training materials, they assigned the blame to the individual officers involved in the case. The warning label, the family contended, was "known to the Police Defendants" and made clear that

> the device can cause "serious injury or death . . . especially at risk are persons . . . who are physically infirm." The label also warns of dangers to "physiologically or metabolically compromised persons." Finally the label also warns of dangers to "sensitive body parts" including the "chest or breast." Defendants ignored all of these product warnings.

This was precisely the scenario that had so concerned police officers after the September 2009 product bulletin. The warning label had essentially shifted the liability from Taser International to the police. Rick Smith had said, during the conference call, that this could happen only to a "one-in-a-million person"—and now, less than three months later, here was that person. The Brinson family eventually settled with the University of Cincinnati police and University Hospital for $638,000. Taser, meanwhile, was nowhere to be found. Despite Rick Smith's commitment to "stand up for our technology and for officers," and Doug Klint's pledge to "do everything we can to defend law enforcement," Taser appeared to remain completely uninvolved.[32]

Other cases soon materialized. It seemed there were quite a few "one-in-a-million" people.

In April 2010, Craig Prescott was incarcerated at the Stanislaus County jail in Modesto, California, when police Tasered him multiple times. He died soon afterward and the family sued, resulting in a $600,000 settlement.

In June that year, Daniel Sylvester had an adverse reaction to a psychiatric medication early one morning before his local mental health facility opened. He called 9-1-1, but when the Del Norte Police Department arrived, Sylvester ran into his house—seemingly a misunderstanding. Officers entered the house and shocked Sylvester repeatedly with a Taser to subdue him for reasons that remain unclear. He died at the scene. After suing, his mother eventually settled with Del Norte for $550,000.

In August, the family of Andrew Torres—a thirty-nine-year-old diagnosed with schizophrenia—obtained a court order to have him involuntarily committed. They asked police in Greenville, South Carolina, to send plainclothes officers to pick him up, but none were available. Instead, uniformed police showed up at the house, where they charged Torres and chased him into the bedroom. They ended up shocking him with Tasers eighteen times in the space of a minute, which eventually killed him. His family sued, and the case resulted in a $500,000 settlement.

One after another, these cases transpired, costing police departments (and ultimately taxpayers) hundreds of thousands or, in some cases, millions of dollars each: officers would use Tasers, people would die, and police agencies would be held financially accountable. In each of these cases, Taser failed to come to the rescue as Smith and Klint had claimed it would.

On November 27, 2013, Taser International submitted a "current report" document with the SEC that disclosed to its shareholders that the company would accept some liability in certain lawsuits associated with Taser-related wrongful deaths, paying out a total of $2.3 million in settlements to the families involved.[33] The filing didn't specify which cases these payouts were related to, and it made clear that this was the last time Taser would accept any liability for deaths. Taser had been trying to rid itself of this legal nightmare ever since the 2008 Heston decision. Now Taser made its position clear: from this point forward, any further wrongful death lawsuits would not be the company's problem—it would be up to the individual police departments to defend themselves. After all, they had been warned.

In short, the strategy worked. Taser International's legal expenses, which just a few years prior had seemed severe enough to potentially sink the company, began to steadily decline. After facing dozens of lawsuits in 2009,[34] Taser was down to just eight in 2016.[35] But the liability on police remained. Each and every year, police departments nationwide continued to face hundreds of lawsuits related to Taser use, and paid out millions in settlements and legal fees connected to Taser-related deaths.[36]

The company's history wasn't over. Whatever lies, misrepresentations, and questionable relationships it had used to get Tasers into most of the nation's police departments, the company would live on and continue to grow. The liability for Taser use would fall not on the company but to police departments. Taser International—and Rick Smith—had won.

CHAPTER 7

THE GOOD SHEPHERD WATCHING
OVER THE FLOCK

The state-of-the-art surveillance apparatus that Ray Kelly and the NYPD built for the 2004 Republican National Convention didn't disappear when the event packed up and left town. Instead, it would go on to shape some of the NYPD's most prominent and controversial investigative work in the years that followed.

In August 2006, as tensions between the United States and Iran grew ever higher following the election of the hard-line president Mahmoud Ahmadinejad one year earlier, the Bush administration condemned Iran's uranium enrichment program and threatened "consequences" if the country continued pursuing nuclear weapons. In September, fearing that the harsh warning might provoke a retaliation from Iranian nationals or Iranian Americans living in New York City, the NYPD's counterterrorism bureau compiled an intelligence report specifically addressed to the NYPD police commissioner Ray Kelly that recommended surveilling Shi'a Muslims.[1]

The Associated Press noted that the report encouraged targeting people "based solely on their religion," which was prohibited by local law, FBI guidelines, and the department's own internal guidelines.[2] Ray Kelly dismissed the report as a "contingency plan" and, according to the AP, claimed that "police go only where investigative leads take them"—yet at the same time, "the document described no leads to justify expanded surveillance at Shiite mosques." Under former CIA officer David Cohen, the NYPD's counterterrorism bureau would increasingly focus on this kind of aggressive, preemptive surveillance. While these programs may have given comfort to some, they required intensive commitments in terms of resources and manpower, with dozens of undercover officers sent into communities to make contacts and build sources.

News of the NYPD's focus on "intelligence collections at Shi'a mosques" understandably shocked civil libertarians concerned about government overreach and discriminatory policing. But many police leaders in smaller departments around the country were impressed by what they saw as the great lengths to which the NYPD had gone to protect against terrorism—and they were wondering how they might pull off something similar with fewer resources. Fortunately for them, technological advances would make that task considerably easier.

ONE OF THE most basic spying tools used by local police in the mid-2000s was the surveillance camera, which had by that point been around for more than half a century. Brought into existence in the 1930s by the Nazis, closed-circuit television was invented for the purpose of allowing German engineers to observe secret missile tests without having to be present at the launch site, in case of an accidental detonation at liftoff. Broadcast television had been around for years,[3] but in this case the images were too sensitive to be transmitted by a method that was susceptible to interception. So the Nazis enlisted a pioneer of German television, Walter Bruch, as well as specialists with the electrical engineering company Siemens Schuckert, to devise a viewing solution—a way to watch live video from afar on a closed, secure channel.[4] The missile program's managers had been justified in their caution: the first launch exploded on the platform and was a disastrous failure. But it was the first time in recorded history that any person or group was able to watch an event happening elsewhere on a secure monitor that no one else could see. The viewing was, as Bruch would later boast, "strictly confidential." Closed-circuit television, or CCTV, was born.[5]

After the Second World War ended, CCTV was put to use in a number of different settings, including by at least one American company, which created a system it called Vericon. Making no reference to its Nazi origins, a feature on Vericon in the February 1949 issue of *Popular Science* magazine explained that it "requires no government permit" and could be used, for example, to "keep an eye on dangerous industrial processes or bring a close-up of demonstrations and surgical operations to large groups of students." For decades, the technology was used almost exclusively by private businesses. By the 1960s, CCTV technology was being used widely. Boxing promoters would rent out halls far away from arenas to show major bouts to paying audiences in a closed-circuit broadcast.[6] Stock traders used CCTV to send live updates from the trading floor to their offices.[7] Hospitals used the technology to monitor patients.[8]

Law enforcement wasn't far behind.

In 1964, across the Atlantic, in Liverpool, Herbert R. Balmer had just[9] taken the reins at the city's police department, which was busy contending with a rising crime rate. Reports of thefts and assaults were up by 100 percent over the preceding two years—and only 18 percent of those crimes had been prosecuted. What's more, the department was 540 officers short.[10] So, that year, Balmer announced to the local press that his department would install closed-circuit cameras in unspecified high-crime locations throughout the city—on tall buildings or behind signs, for example. He sent teams of young officers with wireless radios, or walkie-talkies, to stand by in areas near the cameras. The commandos, as they were known, would wait until officers monitoring the cameras from headquarters notified them of crimes in process—then they would pounce. In the months after this strategy was implemented, the crime rate went down by 54 percent.

Before long, Balmer's CCTV innovation spread overseas to the United States. This was a time when much attention was focused on the national crime rate—in 1965, President Lyndon B. Johnson made his impassioned crime speech in which he called for bold experiments in policing to combat the rising tide of crime. Balmer's CCTV program seemed to many American police leaders a promising starting place for such experiments, and shortly thereafter, police in both New York and Chicago announced that they were studying the possibility of using CCTV to fight crime.[11]

The notion of police surveilling people was nothing new—they had been wiretapping and listening in on phone conversations at least since the turn of the century.[12] And in 1928, the landmark U.S. Supreme Court decision in *Olmstead v. United States* made that practice constitutional, so long as police obtained a warrant to do so.[13] But CCTV cameras were a completely different kind of technology and posed a different set of ethical and constitutional questions. They were used to target not a specific person or group but a place.

In 1966, as the idea spread to more police departments around the country, the Supreme Court hadn't yet considered its constitutionality. But police weren't about to wait for the court.

Around this time, the Johnson administration published its report "The Challenge of Crime in a Free Society," following up on the president's speech the previous year. CCTV was mentioned only twice, briefly, as a technology that was "being explored,"[14] but surveillance in general was clearly a significant concern. "In a democratic society privacy of communication is essential if citizens are to think and act creatively and constructively," the report read. "External restraints, of which electronic surveillance is but one possibility, are thus repugnant to citizens of such a society."[15] Nevertheless, it went on to praise investigations that used electronic surveillance to target organized crime—a mixed message that effectively gave police a green light to continue pursuing the latest trend in high-tech law enforcement: CCTV.

In the 1972 case *Laird v. Tatum*, the U.S. Supreme Court dealt a victory for police who wanted to use CCTV. A group of political activists teamed up with the American Civil Liberties Union to sue the Department of the Army for surveilling them by means that included monitoring with CCTV cameras,[16] arguing that the surveillance kept them from exercising their First Amendment rights. The justices' decision didn't specifically address public video surveillance by cops, but it did reject the argument that protesters' First Amendment rights could be curtailed by "the mere existence . . . of a governmental investigative and data-gathering activity."[17] For police, that was good enough; departments across the country took the ruling as confirmation that CCTV surveillance was constitutional.[18]

A YEAR LATER, in 1973, a cadre of New York City business owners from around Times Square and the Broadway theater district pooled their resources and paid more than $15,000 to install cameras throughout the neighborhood, which the NYPD agreed to monitor. The cameras would be supplemented with ominous signs on lampposts announcing their presence: THIS BLOCK IS BEING MONITORED BY THE NEW YORK CITY POLICE DEPARTMENT BY MEANS OF CLOSED-CIRCUIT TV. The endeavor, which the business owners hoped would keep prostitution away from their storefronts, was an almost exact re-creation of Balmer's Liverpool experiment.[19] The New York Civil Liberties Union responded with a statement arguing that the system was "potentially abusive" and could "lead to the keeping of permanent records of persons engaged in legal private behavior." Police dismissed such concerns out of hand, claiming they were acting only to protect the interests of the people. As one officer put it, "We consider ourselves as the good shepherd watching over the flock."

Regardless of concerns about the potential threat posed to civil liberties, there was another, more significant problem with the cameras: they just didn't do what they were supposed to do.

Though coverage of their failure wasn't widespread, the *New York Times* reported that after twenty-two months in operation, the cameras were taken down and the program unceremoniously discontinued. "It may go down in police records as one of the [biggest] flops" on Broadway, *Times* columnist Richard Haitch wrote in October 1975. The CCTV effort had accounted for fewer than ten arrests, he continued—and none related to prostitution.

Maybe the problem was the footage itself—which at the time was still extremely grainy and low-resolution, making it difficult to identify suspects. Or maybe the inability to record without significant expense made the fleeting nature of the footage useless. (Most law enforcement CCTV setups didn't have the ability to record and replay video until well into the 1980s.) But the most significant problem, according to media reports, was that the cameras simply weren't as effective as assigning a cop to patrol the same area. A police commander who spoke with Haitch explained that ending the program was entirely a question of efficiency: "We felt it would be more productive to have the men on patrol."[20]

In 1981, there was another flop. The city shelled out $500,000 for seventy-six cameras to be installed at the Columbus Circle subway station, near the southwest entrance to Central Park. After a year of having these cameras installed and monitored, crime at the station actually increased by 30 percent. That's not to say the cameras *contributed* to the crime; this was, after all, a time when crime rates were climbing every day. But the cameras also didn't seem to do much to prevent crime. The city's baffling response was to spend an additional $1.2 million installing another round of cameras, this time in Times Square. Those went into operation in March 1983.

The introduction in 1977 of VHS recording technology into the

U.S. market transformed the surveillance industry. Cops no longer needed to monitor CCTVs constantly in order to spot crime; in many cases, they could simply record onto VHS tapes and then go back and review the footage after the fact if a crime was reported. Whatever useful footage emerged could be used as evidence in court. Improved picture quality helped, too.

By the mid-1980s, police departments in Chicago, Seattle, Washington, D.C., and Charleston, West Virginia, had developed robust CCTV systems as well. The cameras were soon seen as an inevitability—so ubiquitous in certain places that "people don't pay any attention to them," as Charleston's police chief said.[21]

WHILE SURVEILLANCE CAMERAS spread throughout the United States and the world, another technology, mobile phones, grew at an even faster rate. Police were, of course, eager to see how the devices could be applied to law enforcement. Before long, however, they discovered something even better, a related invention that could give them previously unimaginable surveillance capabilities—but only if they were able to keep it secret.

By the early 1990s, several years after Motorola had introduced the first mass-market cellular phones, the devices were still heavy and bulky, and their charges lasted for only a very short time. Before shipping them out to retailers, technicians would test the mobile phones using something called a "cell-site simulator." A cell-site simulator, as the device's name implies, imitates the signal of a cellular tower and forces any mobile phones within its range to connect to it rather than cell towers. But the devices do more than just test a cell phone's ability to connect. When a cell phone connects to a tower, ordinarily that phone shares certain information about the customer, such as the phone number and the International Mobile Subscriber Identity (IMSI) number, a unique code assigned to every cellular customer.

Because cell-site simulators act almost exactly like cell phone towers, they also collect user data, allowing whoever is using them to see the personal information of all cell phone users in the vicinity.

Federal agencies tend to keep their investigative strategies secret, so it's not clear when exactly the FBI, the DEA, and the Secret Service began using these cell-site simulators, but one of the first and most widely discussed cases was documented in detail in the pages of *Wired* magazine in February 1996.[22] It involved Tsutomu Shimomura, a computational physicist who had immigrated to the United States from Japan when he was a child and grown up in Princeton, New Jersey, where his father was a renowned chemist. While working as a research scientist in the University of California at San Diego's physics department, he, like many other Silicon Valley researchers and businesspeople at the time, found himself the victim of cyberattacks conducted by the infamous hacker Kevin Mitnick.

Mitnick had become a legend in hacking circles for using what's known as social engineering to game his way into secure corporate computer systems. Rather than exclusively using computer code to break into those systems, he would call people who worked at the companies on the phone, pretending to be people of authority and using a variety of psychological manipulation techniques to convince representatives to divulge passwords and other sensitive information. Shimomura had been aware of Mitnick's reputation for some time, but when he learned that his own computer system had been targeted, he became determined to fight back.

Mitnick was considered a "black hat," or malicious, hacker, and by the time he attempted to break into Shimomura's system, he had been on the run for more than two years as federal authorities pursued him for an earlier hack into the phone company Pacific Bell. Shimomura was something of a hacker himself, but he was a "white hat" hacker, meaning he would alert companies and law enforcement when he discovered vulnerabilities in computer systems. Because of his work, Shimomura had connections with the FBI, and he was able to convince the agency to help him arrange an operation to track Mitnick. Since Mitnick's weapon of choice was a cell phone, Shimomura and the FBI agents teamed up with cellular technicians to catch Mitnick using a cell-site simulator.

First, using a network of forums called the WELL, one of the oldest virtual communities on the Internet, to track Mitnick's online activity, Shimomura and his team determined that at least one of Mitnick's cellular phones was located in a large apartment complex in Raleigh, North Carolina. Next, they had the cell-site simulator page Mitnick's phone, which allowed another device known as a Trigger-Fish to pinpoint the phone's exact coordinates within the compound. Just hours after their arrival in Raleigh, they had his precise location. The FBI agents then raided the complex and had Mitnick behind bars that same night.[23]

The Mitnick-Shimomura chase became legendary in the pages of *Wired*, and not long afterward Shimomura published a book about the pursuit, which he wrote with *New York Times* reporter John Markoff.[24] For readers, it was a fascinating story that demonstrated the power of technology to fight crime, and perhaps also the dangers posed by those same technologies. For police, however, it served as a model: if Shimomura could use this technology to track down a criminal as sophisticated as Mitnick, surely it could help police catch everyday, run-of-the-mill criminals as well.

Maybe it could even be used to track noncriminals.

Right around the time *Wired* published its article about the Mitnick-Shimomura chase, a number of companies began marketing cell-site simulators designed specifically for law enforcement. (Up until then, law enforcement agencies had no choice but to use devices intended for testing phones, which were functional but not ideally suited to fighting crime.) One of these companies was the Harris Corporation, a Florida-based military contractor and maker of the

TriggerFish device that FBI agents had used in the Mitnick case. By 1996, the company's patent for a "multi-channel cellular communications intercept system"[25]—one that would be customized for law enforcement use—was approved.

The Mitnick-Shimomura case seemed to prove that the public was sold on the idea of police using this high-tech device to fight crime—and yet the possibilities for law enforcement use extended far beyond the clear-cut targeting of a malicious hacker hell-bent on compromising computer systems. Such a tool could in fact be used to indiscriminately spy on everyone with a cell phone in a certain geographical area.

IN NOVEMBER 2003, TRADE ministers from thirty-four countries met in Miami, Florida, to discuss expanding the North American Free Trade Agreement to include nearly every country in the western hemisphere besides Cuba. A large number of activists and labor groups found the proposed agreement, known as the Free Trade Area of the Americas, or FTAA, objectionable, as they felt it exploited Latin American resources[26] and allowed too many concessions for corporations.[27] As had happened at other free trade meetings such as the 1999 WTO conference in Seattle, massive protests were planned.

With memories of 9/11 still fresh, law enforcement leaders in Miami organized a robust response to the protests, including riot control and SWAT teams. One element of their preparations was a plan to determine the identity of those who were present by tracking their cell phones. The Miami Police Department already had an older model TriggerFish from the Harris Corporation, but it was only able to track calls made through two wireless carriers, Cingular and AT&T. However, by that time, Harris had a newer model on the market, a device it was calling the StingRay, which was able to gather calls from Metro PCS, Sprint, and Verizon as well—all together about 90 percent of cell phone traffic in the Miami area. With the FTAA protests looming, the extra capability was too much to pass up. Miami PD leaders didn't even wait for official approval to purchase the device—at a price of $115,000.[28]

"Based on the history of these conferences, the department anticipated criminal activities directed at attendees and conference sites facilitated by the use of cellular phones," a police official later wrote in a document retroactively approving "emergency purchases" for security during the FTAA event. The statement continued: "Wireless phone tracking systems utilized by law enforcement have proven to be an invaluable tool in both the prevention of these offenses and the apprehension of individuals attempting to carry out criminal activities." The Miami Police Department's use of the Harris Corporation's StingRay during those protests was kept secret—along with every other instance in which police across the country used the product—for a full decade afterward at the request of Harris executives, who wanted to avoid associating the company with potentially scandalous investigations. Likely because it knew that its cell-site simulation products had the potential to raise significant civil liberties questions—and because the Harris Corporation was publicly traded and feared the possible backlash if such questions were to stir a controversy—the company included language in its contractual agreements for cell-site simulator sales that prohibited its customers (e.g., police departments) from disclosing anything about the cell-site simulator's use.

Miami was far from the only police department to be muzzled by such an agreement. One of Harris's contracts, with the City of Tucson, was uncovered only because of a lawsuit brought by the ACLU of Arizona, years later, in March 2014. That agreement stated that the City of Tucson:

> . . . shall not discuss, publish, release or disclose any information pertaining to the Products . . . In the event that the city receives a Public Records request from a third party relating to any Protected Product, or other information Harris deems confidential, the City

will notify Harris of such a request and allow Harris to challenge any such request in court. The City will not take a position with respect to the release of such material, beyond its contractual duties, but will assist Harris in any such challenge.[29]

The secrecy didn't seem to bother leaders in many jurisdictions. Cell-site simulators, especially in the technology's early days, carried hefty price tags, retailing for as much as $169,000 apiece.[30] Even so, Harris sold dozens, if not more, of the devices to local law enforcement agencies.[31] But because of that secrecy, there have been few public accounts of specific uses of cell-site simulators.

More than three years passed, in fact, between the FTAA protests in Miami and the next documented incident in which police used the devices: a 2006 criminal investigation by the Palm Bay Police Department in East Central Florida. In that case, officers were trying to figure out who had made a false bomb threat in October 2006 to the local public high school. They already had some information to narrow their search, but police were stuck.

"The caller's voice was consistent with a young white male who was making an attempt to disguise his voice by lowering the tone and drawing out the pronunciation . . . a theatrical animation consistent with a horror movie character," one Palm Bay officer wrote in an incident report. To emphasize that the person making the threats was very likely some goofball kid trying to get out of school for an afternoon, the officer wrote that the "caller's time on the phone was not quick and to the point, but rather longer where he spent time making grunting sounds and moans."[32] The officer took the call very seriously, but when he asked the FBI for assistance in analyzing and tracing the call, the agency was unhelpful. The case didn't qualify as terrorism in its eyes, and, according to the Palm Bay officer, the FBI agents' "criteria were too restrictive to be of any use for this case."[33] The officer then went to Cingular, the cellular provider for the number that had been used to make the threat. That too was fruitless. Cingular representatives told the officer that "the company would need to be subpoe-naed" for it to divulge any subscriber information. The officer did file a subpoena, but he knew that the court process could be lengthy.

Having been blocked at every turn, it seemed there was simply no way to track down the caller. However, Palm Bay PD was headquartered less than ten miles south of the Harris Corporation's Melbourne base of operations. Determined to solve the case, the officer later wrote in an incident report, he simply called up the company and arranged to borrow "some of their technology and engineers to track the cell call."

No warrant. No subpoena.

The details of the Palm Bay case, like the Miami PD case, would not be disclosed to the public until almost a full decade later—and only after the ACLU sued to have the information released. In Florida alone, the ACLU found nearly two thousand cases in which local police departments used Harris Corporation cell-site simulators. While the FBI's disinterest in the Palm Bay case indicated that it had high standards for when it would deploy cell phone surveillance, these departments apparently did not.[34]

BECAUSE CELL-SITE SIMULATORS were still a relatively new technology well into the 2000s, police leaders felt it unnecessary to obtain warrants when using them to track cell phone signals. The 1928 U.S. Supreme Court decision in *Olmstead v. United States* had established that cops were permitted to listen in on private conversations as long as they obtained a warrant to do so. Once police decided that they didn't need a warrant to track someone with a simulator, use of the devices quickly became ubiquitous and indiscriminate, used to cast a wide net and collect a list of every person present at an event who had a cell phone—which increasingly meant just about everyone. As the 2000s rolled on and the 2010s began, activists and advocacy organizations raised concerns with law enforcement agencies about their use of cell-site simulators. In Chicago, privacy activist and security engineer Freddy Martinez, with the help of his lawyer Matt Topic, bombarded the Chicago Police Department with records requests and appeals to identify when and how cell-site simulators were used, how they were paid for, and which agreements the CPD had signed.[35] In Los Angeles, activists organized under the First Amendment Coalition unearthed records pertaining to cell-site simulators used by the LAPD.[36] Similar records sleuthing in St. Louis, Baltimore, and Erie County, New York, forced prosecutors to drop charges in cases in which police used cell-site simulators, rather than go against nondisclosure agreements with manufacturers.[37]

The secrecy of these agreements raised much broader and more troubling questions as well. What did it mean for democracy in the United States if a few lines from a contractual agreement between a corporation and a police department could obscure the use of technologies that violated civil rights? And if a corporation could keep these technologies secret so easily, how many other potentially abusive tools were being used among the approximately eighteen thousand law enforcement agencies in the country?

Because of private nondisclosure agreements like the Harris Corporation's, it was difficult to know. How many other companies pursued similar agreements with law enforcement agencies? Without scrutiny of such agreements and their underlying technologies, the profit motives of the companies began to exercise influence over how police operated.

"The relationships between surveillance technology vendors and police departments show the increasing degree to which private companies can guide, shape, and limit what the public police do," wrote Elizabeth Joh, a law professor at the University of California at Davis who studies police technology. "That police rely on private vendors is unremarkable as a general proposition," she conceded. But what she found most troubling was "when the product itself is central to the development of the governmental suspicion that underlies so many enforcement decisions." Joh went on:

> The typical approach to the use of new police technologies involves the oversight of courts, legislatures, and local government bodies through judicial opinions, statutes, and local ordinances. The Supreme Court has weighed in, for example, on the police use of manned overhead surveillance, thermal imaging devices, and GPS trackers. Congress and state legislatures have created legal standards for investigative techniques like electronic eavesdropping. Cities and counties can oversee local law enforcement agencies through budgetary decisions. When private companies influence policing through their role as vendors, the usual mechanisms of oversight do not easily apply; they have little obligation to permit public access, and the usual constitutional constraints over the police do not regulate them at all.[38]

CHAPTER 8

TRANSPARENCY AND OPENNESS

After the killing of Michael Brown and the intense unrest it caused in Ferguson and across the country in 2014, something had to change. Protesters and activists who already distrusted the police after years of harassment and neglect would not allow the shooting to fade into memory as yet another unfortunate encounter between a police officer and an unarmed black man. Even the police must have known on some level that the protests signaled a major change in how the public viewed their profession.

In the incident's aftermath, something surprising happened: just about everyone—protesters, cops, even such politicians as President Obama—agreed on a course of action. It wasn't exactly a solution, but it was something that most people thought would go a long way toward improving relations between police and the communities they serve: equipping officers with body cameras.

Body cameras hadn't been around all that long; they'd been available for purchase for less than a decade and a realistic concept in the minds of police leaders and corporate executives for only a few years.

A few companies—Vievu, Digital Ally, WatchGuard, and Taser International, among others—produced body cameras for cops by that point, but the market was still quite small: Taser was by far the most visible body-camera maker in the United States, and in the previous year, 2013, it had sold fewer than five thousand units. By comparison, the company sold nearly 1.6 million cartridges for its Taser weapons in 2013.[1]

In the wake of Ferguson, however, body cameras started to receive serious consideration nationwide. The cameras would, the thinking went, hold police accountable, establish trust, and also protect police from baseless accusations. With direct input from corporate representatives of body-camera makers, a 2014 report from the Justice Department's Office of Community Oriented Policing Services (also known as the COPS Office) issued a bold pronouncement in favor of open government and transparency: "A police department that deploys body-worn cameras is making a statement that it believes the actions of its officers are a matter of public record."[2] Less than three months later, as part of a nationwide community policing initiative, President Obama asked Congress to fund a three-year, $75 million program to help police departments purchase body cameras.[3] It was a remarkable point of agreement amid a tumultuous and fiercely antagonistic debate, as everyone from Black Lives Matter activists to district attorneys, and even some police unions, lined up to support the idea.

City councils began approving millions in funding for body cameras and storage fees to keep video footage on file. New companies emerged with new features, and their sales representatives offered incentives for police leaders who pushed to outfit their entire force with body cameras. The body-camera market grew and grew and showed no signs of slowing down.

THE IDEA OF police officers carrying around video cameras while on duty to document their work in real time was featured in the September 1939 issue of *Popular Science* magazine. A California High-way Patrol officer named R. H. Galbraith, the article reported, had installed a "motion-picture camera" on "the dashboard of his patrol car, with its lens pointing forward through the windshield," which he used to "[take] photographs of the automobiles he trails along the high-ways." Galbraith's goal, the magazine went on, was to create "a perma-nent film record of any traffic violations for possible later use in court."[4] Galbraith's invention was far ahead of its time—an unusual idea, rigged up by a motivated tinkerer—and it seems unlikely that anyone else tried out the idea for many years after.

By the 1960s, the concept was becoming more realistic—and was, by then, known as the dashboard camera, or "dashcam." In 1968, a lengthy *Popular Mechanics* article touted "a new weapon" that "pro-vides damning evidence." Throughout the late 1960s and 1970s, these cameras were rare and expensive. The *Popular Mechanics* arti-cle noted that the device used by one highway patrolman cost about $2,000—the equivalent of a new car in 1968.[5] Dashcams were not widespread. But by the 1980s, when VCR technology became cheap and CCTV cameras began to be implemented widely, so too did dashcams.

As the use of dashcams spread, they were most often used as a means of protecting cops. A 1983 wire service article described the case of a woman in Houston, Texas, who was indicted by a grand jury for falsely suggesting that an officer tore her coat during an arrest. The police department was able to use video "shot from a camera mounted on the dashboard of the officer's patrol car" to show otherwise. "It's about the best evidence you can get," said a local assistant district attor-ney. "We always tell juries we wish they could have been there at the time of the crime. This is pretty close to being there."[6]

By the 1990s, video from police dashcams and CCTV had devel-oped into a full-blown propaganda mechanism: two of the nation's top prime-time television series in 1990 and 1991—*COPS* and *Top Cops*—were "reality-based" shows that used dashcam footage to show police officers going about their duties (though camera crews were also used).[7]

In November 1993, a freelance writer named Debra Seagal went undercover to work as a "story analyst" for a competing prime-time cop show, *American Detective*, that used a similar production process. She described sifting through thousands of hours of film to find the kinds of stories that the show's producers sought to air.

"By the time our 9 million viewers flip on their tubes, we've reduced fifty or sixty hours of mundane and compromising video into short, action-packed segments of tantalizing, crack-filled, dope-dealing, junkie-busting cop culture," she wrote.

> How easily we downplay the pathos of the suspect; how cleverly we breeze past the complexities that cast doubt on the very system that has produced the criminal activity in the first place. How effortlessly we smooth out the indiscretions of the lumpen detectives and casually make them appear as pistol-flailing heroes rushing across the screen.[8]

This was, of course, TV. Ordinary cops did not have the opportunity to carefully pick through and edit their dashcam footage before submitting it to be used in court. But the cameras did show incidents from their perspective and were intended, ultimately, to show their side of an encounter—to shield them from accusations of misconduct rather than hold them accountable for their actions.

This had been the idea behind Taser International's Taser Cam,[9] the ill-fated product the company had rolled out in 2006 as it was fighting the SEC investigation and an onslaught of lawsuits.

"With Taser Cam, our first goal is we can protect our officers from allegations of misuse," Rick Smith said. "And then, number two, it's— if there is somebody who dies after a Taser use, we're going to be able to see what happened."

However, the Taser Cam was bulky and inconvenient and overly expensive both for Taser International to produce and for police departments to buy. It was not the solution that Rick Smith had envisioned. Then, after about eight months of investigation, the SEC quietly ended its inquiry into Taser in May 2006—no charges filed, no regulatory action taken. It was a huge, if unexpected, victory for the company. Still, the damage was done. Taser's stock value had been obliterated. It was dealing with declining revenues in four straight quarters.[10] The company needed something to reinvigorate its business.

STEVE WARD BEGAN working for Taser the same way many others had: he was an officer with the Seattle Police Department's SWAT team and in 1999 signed on to be a Taser master instructor, one of the cops who were paid to train other officers to use Taser International's weapons. After working as a master instructor for a few years while also continuing his job with the Seattle PD, Ward established a reputation among his peers in the Seattle region as an expert in nonlethal weapons, including Tasers, pepper spray, rubber bullets, and batons. He also fancied himself a salesman and entrepreneur.

"Taser had a good product, but when I started they had no idea how to sell it," Ward said, referring to Rick Smith and his brother, Tom. "These guys had no understanding of the police world."

So, as Ward explained it, he did his best to establish a working relationship with Rick while working as a master instructor. By January 2004, Rick was so impressed with Ward that he offered him a job as Taser's vice president of international sales in Europe. In his new position, Ward helped to build Taser International's sales outside the United States—which had never been strong, despite the international focus the company's name implied. In 2006, Ward transitioned from international sales to a marketing job with Taser—a position in which he would be helping rebuild the company's product sales after its disastrous period facing an SEC investigation.

As a former cop, Ward had a hunch that the next innovation in police surveillance would be an extension of the cameras mounted on buildings and affixed to cruiser dashboards—it was time, he thought, for a camera that cops would wear and take with them everywhere they went. He saw the Taser Cam as an interesting step in the right direction, but Ward wondered why it had to be connected to the weapon at all. Why couldn't it instead be mounted on an officer's sunglasses or on the breast pocket of an officer's uniform?

According to Ward, he had been contemplating the idea since 1997. The benefits of such an invention, he believed, would be obvious to cops. The only thing that was needed was technological progress. Cameras would have to be cheap enough that the price tag wouldn't scare away public officials and small enough to fit comfortably on a cop's uniform—and for a long time, that wasn't the case. But by 2007, the technology was there.

So in 2007, after only a year or so in his new role, Ward left Taser International to start a new company called Vievu that would do exactly what he envisioned.

Rick did not take kindly to the departure; as he saw it, Ward was betraying the company. Ward, he claimed, was taking advantage of insider information and internal discussions at Taser International about where to take the Taser Cam.

"The way I look at it, [Ward] was supposed to be spearheading internal research into a camera product for Taser," Rick said.

> Unbeknownst to me, Steve was already starting Vievu and building a camera for his own benefit. And the reason I was upset about that was that it was in direct competition with what he was supposed to be doing here—it was a task for which we were paying him a salary and stock options. And while he was an officer of this company, he was secretly competing with us. . . . [Ward] had asked me at one point, "Hey, do you mind if I go and do this camera on my own?" To which I said, "Yes, I would mind that."[11]

A lawsuit followed. Taser won an initial summary judgment finding that Ward had misappropriated trade secrets. But an Arizona court of appeals reversed that decision[12]—and by then, Vievu was already ahead of Taser. The company unveiled its first body-worn camera that same year, in 2007. Taser wouldn't release its own camera until 2009.

A battle of body cameras ensued—the former Taser employee versus the company he spurned. In time, it turned out to be an unfair match.

THE SMITHS, AS Steve Ward recalled, may have had difficulty selling to cops back when he started with the company in 1999. By the late 2000s, when they were entering the body-camera market, they had come a long way. The master instructor program had proven wildly successful and became the centerpiece of the company's sales strategy, giving the Smiths a significant boost as they worked to rebound after the SEC inquiry. Even more important, it helped them gain traction and box out competition in the new body-camera market.

Commander Clarence "Ed" Trapp had been working for the Pittsburgh Bureau of Police for nearly twenty years in 2012 when he— nearly by accident—led the bureau into the twenty-first century with one of the first and largest body-camera programs in Pennsylvania. It all started when he was assigned to work in the office of Pittsburgh Police Chief Nathan Harper. Harper had recently attended a policing conference where he met with Taser International salesmen representing the company's Axon camera division. At that point, Axon was a relatively small part of the larger Taser company, selling body cameras and cloud storage space for the video footage they produced on the company's website, Evidence.com. The Taser representatives showed Harper a body camera that could be affixed to an officer's sunglasses, a product they called the Axon Flex. Intrigued, Harper asked his new deputy Trapp to look into getting the cameras for the department and put together a policy for how they might be used.[13]

Taser International provided three cameras to the Pittsburgh police free of charge for a trial and hosted a training session in March 2012 at Pittsburgh police headquarters. After the initial test period, the city ordered fifty body cameras for slightly less than $162,000. The purchase was approved with little fanfare, and Trapp began implementing the city's body-camera program. Trapp's relationship with Taser International soon grew closer, as the company paid his expenses to attend three conferences in 2012 and 2013 at Axon's Scottsdale headquarters, where he gave trainings and did consulting work. In July 2013, Trapp was asked to join the Axon instructor program, the body-camera equivalent of the Taser master instructor program, for which all his expenses would be paid by the company. In this role, he would be showing other police leaders around the country how to implement and use Axon cameras and products.

There was just one problem standing in the way of Axon being able to implement a full-fledged body-camera program in Pittsburgh: Pennsylvania's Wiretap Act, originally passed in 1978,[14] which required all police video units to be mounted inside a vehicle and prohibited officers from recording video footage inside private residences. Trapp had begun the Pittsburgh police bureau's pilot program of thirty-seven cameras by issuing them to bicycle and motorcycle cops who generally did not dismount their bikes to enter civilian homes.[15] But if the cameras were to be implemented department-wide—to officers who *did* enter residences—a more permanent solution would be necessary. Furthermore, the roughly twelve hundred other law enforcement agencies in the state would be essentially off-limits unless Axon could get the law changed; it seemed unlikely that departments would make the effort to outfit cops with cameras if those cops were effectively barred from entering homes while wearing them.

So the company set its lobbying arm into motion, putting Trapp in contact with lobbyists at the Philadelphia-based international law firm Ballard Spahr LLP. An e-mail exchange from around this time, in October 2013, suggests that Axon representatives were specifically urging Trapp to lobby state legislators in Harrisburg by appearing before a state senate committee hearing in his police uniform to argue for changes to the Wiretap Act that would make body cameras legal. By November 2013, Ballard Spahr representatives were providing Trapp with specific talking points via e-mail and putting his name on lobbying material. "Attached is a draft letter for your consideration," one e-mail to Trapp read.

> If you are comfortable with the text, I would like to get this signed by yourself or the appropriate person from the Department on Department letterhead. I would like to send this to both Senators Costa and Vulakovich via e-mail and fax on Friday if possible so they can discuss it on Monday or Tuesday morning and we can push to have the amendment introduced. I plan on drafting a similar letter for other police departments to use as necessary.[16]

These efforts eventually triumphed; in 2016, lawmakers amended Pennsylvania's Wiretap Act to allow for body cameras.[17]

Trapp continued attending Axon conferences through 2014, and by July that year—a month before Michael Brown's killing in Ferguson, Missouri—he was selected to join Taser's Consumer Advisory Board. Though Trapp said that he received only travel-related expenses for his work on the advisory board, e-mails indicate that board members were paid a flat rate of as much as $700 per day while attending conferences, in addition to travel expenses, plus $50 per hour of travel time. It is not clear how many days Trapp provided services for the board, though he said he was not paid for his first meeting in 2014.[18]

In October 2016, having successfully lobbied the state legislature to loosen the Wiretap Act's restrictions on police video recordings, Trapp helped Axon to secure a $1.5 million contract with the City of Pittsburgh for five hundred fifty body cameras—a contract on which no other company was allowed to bid. The city opted not to put the body-camera contract up for bid despite the existence of dozens of

viable competitors in the police body-camera industry—and despite
the fact that the streamlined bidding process didn't seem to provide
the city with the best possible deal. (A number of other police departments had, around that time, signed deals with Axon for the same
amount, $1.5 million, and received considerably more for their
money—the LAPD, for example, got eight hundred fifty cameras, and
the New Jersey State Police got one thousand cameras.) By that point,
Trapp had served in both official and unofficial capacities as an Axon
product consultant and had received thousands of dollars in travel-
related expenses from the company. All the while, he had also been
serving as a sworn police officer, receiving a salary funded by taxpayers.

Trapp's cozy relationship with Axon seems not to have been the
only instance in which the company used questionable practices to
win contracts. In Albuquerque, the city's chief of police, Ray Schultz,
accepted travel expenses and other gifts from Axon, and was then
accused by the New Mexico state auditor of rigging the city's 2013
body-camera contract before retiring to work as an Axon contractor.[19]
New Mexico's attorney general opened a criminal investigation into
Schultz's relationship with Axon but never filed charges. Albuquerque's
city council later ignored complaints about Axon salespeople court-
ing Schultz with gifts and awarded the company a $4.4 million body-
camera contract anyway.[20]

In 2015, the Associated Press reported that chiefs of police in Fort
Worth and Salt Lake City had accepted travel expenses and taken contract work with Axon while overseeing the implementation of Axon
body-camera programs.[21] In Memphis, Axon paid $880,000 to the
mayor's campaign manager at the same time it signed a $9.4 million
body-camera contract with the city. The revelation of that payment
caused the city to temporarily suspend its body-camera expansion, but
it then moved forward with the contract. A patent infringement lawsuit filed by body-camera competitor Digital Ally listed more than ten
cities whose contracts were reportedly directed by government representatives who had financial ties to Axon.[22]

In short, Axon was engaged in a no-holds-barred effort to elbow out its competitors using the same tactics that had helped the company sell its Tasers to nearly every police department in the country.

BY THE TIME Michael Brown was shot dead in Ferguson in 2014, Steve Ward's body-camera company, Vievu, was pulling ahead in its competition with Taser International, having sold about twenty-four thousand more body cameras than its rival.[23] Rick Smith was determined to fight back, and as he saw it the furor that had erupted over Brown's killing presented an ideal opportunity to get ahead. His company soon embarked on a marketing blitz, targeting police departments across the country that were eager to avoid the fate of Ferguson.

When President Obama made his request to Congress for the three-year, $75 million body-camera program to help police departments purchase body cameras, Rick knew this was his chance. If approved, that federal money would be available to fund body-camera programs all over the country, and perhaps even those departments that weren't chosen to receive federal funding could be convinced to pursue body-camera programs, given all the hype.

Rick Smith's tenure as an entrepreneur with Taser International had been long and fraught with controversial decisions, massive losses, and numerous product failures. But that history had given him a close view of more than two decades of the U.S. police business as it progressed through the late twentieth century and into the twenty-first. In addition to essentially building the electroshock weapons market from the ground up, he had seen firsthand the rise of surveillance in U.S. policing. He watched data become more and more relevant and concepts such as facial recognition move from the realm of science fiction into reality.

In body cameras, politicians and civil rights groups saw a technology that would encourage, perhaps even force, transparency, allowing police and civilians alike to consider interactions after the fact.

Rick Smith and the executives at Taser International saw something different: a way to rebuild their company around data and surveillance. In an article published less than three months after Michael Brown was killed, Rick told *Forbes* magazine that he envisioned a "Dropbox for cops"[24]—a camera and cloud storage system that would allow the company to charge police departments for server space as well as hardware.

In time, that "Dropbox for cops" vision expanded beyond cameras and storage. Facial recognition, while still imperfect, had improved significantly since the 2001 Super Bowl, to a degree such that the Smiths' company could potentially use it to analyze faces caught on body cameras. The company saw so much promise in the market for data and surveillance that it changed its name from Taser International to Axon Enterprise[25]—a change that carried the added benefit of beginning to distance the company from the controversy surrounding Taser-related deaths. It also represented a prediction that data and surveillance would comprise the bulk of the policing market going forward.

As Axon worked to implement this vision, it continued to use the same ruthless sales tactics. The New York Police Department's stop-and-frisk program—which descended from the broken windows policing efforts Bill Bratton and Jack Maple set in motion twenty years earlier—was found by a federal district court judge to have unfairly targeted people of color. To remedy the systemic bias, the judge ordered that all NYPD officers be outfitted with body cameras. The NYPD employed more than twenty thousand officers, meaning that whichever body-camera company won the contract would receive a massive windfall. Not only would each of those officers need a camera; they would also need cloud storage and, potentially, the ability to integrate that video storage system with data systems used by other municipal departments. In February 2017, the city awarded a five-thousand-camera pilot program contract to Vievu—which Steve Ward had, by then, sold to tactical equipment company Safariland.[26] Axon cried foul, claiming that Vievu had rigged the deal by selling its cameras below cost, and then, according to New York mayor Bill de Blasio, Axon worked behind the scenes to cast doubt on Vievu's reliability.[27] When that didn't work, Rick Smith offered to outfit NYPD officers with Axon cameras for free, stipulating that the department would only have to pay for cloud storage. Amazingly, the city's leaders turned down the offer, but the gesture was enough to put Axon on the front pages of the *New York Times* and the *Wall Street Journal*.[28] It was certainly a victory for Vievu—an indication that Axon wasn't the only player in the body-camera market and that one of the nation's largest police departments had sided with a competitor. But the win would be short-lived: fifteen months after Vievu inked its NYPD deal, Axon acquired the company from Safariland for an undisclosed sum.[29]

While all this played out, another Axon competitor, the Kansas-based Digital Ally, brought a patent-infringement lawsuit against Axon after losing out to the Smith brothers on a number of contracts—including one for the nearby Kansas City Police Department. Digital Ally's lawsuit claimed that it owned the rights to a so-called auto-activation system—a body-camera feature that would automatically engage a recording when an officer opened a police cruiser's door, for example, or turned on its siren. The lawsuit also leveled a number of unrelated accusations at Axon, including that it won at least ten body-camera contracts with major police departments by either directly paying government officials, paying friends of officials, or promising jobs to police officers nearing retirement.[30]

Similarly, Utility Associates, Inc.—a body-camera company in Decatur, Georgia—made news when it sued the city manager of Austin, Texas, after losing out on a contract with the city's police department. According to the lawsuit, the Austin city manager had chosen Axon even though its products did not meet the city's own technical specifications and despite its bid being $3 million higher than Utility's. Furthermore, Utility claimed that there had been an "illegal and impermissible 'non-competitive bidding process'" set in Axon's favor.

A judge dismissed the lawsuit, finding that it was the role of Texas's legislature, not the courts, to step in if the process was unfair. The legislature did nothing, and Austin's $12 million body-camera contract went to Axon.[31]

BODY CAMERAS HAD been sold to police—by Axon and others—as a way of proving officers' innocence by demonstrating that uses of force were in fact justified. But now an increasing number of cops were being publicly lambasted after body-camera footage caught them in the wrong. In Baltimore, a cop's body camera caught him planting drugs to falsely accuse a suspect.[32] In Idaho, body-camera footage recorded an officer saying, "If I could get away with it, I would've put a bullet in the center of each one of their heads," referring to suspects who didn't respond politely to his questioning.[33] All over the country, cops were caught lying about suspects and crimes on camera.[34]

Even under circumstances in which cops technically acted within the boundaries of their sworn duties, there was a significant risk of public outcry. Police are permitted—and are in fact trained—to kill when they feel their life is in danger. Because the standard for determining when an officer feels he is in mortal danger is largely determined by the officer himself, police killings that would strike many as outrageous offenses are perfectly acceptable in the eyes of the law. Now, with the proliferation of body cameras, the public increasingly had the chance to observe these encounters and make their own determination about whether a killing was "justified"—and predictably, this led to more and more outrage in the streets.

The way police officers saw it, their work could often be ugly. The public simply wasn't ready for an insider's view. As body-camera programs multiplied in the aftermath of Ferguson, police started to push back. The police union in Boston even filed a lawsuit against the city when it introduced a body-camera pilot program, going so far as to imply that officers were getting assaulted on duty more frequently because of body cameras.[35]

For Axon, these protests represented a potentially catastrophic threat, so once again the company turned to Clarence Trapp, the Pittsburgh police commander, for lobbying help. This time, the objective was to amend Pennsylvania state law to effectively make body-camera footage secret and inaccessible to the public. That change was representative of a shift that was beginning to take place: body cameras weren't really for building community trust. In large part, they were for public relations.

IN MAY 2017, THE *New York Times* published an article headlined "Hollywood-Style Heroism Is Latest Trend in Police Videos," about a wave of body-camera videos that showed police officers performing various acts of bravery and integrity. One video, from the Hamden Police Department in Connecticut, showed an officer pulling a troubled man away from the edge of a building. Another, from the Topeka Police Department in Kansas, showed an officer rescuing a drowning boy from a pond. These videos were not released because of public records requests from journalists—and they did not go viral by mere happenstance. They were, in fact, released and promoted by police employees as counterprogramming against the overwhelming tide of videos showing abuse and misconduct. "The chief talked to me about how Topeka was really getting beat up in the news with some shootings, some homicides," an officer told the *Times*. "Topeka really needed a good story."[36]

These positive videos appeared especially propagandistic to many observers because they were emerging just as states such as Pennsylvania were passing laws to keep less flattering videos hidden. North Carolina, for example, passed legislation in 2016 excluding body-camera video from the public record, meaning footage would not be available through the state's Public Records Act. Louisiana soon followed suit, and South Carolina amended its laws so that body-camera footage would be available only to criminal defendants and the subjects of recordings.

This opaque state of affairs stood in stark contrast to the way body cameras were understood just a few years earlier during the aftermath of Michael Brown's killing. As people around the world were trying to piece together what exactly had happened between Darren Wilson and Michael Brown, civilians and police alike began to see body cameras as a solution. For the civilians who saw the cameras as a tool for holding police accountable, there was an underlying assumption on which their support hinged—the videos would have to be available to the public at large.

At first, police leaders had been willing to go along with this. In a 2014 report from the Police Executive Research Forum—a national membership organization of police leaders mostly from big city and state law enforcement agencies in the United States—the group's executive director, Chuck Wexler, wrote that "body-worn camera video footage should be made available to the public upon request not only because the videos are public records but also because doing so enables police departments to demonstrate transparency and openness in their interactions with members of the community."[37]

That report, released by one of the most respected law enforcement groups in the world, made it clear that body cameras could help police leaders build trust with the communities they served by documenting both the good and the bad. Unflattering videos, including ones that forced indictments, would have to be released along with the flattering ones or the ones that exonerated cops wrongly accused of misconduct. Transparency was worth it for everyone.

For a while, the rules governing how this would work were written by local or municipal lawmakers. There were good policies and bad, with some cities making it easier than others for civilians to obtain police video. But—as more police departments spent larger and larger sums on body cameras and video storage—police unions, district attorney associations, and law enforcement lobbying groups began to push for statewide laws restricting transparency. North Carolina, Louisiana, South Carolina, and Kansas, among others, instituted countertransparency body-camera laws. Even Missouri—home of Ferguson—classified body-camera footage as a "closed record."

In Pennsylvania, the story was similar. Police leaders such as Trapp argued for the most restrictive option—excluding body-camera footage from the commonwealth's public records law. Pennsylvania's legislature and its governor went along and, in July 2017, passed Act 22, a law that followed the restrictive requests of police leaders. Whereas journalists and others seeking documents through Pennsylvania's public records law could ordinarily appeal rejected requests with an independent state agency called the Office of Open Records, there would be no appeals process to contest sealed body-camera footage. Civilians would have to file a lawsuit if they disagreed with a police department's decision to withhold body-camera footage.[38]

Pennsylvania's body-camera law thus made access to footage basically impossible—just as it was in North Carolina, Louisiana, South Carolina, and Kansas. The trend would continue as time passed and body-camera programs proliferated across the country.

THE PROBLEM WITH SOLUTIONISM

It's certain that Jack Cover will go down in history for the importance of his groundbreaking invention, the Taser—a technology that, for all its faults, is considered indispensable by most police today. But his greatest legacy may be that he precipitated a philosophy of American policing that sees technology as the solution to all, or at least most, of the problems cops face. Rejecting substantial institutional reform—which can be messy and requires a tough accounting of what's working and what isn't in a police department—adherents of this philosophy have looked to electroshock weapons, statistical analysis, CCTV, facial recognition, cell-site simulators, body cameras, and a host of other technologies to supposedly make policing more efficient and humane.

This philosophy persisted well after Cover sold his Taser to the LAPD, and well after he retired to the quiet suburbs of Tucson, Arizona. In fact, it flourished—largely thanks to the efforts of Rick Smith and his family. By popularizing Cover's invention, Taser International continued to grow the philosophy of technological solutionism, bringing it to virtually every police department in the country.

This philosophy isn't unique to policing, of course. In his 2013 book *To Save Everything, Click Here*, the Belarusian writer, researcher, and self-proclaimed "digital heretic" Evgeny Morozov argued that the Silicon Valley tech industry is defined by innovators who see every problem as an invitation for a simple solution. To illustrate this point, he cited a number of patently absurd projects that sought to harness technology to solve various problems. One team of researchers planned to use smartphone cameras to surveil people in the act of throwing away garbage and shame them into separating recyclables from trash. Another proposal encouraged tea drinkers to be more conscious of their energy consumption by sending them an alert through their electric kettles at times when the electrical grid was overburdened. While these projects may have been guided by noble intentions, Morozov writes, their solutions reflect an oversimplified view of the problems they sought to address. He continues:

> Recasting all complex social situations either as neatly defined problems with definite, computable solutions or as transparent and self-evident processes that can be easily optimized . . . is likely to have unexpected consequences that could eventually cause more damage than the problems they seek to address.[1]

This is precisely what happened with Cover's Taser—a supposedly nonlethal weapon developed to solve the problem of police shootings and beatings. In fact, there's no evidence that the Taser has solved anything. As more and more police departments began using the devices over the last several decades, they did not cause any reduction in the number of lethal police shootings, as many had hoped. As it turned out, Tasers contributed to the very problem it was hoped they would solve; many civilians died after being shocked, and the presence of electroshock weapons on officers' duty belts created a multitude of additional possibilities for abuse and even torture. The result is that

Tasers have, in fact, exacerbated the feelings of unrest and distrust that set off the 1965 uprisings in Watts and spurred the protests that followed Rodney King's beating in 1991. What happened in Ferguson in 2014 was yet another reminder that no technological solution can bring peace between police and the public.

Police leaders have, regardless, stuck to the philosophy of technological solutionism with steadfast conviction, looking to the inventions of outsiders to address the problems that police seem unable or unwilling to solve internally.

TAKE THE CASE of Laquan McDonald.

During a traffic stop in October 2014, Chicago Police Department officer Jason Van Dyke shot the black seventeen-year-old McDonald sixteen times in fifteen seconds, killing him in the middle of a four-lane thoroughfare. The incident was recorded by a dashboard camera, but it wasn't until thirteen months later, after at least one lawsuit, that city administrators finally released the footage to the public. McDonald's killing was an example of an officer killing another person, allegedly with wanton disregard for the law. This was not a simple problem by any stretch of the imagination.

Amid justified outrage and the protests that erupted after the video went public, however, Chicago mayor Rahm Emanuel announced a simple solution: he would confront the turmoil with technology. Though camera footage of McDonald's killing was clearly available—and had done nothing to alleviate the situation—the city would spend $2.2 million outfitting Chicago police officers with fourteen hundred police body cameras.[2] A month later, Emanuel doubled down on the approach, devoting millions of dollars more from the city's coffers to outfit every Chicago Police Department officer with a Taser.[3]

Body cameras have simply not been proven to keep officers honest. In fact, the largest study of their use to date found that when more than two thousand cops were outfitted with body cameras in Washington, D.C., there was no change in their use of force or the number of citizen complaints.[4]

The Taser—once marketed as a nonlethal device—had played a role in the deaths of more than one thousand people by the time Emanuel made his spending announcement, according to the website Truth . . . Not Tasers, which documents lethal police encounters involving Tasers.[5] That number was backed up in 2017 by an exhaustive investigation by Reuters journalists.[6] The Reuters team also found that law enforcement agencies had shelled out more than $172 million in 232 judgments or settlements for plaintiffs who sued over an officer's use of a Taser.[7] In the relatively rare occasions when Taser use had been independently evaluated in the field, the device often proved to be ineffective in immobilizing suspects. According to a 2015 LAPD use-of-force report, officers activated Tasers 1,101 times that year, and the weapons failed in 516 cases—nearly 47 percent of the time—because suspects wore thick clothing, or the darts didn't fully impale a suspect's skin, or for any number of other completely mundane reasons.[8] A commander with the Los Angeles Sheriff's Department was quoted in the Los Angeles Times reacting to the statistics. "It's going to create a predisposition that you're expecting a Taser failure," the commander said. "I'm not going to risk my life for a 50 percent success rate."[9]

Would devoting millions of dollars to buying police equipment change the way Chicago police officers did their jobs? Would it improve how they interacted with citizens on the streets? Would those millions do anything to change the underlying conditions that might have led an officer to shoot an unarmed person sixteen times? Not likely.

Yet some police companies with questionable pasts, such as Axon Enterprise, became the perceived antidote to police killings and the justified indignation they sparked. These companies gave politicians like Emanuel an easy path to follow—one that collapsed the multitude of simmering tensions and underlying social problems into a singular challenge that could be overcome with decisive action—and money.

Emanuel wasn't the only civic leader to follow this path.

When protests erupted after surveillance video captured officers with the Cleveland Police Department mistaking twelve-year-old Tamir Rice's toy gun for the real thing and killing the boy, city leaders responded by spending $2.4 million to outfit the city's officers with Axon-brand body cameras.

Even though the body cameras worn by Baton Rouge police officers in July 2016 fell off during an altercation with Alton Sterling, a man suspected of carrying a gun and possibly yelling at someone on the street while selling CDs, the city nevertheless paid $2.25 million to outfit the rest of its officers with bodycams in response to the incident.[10]

It was a similar story when North Charleston police officer Michael Slager shot and killed Walter Scott after Slager's Taser failed and Scott ran from him: in response to the shooting, which sent shock waves across the country, North Charleston ponied up for hundreds more body cameras.[11] (Already flush with Tasers, North Charleston was known to some locals as "Taser Town" because of its officers' overuse of the weapons.)[12]

It's important to remember that when politicians and police leaders pursued technological solutions in each of these cases, they were not going against the will of the people. The idea of police using technology to solve their problems is, in fact, overwhelmingly popular. In a 2016 criminal justice survey, the Cato Institute found that 89 percent of Americans supported equipping police with body cameras.[13] Even more extreme proposals also enjoyed broad support. Fifty-nine percent of respondents, for example, supported police "regularly" using drones for surveillance purposes. About 50 percent approved of police departments purchasing other military-inspired technologies such as predictive tools to identify individuals who might potentially commit crimes in the future.

But despite the popularity of these technologies, the confidence that politicians place in them reflects an oversimplified understanding of the underlying difficulties.

When people protest shootings such as Laquan McDonald's, they protest serious, deeply entrenched problems: the leniency given to officers who instigate violence, the disparity in arrest rates between blacks and whites, the overpolicing of the poor, and the lack of transparency in any situation deemed by prosecutors to involve potential investigative evidence. In essence, they protest unfairness. These are problems that technology will never be able to solve.

AUGUST VOLLMER WAS not a perfect lawman.

As we have seen, he was a man of many flaws, but most significantly he contributed to an early form of technological solutionism, advancing the idea that new technologies like the lie detectors he helped to popularize could help police overcome the massive, seemingly intractable challenges they faced.[14]

But many of Vollmer's ideas were astoundingly forward-thinking and smart. Though he possessed only a grade-school education, he was the first chief in recorded history to actively recruit college-educated police officers and encourage continuing education for anyone working in his department.[15] He actively pushed to root out corruption from the department's ranks in the early years of the twentieth century, at a time when San Francisco cops were deeply involved with organized crime. He was an early proponent of collecting police data and making it available for investigative purposes. He believed in compensating officers generously so as to encourage them to see policing as a viable career.

These are the ideas that define Vollmer's legacy in American policing. But one of his lesser-known ideas may be most instructive for an era when police are seen by many as unfair, overbearing, and discriminatory.

Vollmer wanted officers to think of themselves not as soldiers or as high-tech enforcers or thugs, but as social workers—public servants on duty to help people. One of his officers paraphrased a speech he would give to new recruits. "I'll admire you more if in the first year you don't make a single arrest," he told them. "I'm not judging you on arrests. I'm judging you on how many people you keep from doing something wrong. Remember you're almost a father-confessor," he went on. Officers were, he said, on duty "to listen to people"—"to advise them."[16]

Technology can be useful, of course; there are circumstances in which Tasers have helped to de-escalate confrontations, in which body cameras have helped to clarify details of tense interactions, in which data have helped to better target crime hot spots. But an overreliance on these technologies elides what Vollmer attempted to communicate to his recruits: that police aren't warriors. They are public servants hired to make communities livable and safe. Instilling and encouraging a sense of empathy and inquisitiveness and compassion among cops should therefore be the focus of police leaders' attention, rather than which technologies they might use to make law enforcement simpler and more convenient.

More than sixty years after Vollmer's death, it's a wonder why so few police leaders have taken his best advice.

NOTES

INTRODUCTION: WHEN PUBLIC ORDER BREAKS DOWN

1. U.S. Census Bureau, "QuickFacts: Ferguson City, Missouri: Population Estimates, July 1, 2017," retrieved from https://www.census.gov/quickfacts /fact/table/fergusoncitymissouri.
2. Samuel H. Kye, "The Persistence of White Flight in Middle-Class Suburbia," *Social Science Research* 72 (May 2018): 38–52.
3. Elizabeth Kneebone, "Ferguson, Mo. Emblematic of Growing Suburban Poverty," Brookings, August 15, 2014, https://www.brookings.edu/blog/the -avenue/2014/08/15/ferguson-mo-emblematic-of-growing-suburban -poverty/.
4. Katie Sanders, "Ferguson, Mo., Has 50 White Police Officers, Three Black Officers, NBC's Mitchell Claims," Politifact, August 17, 2014, https://www .politifact.com/punditfact/statements/2014/aug/17/andrea-mitchell /ferguson-police-department-has-50-white-officers-t/.
5. U.S. Department of Justice, "Department of Justice Report Regarding the Criminal Investigation into the Shooting Death of Michael Brown by Ferguson, Missouri, Police Officer Darren Wilson," March 4, 2015.
6. Alan Scher Zagier, "Missouri Crowd after Shooting: 'Kill the Police,'" Associated Press, August 10, 2014.

7. J. David Goodman, "Difficult Decisions Ahead in Responding to Police Chokehold Homicide," *New York Times*, August 4, 2014.

8. Department of Justice, Civil Rights Division, "Investigation of the Ferguson Police Department," March 4, 2015.

9. Kneebone, "Ferguson, Mo. Emblematic of Growing Suburban Poverty."

10. Department of Justice, Civil Rights Division, "Investigation of the Ferguson Police Department."

11. Lyndon B. Johnson, "Special Message to the Congress on Crime in America," February 6, 1967, retrieved from the American Presidency Project, http://www.presidency.ucsb.edu/ws/?pid=28394.

12. President's Commission on Law Enforcement and Administration of Justice, "The Challenge of Crime in a Free Society," 1967.

13. Ibid.

14. Ibid.

15. Ibid.

16. Ibid.

17. Bureau of Justice Statistics, "Justice Expenditure and Employment Extracts: 1980 and 1981," March 1985, 1, https://www.bjs.gov/content/pub/pdf/jeee -8081dagfes.pdf.

18. John S. Dempsey, Linda S. Forst, and Steven B. Carter, *An Introduction to Policing*, 9th ed. (Boston: Cengage Learning, 2018), 50.

19. Joel Currier, "Police Should Be Required to Wear Body Cameras, Ferguson Group Says," *St. Louis Post-Dispatch*, June 23, 2015.

20. Phillip Swarts, "Grand Jury Files Show Ferguson Cop Shunned Taser, Renewing Debate over Nonlethal Weapons," *Washington Times*, November 26, 2014.

21. Thomas Franck, "There's 'No Evidence' Tasers Reduce Police Use of Firearms, New Study Shows," CNBC, January 18, 2018.

22. Department of Justice, "Justice Department Awards over $23 Million in Funding for Body Worn Camera Pilot Program to Support Law Enforcement Agencies in 32 States," press release no. 15-1145, September 21, 2015, https://www.justice.gov/opa/pr/justice-department-awards-over-23-million -funding-body-worn-camera-pilot-program-support-law.

1: CONFRONT AND COMMAND

1. Gene E. Carte, "August Vollmer and the Origins of Police Professionalism" (Ph.D. diss., University of California at Berkeley, 1972), 1.

2. O. W. Wilson, "August Vollmer," *Journal of Criminal Law and Criminology* 44 (1953): 91.

3. "Casualties and Damage after the 1906 Earthquake," United States Geological Survey, accessed July 31, 2018, https://earthquake.usgs.gov/earthquakes /events/1906calif/18april/casualties.php.

4. Jack London, "The Story of an Eyewitness," *Collier's*, May 5, 1906.

5. Carte, "August Vollmer and the Origins of Police Professionalism," 62.

6. Ibid., 63–64.

7. Ibid., 62–63.

8. Gordon Thomas and Max Morgan Witts, *The San Francisco Earthquake* (New York: Stein and Day, Souvenir Press, 1971), 256.

9. Carte, "August Vollmer and the Origins of Police Professionalism," 61–62.

10. Bruce L. Berg, *Policing in Modern Society* (Oxford: Butterworth-Heinemann, 1999), 145.

11. *August Vollmer: Pioneer in Police Professionalism: Oral History Transcript / and Related Material, 1971–1972* (Berkeley: University of California, 1971), viii.

12. Ezra Carlsen, "Truth in the Machine: Three Berkeley Men Converged to Create the Lie Detector," *California Magazine*, Spring 2010.

13. United States, Wickersham Commission, *Full Text of the Wickersham Commission Report on Prohibition* (Girard, Kans.: Haldeman-Julius, 1931), 1, 3, 4.

14. Albert Deutsch, *The Trouble with Cops* (New York: Crown Publishers, 1955), 150.

15. Randall G. Holcombe, "The Growth of the Federal Government in the 1920s," *Cato Journal* 16 (Fall 1996): 175–99.

16. Ken Burns, "Prohibition: Unintended Consequences," accessed July 19, 2018, www.pbs.org/kenburns/prohibition/unintended-consequences/.

17. Lawrence Rosen, "The Creation of the Uniform Crime Report: The Role of Social Science," *Social Science History* 19, no. 2 (Summer 1995): 215–38.

18. U.S. Census, 1920, available at https://www.census.gov/population/www /documentation/twps0076/twps0076.html.

19. August Vollmer, *The Police and Modern Society* (Berkeley: University of California Press, 1936).

20. Franklin D. Roosevelt, "Executive Order 8802: Reaffirming Policy of Full Participation in the Defense Program by All Persons, Regardless of Race, Creed, Color, or National Origin, and Directing Certain Action in Further-ance of Said Policy," The White House, June 25, 1941.

21. Dominic J. Capeci Jr. and Martha Wilkerson, "The Detroit Rioters of 1943: A Reinterpretation," *Michigan Historical Review*, January 1990.

22. William P. Jones, *The March on Washington: Jobs, Freedom, and the Forgotten History of Civil Rights* (New York: W. W. Norton, 2013), 66.

23. Vivian M. Baulch and Patricia Zacharias, "The 1943 Detroit Race Riots," *Detroit News*, February 10, 1999.

24. John Hollitz, *Thinking Through the Past, Volume 2: Since 1865* (Boston: Cengage Learning, 2014), 192.

25. Baulch and Zacharias, "The 1943 Detroit Race Riots."

26. Ibid.

27. Thurgood Marshall, "The Gestapo in Detroit," *Crisis*, 1943.

28. Baulch and Zacharias, "The 1943 Detroit Race Riots."

29. J. E. Weckler and Theo E. Hall, "The Police and Minority Groups: A Program to Prevent Disorder and to Improve Relations Between Different Racial, Religious, and National Groups," International City Managers' Association, 1944.

30. Ibid.

31. Ibid.

32. Walter White, "Behind the Harlem Riot," *New Republic*, August 16, 1943, 220–22.

33. Weckler and Hall, "The Police and Minority Groups."

34. Ibid.

35. David Alan Sklansky, "Not Your Father's Police Department: Making Sense of the New Demographics of Law Enforcement," *Journal of Criminal Law and Criminology* 96, no. 3 (Spring 2006): 1209–43.

36. "Historical Census Records Ethnic Groups in Los Angeles County 1850 to 1960," Los Angeles Almanac, accessed July 31, 2018, www.laalmanac.com /population/po20.php.

37. Peter J. Boyer, "Bad Cops," *New Yorker*, May 21, 2001.

38. "Historical Census Records Ethnic Groups in Los Angeles County 1850 to 1960," Los Angeles Almanac.

39. Joe Domanick, *To Protect and to Serve: The LAPD's Century of War in the City of Dreams* (New York: Pocket Books, 1994), 401.

40. John Buntin, *L.A. Noir: The Struggle for the Soul of America's Most Seductive City* (New York: Broadway Books, 2010), 254.

41. Jerry Cohen and William S. Murphy, "Burn, Baby, Burn!" *Life*, July 15, 1966.

42. Ibid.

43. Ibid.

44. "Watts Riots," Digital Library of Georgia, accessed December 1, 2017, crdl .usg.edu/events/watts_riots/?Welcome/.

45. Domanick, *To Protect and to Serve*, 185.

2: A MAN OF IDEAS

1. President's Commission on Law Enforcement and Administration of Justice, "The Challenge of Crime in a Free Society," 1967.
2. Ibid.
3. *Who's Who in America*, 40th Edition (Chicago: Marquis Who's Who Inc., 1978).
4. Interview with Ginny Cover, November 16, 2016.
5. John H. Cover, "Resume—Detailed Summary of Concepts, Developments, and Inventions," accessed July 31, 2018, https://www.documentcloud.org /documents/4623912-Jack-Cover-Resume.html.
6. Tom Zito, "Tom Swift's Electric Rifle Is Here," *Washington Post*, January 14, 1976.
7. John Murray and Barnet Resnick, *A Guide to Taser Technology: Stunguns, Lies, and Videotape* (Whitewater, Colo.: Whitewater Press, 1997), 22.
8. Zito, "Tom Swift's Electric Rifle Is Here."
9. H. B. Whitaker, *Electric Shock as It Pertains to the Electric Fence* (Chicago: Underwriters' Laboratories, 1941), 27–28.
10. Murray and Resnick, *A Guide to Taser Technology*, 22.
11. President's Commission, "The Challenge of Crime in a Free Society."
12. Abraham Flatau, Miles C. Miller, and Donald N. Olson, "Non-hazardous Ring Airfoil Projectile for Delivery of Non-lethal Material," U.S. Patent 3,898,932 A, August 12, 1975.
13. Jack E. Lewis, "Nunchaku," U.S. Patent 4,023,803, May 17, 1977.
14. Murray and Resnick, *A Guide to Taser Technology*, 26.
15. Interview with Ginny Cover, November 16, 2016.
16. Brendan I. Koerner, *The Skies Belong to Us: Love and Terror in the Golden Age of Hijacking* (New York: Broadway Books, 2014), 80.
17. Murray and Resnick, *A Guide to Taser Technology*, 25.
18. Ibid., 26.
19. John Nadel, "Stun Gun Is Getting Another Look by Law Enforcement Officials," Associated Press, May 4, 1977.
20. Murray and Resnick, *A Guide to Taser Technology*, 28.
21. Ibid., 32.
22. Ibid.
23. Gladwin Hill, "Los Angeles Police Criticized in Killing," *New York Times*, October 7, 1979.
24. Gladwin Hill, "Citizens to Review Police Shootings in Los Angeles," *New York Times*, October 22, 1979.

25. Interview with Greg Meyer, November 16, 2016.

26. Joel Kotkin, "Upstart Paper Challenges 'Juggernaut' Los Angeles Times; Gossipy *Herald* vs. Powerful *Times*," *Washington Post*, November 23, 1979.

27. Richard Simon, "The Planning and Research Division of Los Angeles Police Department," *Journal of Criminal Law and Criminology* 44, no. 3 (1953): 365.

28. James A. Inciardi, *Handbook of Drug Control in the United States* (New York: Greenwood Press, 1990), 16.

29. Matthew L. Wald, "Sale of Mace to Public Worries Connecticut Police," *New York Times*, December 10, 1981.

30. Interview with Dan Watson, November 17, 2016.

31. Murray and Resnick, *A Guide to Taser Technology*, 36.

32. "Plant Industries Proposes Exchange Offer," *Securities and Exchange Commission News Digest*, January 17, 1969.

33. Interview with James McNulty, November 18, 2016.

34. Murray and Resnick, *A Guide to Taser Technology*, 117.

35. Interview with James McNulty, November 18, 2016.

36. Nova USA, "Executive Summary—History and Description of Business," accessed July 31, 2018, https://www.sec.gov/Archives/edgar/data/1405048/000121478207000227/ex99-1.htm.

37. J. Michael Kennedy, "Device Designed to Deliver 45,000-Volt Jolt to Attacker: Stun Gun Pleases Buyers, Shocks Critics," *Los Angeles Times*, March 31, 1985.

38. Murray and Resnick, *A Guide to Taser Technology*, 39.

39. Interview with Jim Scroggins, June 4, 2017.

40. Murray and Resnick, *A Guide to Taser Technology*, 39.

41. Ibid., 38.

42. Ibid.

43. Sherri Sweetman, "Report on the Attorney General's Conference on Less Than Lethal Weapons," U.S. Department of Justice, National Institute of Justice, Office of Communication and Research, March 1987.

44. Selwyn Raab, "Police Sergeant and Officer Are Charged with Torturing Youth after Arrest," *New York Times*, April 23, 1985.

45. Ruth Marcus, "Controversy Accompanies Popularity of Cheap Electric Stun Guns," *Washington Post*, May 6, 1985.

46. Scott Armstrong, "Stun Guns Getting More Popular—and Controversial," *Christian Science Monitor*, May 16, 1985.

47. Darius Rejali, *Torture and Democracy* (Princeton, N.J.: Princeton University Press, 2009), 242.

48. Marcus, "Controversy Accompanies Popularity."

49. "A Violent Man Possibly under the Influence of the Hallucinogenic Drug PCP Was Stunned by Police Officers Using a Supposed Non-lethal Taser Dart Gun and Later Died Wednesday," United Press International, August 10, 1983.

50. Howard E. Williams, *Taser Electronic Control Devices and Sudden In-Custody Death: Separating Evidence from Conjecture* (Springfield, Ill.: Charles C. Thomas Publisher, 2008), 36–39.

51. Richard Simon, "L.A. Will Pay $585,000 in Chokehold Death," *Los Angeles Times*, April 3, 1986.

52. "Preliminary Autopsy Findings Failed to Reveal the Cause of Death of Lannie S. McCoy, 35, Who Died after Being Shot by Los Angeles Police with a High-voltage Taser Gun," *Los Angeles Times*, August 30, 1985.

53. Daryl Kelley, "Inventor Had Warned Taser Unsafe for Cardiac Patients," *Los Angeles Times*, March 18, 1990.

54. "NAACP Calls for Federal Investigation in Waynesboro Death," Associated Press, September 21, 1984.

55. Phillip Hager, "Court Limits Police Use of Deadly Force: Fleeing Suspects May Not Be Shot Unless They Pose a Danger," *Los Angeles Times*, March 28, 1985.

56. "Rodney King Video: Video Footage of Arrest by Los Angeles Police Officers on March 3, 1991," FBI Records: The Vault, accessed July 31, 2018, https://vault.fbi.gov/rodney-king/video/rodney-king-video.

57. Seth Mydans, "Tape of Beating by Police Revives Charges of Racism," *New York Times*, March 7, 1991.

58. "Official: L.A. Detective from King Trial Kills Self," Associated Press, July 7, 2009.

59. Leslie Berger and Eric Malnic, "Arrest Puts King's Parole in Jeopardy," *Los Angeles Times*, May 31, 1991.

60. Stacey Koon, *Presumed Guilty: The Tragedy of the Rodney King Affair* (Washington, D.C.: Regnery Publishing, 1991), 52.

61. Ibid., 33.

62. Interview with Greg Meyer, November 16, 2016.

63. Rejali, *Torture and Democracy*, 236.

64. Greg Meyer, *Nonlethal Weapons versus Conventional Police Tactics: The Los Angeles Police Department Experience* (Los Angeles: Department of Political Science, California State University in Partial Fulfillment of the Requirements for the Degree Master of Science, 1991), 44.

65. The Independent Commission on the Los Angeles Police Department, "Report of the Independent Commission on the Los Angeles Police Department," July 10, 1991.

66. Howard E. Williams's book *Taser Electronic Control Devices and Sudden In-Custody Death: Separating Evidence from Conjecture* put the number at twenty-four by the end of 1991. A website devoted to counting the number of in-custody Taser deaths, TNT—Truth . . . Not Tasers, put it at twenty-six.

3: CHARTS OF THE FUTURE

1. Richard Stengel, Marcia Gauger, and Barry Kalb, "A Troubled and Troubling Life," *Time*, April 8, 1985.
2. Larry McShane, "For One Goetz Victim, Suffering Won't End," Associated Press, January 8, 1995.
3. Philip Lentz, "Victim of Goetz Refuses to Testify," *Chicago Tribune*, May 6, 1987.
4. Stengel, Gauger, and Kalb, "A Troubled and Troubling Life."
5. "Crime and Justice Atlas 2000," Justice Research and Statistics Association, accessed July 31, 2018, www.jrsa.org/projects/Historical.pdf.
6. Patrick A. Langan and Matthew R. Durose, "The Remarkable Drop in Crime in New York City," Bureau of Justice Statistics, U.S. Department of Justice, October 2004.
7. Leonard Buder, "1980 Called Worst Year of Crime in City History," *New York Times*, February 25, 1981.
8. Vincent Canby, "They Make Movies Look Good," *New York Times*, August 2, 1981.
9. Jen Carlson, "The 1970s Pamphlet Aimed at Keeping Tourists out of NYC," *Gothamist*, September 16, 2013.
10. Darrell Moore, dir., *The Confessions of Bernhard Goetz* (Orland Park, Ill.: MPI Home Video, 1987).
11. Joe Starita, "N.Y. 'Vigilante' Sparks Wave of Hero Worship," *Miami Herald*, January 6, 1985.
12. Isaac Ehrlich, "The Deterrent Effect of Capital Punishment: A Question of Life and Death," *American Economic Review*, June 1975.
13. Rick Nevin, "How Lead Exposure Relates to Temporal Changes in IQ, Violent Crime, and Unwed Pregnancy," *Environmental Research*, May 2000.
14. David Burnham, "Graft Paid to Police Here Said to Run into Millions," *New York Times*, April 25, 1970.
15. Jack R. Greene, *The Encyclopedia of Police Science, Volume 1* (Athens, Ga.: New Georgia Encyclopedia, 1989), 844.
16. Douglas Martin, "Jack Maple, 48, a Designer of City Crime Control Strategies," *New York Times*, August 6, 2001.

17. Jack Maple and Chris Mitchell, *The Crime Fighter* (New York: Doubleday, 1999), 13.

18. Richard Levine, "Decoy Unit Halted by Transit Police in Arrests Dispute," *New York Times*, December 3, 1987.

19. "Jack Maple—Part 1—Speaking to MTA Training Program," accessed July 31, 2018, https://www.youtube.com/watch?v=kNEzAaql8qc.

20. Maple and Mitchell, *The Crime Fighter*, 30.

21. Ibid.

22. Interview with Vertel Martin, August 22, 2017.

23. Ibid.

24. Raymond Dussault, "Jack Maple: Betting on Intelligence—Former NYPD Map Master Jack Maple Puts His Money Where His Crime Stats Are," *Governing*, March 31, 1999.

25. Calvin Sims, "With Subway Crime Up, Transit Police Get a New Chief," *New York Times*, April 12, 1990.

26. William Bratton, *Turnaround: How America's Top Cop Reversed the Crime Epidemic* (New York: Random House, 1998), 36.

27. "The LAPD: Chief Bratton," History of the LAPD, accessed July 31, 2018, www.lapdonline.org/history_of_the_lapd/content_basic_view/1120.

28. Interview with William J. Bratton, October 18, 2017.

29. Bratton, *Turnaround*, 99.

30. Ibid.

31. Ibid., xii.

32. Jack Curry, "Tourist Slain in a Subway in Manhattan," *New York Times*, September 4, 1990.

33. Joyce Wadler, "Death of an Out-of-Towner," *People*, September 24, 1990.

34. Bob Greene, "For New York, the End Is Here," *Chicago Tribune*, September 9, 1990.

35. George L. Kelling and James Q. Wilson, "Broken Windows: The Police and Neighborhood Safety," *Atlantic Monthly*, March 1982.

36. Maple and Mitchell, *The Crime Fighter*, 154.

37. Ibid.

38. "*Miranda v. Arizona*: The Rights to Justice," U.S. Library of Congress, accessed July 31, 2018, https://www.loc.gov/law/help/digitized-books /miranda-v-arizona/miranda-overview.php.

39. Maple and Mitchell, *The Crime Fighter*, 155.

40. Ibid., 157–58.

41. W. Chan Kim and Renee Mauborgne, "Tipping Point Leadership," *Harvard Business Review*, April 2003.

42. "About the Commission," Citizens Crime Commission of New York City, accessed July 12, 2018, www.nycrimecommission.org/about.php.

43. Brian McGrory, "Tough Role Awaits Bratton's Return," *Boston Globe*, January 26, 1992.

44. Bratton, *Turnaround*, 74.

45. Ibid., 73.

46. William J. Bratton, "Transit Police Enforce Subway Rules While Helping Homeless," *New York Times*, February 4, 1991.

47. Martin, "Jack Maple, 48, a Designer of City Crime Control Strategies."

48. Bratton, *Turnaround*, 233.

49. Maple and Mitchell, *The Crime Fighter*, 33.

50. James Lardner, "The CEO Cop: Common Wisdom Has It That the Police Commissioner Can Either Fight Corruption or Win Over the Rank and File. William Bratton Thinks He Can Do Both," *New Yorker*, February 6, 1995.

51. Chris Smith, "The NYPD Guru," *New York*, April 1, 1996.

52. Bratton, *Turnaround*, 237.

53. David Firestone, "The Bratton Resignation," *New York Times*, March 27, 1996.

54. "Compstat: A Crime Reduction Management Tool," John F. Kennedy School of Government at Harvard University, accessed July 31, 2018, https://www.innovations.harvard.edu/compstat-crime-reduction-management-tool.

55. Lardner, "The CEO Cop."

56. Langan and Durose, "The Remarkable Drop in Crime in New York City," appendix, table 1.

57. Ibid.

58. Franklin E. Zimring, *The City That Became Safe: New York's Lessons for Urban Crime and Its Control* (New York: Oxford University Press, 2012), ix.

59. Andrew Karmen, *New York Murder Mystery: The True Story Behind the Crime Crash of the 1990s* (New York: New York University Press, 2000), 25, 31.

60. Suzanne Sataline, "Despite Its Marred Image, NYPD Emulated by Others," *Record*, September 7, 1997.

61. Steve Bailey and Steven Syre, "Former Top Cop's Mission: Securing a Market Niche," *Boston Globe*, April 16, 1996.

62. Alice Lipowicz, "Arresting Results: Bratton Tries to Shift Commish Success to Hotly Contested Investigations Sector," *Crain's New York Business*, May 20, 1996.

63. Carol Robinson, "Police Department Needs Overhaul, Consultants Say Report Cites Lack of Focus, Dissatisfaction," *Birmingham News*, October 16, 1997.

64. Alice McQuillan, "Bratton's Aides: He's Mayor Type," *New York Daily News*, June 18, 1996.

65. "The Business-Cycle Peak of March 2001," *National Bureau of Economic Research*, November 26, 2001.

66. "Justice Expenditure and Employment Extracts: 1980 and 1981," U.S. Bureau of Justice Statistics, March 1985.

67. "Justice Expenditure and Employment in the United States, 2001," U.S. Bureau of Justice Statistics, October 23, 2003.

4: THE TASER REVOLUTION

1. Interview with Patrick W. Smith, February 17, 2015.

2. Ibid.

3. Ibid.

4. Ibid. This story evolved over time. In a June 3, 1996, Associated Press article by Richard Green headlined, "Non-Lethal Gun Marketed for Citizen Self-Protection," Rick said he and his brother "developed the weapon as a way to protect their mother, who lived alone." He told the AP: "First we bought mom a .357 Magnum handgun. She went to an aggressive gun course. They told her that if you shoot someone once, roll him over and shoot him again, even if he's pleading for his life. We knew she could never do that, so we started looking for another way."

5. Ibid.

6. Ibid.

7. *Electronic Medical v. Air-Taser Inc.* (U.S. District Court of the Central District of California, filed February 7, 1995).

8. Rick Smith, "Introducing the Advanced Taser Project," Medical Safety Information, Taser International law enforcement packet, 2000. Many of the details from this section were pulled from notes and internal documents located in the basement of Ginny Cover's home; a trove of documents and letters submitted by Greg Meyer to the Smithsonian; and conversations with Rick Smith, Greg Meyer, and Ginny Cover. For more information, visit officialpolicebusiness.com.

9. Patrick W. Smith, "Advanced Taser M26 Less-Lethal EMD Weapon: Medical Safety Information," Taser International, 2000.

10. Teresa Riordan, "New Taser Finds Unexpected Home in Hands of Police," *New York Times*, November 17, 2003.

11. Interview with Patrick W. Smith, February 17, 2015.

12. Ibid.

13. Ed Taylor, "Scottsdale's Taser Turns a Police Tool into a Profit-making Machine," *East Valley Tribune*, April 11, 2004.

14. "Hans Marrero vs TASER," Air Taser advertisement, accessed July 31, 2018, https://www.youtube.com/watch?v=t2RajoWzz0s.

15. Patti Gillman, "1043+ Dead After Taser Use," TNT—Truth . . . Not Tasers, accessed August 21, 2017, https://truthnotTasers.blogspot.com/2008/04/what-follows-are-names-where-known.html.

16. Daryl Kelley, "Inventor Had Warned Taser Unsafe for Cardiac Patients: Weapons," *Los Angeles Times*, March 8, 1990.

17. Ronald N. Kornblum and Sara K. Reddy, "Effects of the Taser in Fatalities Involving Police Confrontation," *Journal of Forensic Science* 36 (1991): 434–48.

18. "Amnesty Calls for Electro-weapons Suspension," Agence France-Presse, March 3, 1997.

19. Nick Berardini interview with Wayne McDaniel, September 26, 2016.

20. Ibid.

21. Ibid.

22. Interview with Barry Resnick, November 16, 2016.

23. Michael Cooper, "Officers in Bronx Fire 41 Shots, and an Unarmed Man Is Killed," *New York Times*, February 5, 1999.

24. Ginger Thompson and Garry Pierre-Pierre, "Portrait of Slain Immigrant: Big Dreams and a Big Heart," *New York Times*, February 12, 1999.

25. Juan Forero, "Serial Rapist Gets 155 Years; Judge Suggests His Crimes Contributed to Diallo Shooting," *New York Times*, August 2, 2000.

26. Andy Newman, "Disturbed Man Wielding a Hammer Is Killed by Police in Brooklyn," *New York Times*, August 31, 1999.

27. These descriptions and quotes come from promotional videos obtained by filmmaker Nick Berardini.

28. Alex Berenson, "As Police Use of Tasers Soars, Questions over Safety Emerge," *New York Times*, July 18, 2004.

29. Ibid.

30. Taser International, Inc., "Form SB-2—Registration Statement under the Securities Act of 1933," United States Securities and Exchange Commission, February 14, 2001.

31. Julie Cart, "Brothers Stunned by Their New Success in Taser Trade," *Los Angeles Times*, March 21, 2002.

32. "Giuliani's Police Chief Could Be a Problem," Associated Press, October 27, 2007.

33. "Former NYPD Commissioner Bernard Kerik Hosts Panel of Police Chiefs on TASER Deployment," *PoliceOne*, October 20, 2002.

34. "Kerik Made Millions from Agency Contractor," Associated Press, December 9, 2004.

35. Kerik would eventually serve federal prison time for tax fraud and false statement charges.

36. Interviews with Mike Leonesio during the week of July 19, 2016.

37. Ibid.

38. Nick Berardini and Matt Stroud, "A Shot to the Heart," *Intercept*, June 6, 2016.

39. Interviews with Matt Masters, May 25 and 26, 2016.

40. "TASER Certification Lesson Plan," Taser International, Inc., undated.

41. Gary J. Ordog, Jonathan Wasserberger, Theodore Schlater, and Subramaniam Balasubramanium, "Electronic gun (Taser®) Injuries," *Annals of Emergency Medicine* 16 (January 1987): 73–78.

42. Nick Berardini interview with Wayne McDaniel, September 26, 2016.

43. *James F McNulty Jr, et al v. Taser International, et al* (U.S. District Court of the Central District of California, filed April 9, 2001). Quotes are from testimony given on March 20, 2002.

44. Department of Justice, "Attorney General Lynch: Use-of-Force Data Is Vital for Transparency and Accountability," October 5, 2015.

45. Cart, "Brothers Stunned by Their New Success in Taser Trade."

46. Richard Siklos, "Brothers' Stunning Invention Electrifies America," *Telegraph* (UK), April 18, 2004.

47. C. J. Karamargin, "Officer Uses Taser on 9 Year Old Girl," *Arizona Daily Star*, May 25, 2004.

48. "Police Use Stun Gun to Subdue Elderly Woman," Associated Press via *Calgary Herald*, October 21, 2004.

49. "Edited Video Questioned in Police Taser Case," Associated Press, October 29, 2005.

50. "School Official Asks Police to Stop Tasers," United Press International, November 20, 2004.

51. Howard E. Williams, *Taser Electronic Control Devices and Sudden In-Custody Death: Separating Evidence from Conjecture* (Springfield, Ill.: Charles C. Thomas Publisher, 2008), 36.

52. Gillman, "1043+ Dead After Taser Use."

53. Wyatt Andrews and Jamie Holgun, "Tasers under Fire over Deaths," CBS News, April 6, 2004.

54. Steve Tuttle, "TASER Guns Aren't Lethal; There's Proof," *Atlanta Journal-Constitution*, June 8, 2004.

55. Rhonda Brammer, "Bull's Eye, but . . . ," *Barron's*, February 2, 2004.

56. *Malasky v. Taser International, et al.*, 2:05-cv-00115-SRB (U.S. District Court, District of Arizona, Phoenix Division, 2005), information pulled from amended complaints filed August 29, 2005.

57. Nick Berardini interviews with Robert Anglen and Alex Berenson, December 2017.

58. Raksha Shetty, "Report Links Stun Guns to Deaths," Associated Press, November 30, 2004.

59. Nick Berardini interviews with Robert Anglen and Alex Berenson, December 2017.

60. Taser International, Inc., "TASER International, Inc. Demands Amnesty International Withdraw Its Misleading and Defamatory Statements," PR Newswire, June 2, 2004.

61. Documents released by the U.S. Securities and Exchange Commission via Freedom of Information Act request. See officialpolicebusiness.com for complete set of e-mails and related documents.

62. Ibid.

63. Carla Mozee, "Taser's Safety on Kids Questioned," *MarketWatch*, December 6, 2004.

64. Taser International, Inc., "Report: Lab Backs Away from 'Safe' Finding on Tasers," PR Newswire, November 26, 2004.

65. *Malasky v. Taser International, et al.*

66. Interview with Ginny Cover, November 16, 2016.

5: A DIFFERENT WORLD

1. Peter J. Boyer, "Bad Cops: Rafael Perez's Testimony on Police Misconduct Ignited the Biggest Scandal in the History of the LAPD. Is It the Real Story?" *New Yorker*, May 21, 2001.

2. Scott Glover and Matt Lait, "A Tearful Perez Gets 5 Years; Rampart: LAPD Officer Turned Informant Apologizes for His Role in Corruption Scandal," *Los Angeles Times*, February 26, 2000.

3. Violent Crime Control and Law Enforcement Act of 1994, 42 U.S.C. § 14141(a), re-codified as 34 U.S.C. 12601.

4. "The Civil Rights Division's Pattern and Practice Police Reform Work: 1994–Present," United States Department of Justice Civil Rights Division, January 2017.

5. "Appendix F: Timeline of Significant Events," Office of the Independent Monitor: Final Report, June 11, 2009.

6. "Los Angeles Unveils Morale Boosting Recruitment Campaign," Associated Press, May 18, 2001.

7. "Los Angeles Police Department Annual Report 2000," assets.lapdonline.org /assets/pdf/2000_annrprt.pdf, accessed June 14, 2018.

8. Natasha Gregoire, "Software Searches Photos for Suspects," *Tampa Tribune*, December 23, 2000.

9. "Graphco Technologies, Inc. Provides Surveillance for Raymond James Stadium to Identify Known Suspects, Deter Crime," Business Wire, January 29, 2001.

10. Louis Sahagun, "Secret Cameras Scanned Crowd at Super Bowl for Criminals," *Los Angeles Times,* February 1, 2001.

11. Robert Trigaux, "Cameras Scanned Fans for Criminals," *St. Petersburg Times*, January 31, 2001.

12. Ibid.; Sahagun, "Secret Cameras Scanned Crowd."

13. Christopher Slobogin, "Transactional Surveillance by the Government," *Mississippi Law Journal* 75 (2005): 139, 145.

14. Jack Leonard, "Deputies to Join Schools' Anti-Crime Effort," *Los Angeles Times,* January 7, 2001.

15. Andrew Guthrie Ferguson, *The Rise of Big Data Policing: Surveillance, Race, and the Future of Law Enforcement* (New York: New York University Press, 2017), 15.

16. Craig Horowitz, "The NYPD's War on Terror," *New York*, February 3, 2003.

17. Jennifer Steinhauer, "Giuliani Is Resolute on Extending His Term," *New York Times*, October 13, 2001.

18. Ray Kelly, "Bloomberg, as Mayor, Would Bolster NYPD," *Newsday*, November 4, 2001.

19. David Barstow, "After the Attacks: Security; Envisioning an Expensive Future in the Brave New World of Fortress New York," *New York Times,* September 16, 2001.

20. Patrice O'Shaughnessy and Alice McQuillan, "Ray Kelly Returning to Lead City's Police Force," *New York Daily News*, November 12, 2001.

21. Tina Daunt, "NYPD's Ex-Head Eyes Job at LAPD; Police: William Bratton, the Big Apple's Former Police Commissioner, Considers Applying to Become Chief and Sounds Out City Leaders," *Los Angeles Times*, July 14, 2001.

22. Rory O'Connor, "They'll Take Manhattan," *Boston,* October 1999.

23. Joe Domanick, *Blue: The LAPD and the Battle to Redeem American Policing* (New York: Simon & Schuster, 2015), 227.

24. Tina Daunt, "L.A. Police Monitor Issues First Report," *Los Angeles Times*, November 20, 2001.
25. Ibid.
26. B. Drummond Ayres Jr., "Los Angeles Police Chief Will Be Let Go," *New York Times*, March 11, 1997.
27. "The New Iraq; Taxes and Tactics; Newsmaker," *The NewsHour with Jim Lehrer*, May 7, 2003.
28. Beth Barrett, "Contenders Plentiful for LAPD Helm," *Daily News of Los Angeles*, April 10, 2002.
29. Tina Daunt, "LAPD Bid by Ex-N.Y. Chief OK by Hahn," *Los Angeles Times*, July 17, 2002.
30. "Scrutiny for L.A.'s Own Secret Police," *Los Angeles Times*, June 15, 2003.
31. Horowitz, "The NYPD's War on Terror."
32. Beverly Beckham, "Op-Ed: Public Safety Must Trump Privacy," *Boston Herald*, June 26, 2002.
33. David R. Baker, "Pitching Gizmos to Feds; Small Firms to Get Advice on Landing Contracts with U.S.," *San Francisco Chronicle*, June 9, 2004.
34. Anick Jesdanun, "As Tracking Technologies Improve, We're Ever More Constantly Watched," Associated Press, August 29, 2002.
35. "Face-Recognition Software to Fight Crime Proves a Dud," Media General News Service, *Winston-Salem Journal*, August 21, 2003.
36. Robyn E. Blumner, "Face Recognition Has Poor Results," *St. Petersburg Times*, January 13, 2002.
37. Domanick, *Blue*, 236.
38. Walt Schick, "CompStat in the Los Angeles Police Department," *Police Chief*, January 2004.
39. Kevin Herrera, "COMPSTAT: Police, Clergy Reveal Plan to Track Area Crime," *Sentinel*, April 10, 2003.
40. Rachel Uranga, "Bratton Looks Like Shoo-in at LAPD," *Daily News of Los Angeles*, April 30, 2007.
41. Sanford Wexler, "John Miller: LAPD's Counter-Terrorism Bureau Chief," *Law Enforcement Technology*, March 2004.
42. Jay Stanley and Barry Steinhardt, "Bigger Monster, Weaker Chains: The Growth of an American Surveillance Society," American Civil Liberties Union, January 2003.
43. Ibid.
44. Kevin Johnson, "NYPD Adds CIA, Military Experts," *USA Today*, January 29, 2002.
45. Jim Dwyer, "City Police Spied Broadly Before G.O.P. Convention," *New York Times*, March 25, 2007.

46. "Police Surveillance and the 2004 Republican National Convention," *New York Times*, accessed August 1, 2018, www.nytimes.com/ref/nyregion/RNC _intel_digests.html.

47. Jen Chung, "NYPD Releases All 2004 RNC-Related Documents," *Gothamist*, May 17, 2007.

48. "Los Angeles Police Foundation to Announce Partnership Using Black-Berry with Cingular; BlackBerry Devices Enable Senior Lead Officers to Increase Focus on Community Policing," PR Newswire, February 25, 2004.

49. Rick Orlov, "Cop Gadget Flops at Mayor's Demo," *Daily News of Los Angeles*, March 13, 2004.

50. Jeremiah Marquez, "Scandalized LAPD Recruits Pattern-Scanning Computer to Stop Rogue Cops," Associated Press, July 21, 2005.

6: THE WARNING LABEL

1. Alex Berenson, "S.E.C. Looking at Safety Data and Big Order for Taser Guns," *New York Times*, January 8, 2005.

2. Rick Smith, "Dear Entrepreneurs, When the Sky Is Falling, Embrace It," *New York Observer,* December 30, 2016.

3. *Malasky v. Taser International, et al.,* 2:05-cv-00115-SRB (U.S. District Court, District of Arizona, Phoenix Division, 2005).

4. Ibid., from document "In re: Taser International," submitted August 29, 2005.

5. Ibid.

6. Ibid.

7. Nick Berardini interviews with Robert Anglen and Alex Berenson, December 2017.

8. Securities and Exchange Commission, "Form 10-Q: Quarterly Report Pursuant to Section 13 or 15(d) of the Securities Exchange Act of 1934," Commission File Number 001-16391, accessed August 1, 2018, https://www.sec.gov /Archives/edgar/data/1069183/000095015305002014/p71055e10vq.htm.

9. Alex Berenson, "Inquiry into Taser Upgraded, Giving S.E.C. Subpoena Power," *New York Times*, September 28, 2005.

10. Russ Wiles, "Earnings for Taser Decline in 2nd Quarter," *Arizona Republic*, July 21, 2005.

11. Mike Sakal, "Sheriff's Tasers Will Add Video," *East Valley Tribune*, May 24, 2006.

12. "S.E.C. Ends Taser Inquiry," Bloomberg News, May 16, 2006.

13. Nick Berardini interview with Wayne McDaniel, September 26, 2016.

14. Michael Lane, "Is TASER Really Safer Than Tylenol?" Taser Truth,

September 17, 2008, accessed August 1, 2018, tasertruth.blogspot.com /2008/09/is-taser-really-safer-than-tylenol.html.

15. See discussion of average current in chapter 5.

16. Nick Berardini interview with Wayne McDaniel, September 26, 2016.

17. Interviews with Mike Leonesio during the week of July 19, 2016.

18. Nick Berardini interview with Wayne McDaniel, September 26, 2016.

19. Jami R. Grant, Pamela E. Southall, Joan Mealey, Shauna R. Scott, and David R. Fowler, "Excited Delirium Deaths in Custody: Past and Present," *American Journal of Forensic Medicine and Pathology* 30 (March 2009): 1–5.

20. Documents released by the U.S. Securities and Exchange Commission via Freedom of Information Act request. See officialpolicebusiness.com for complete set of e-mails and related documents.

21. Interviews with Matt Masters, May 25 and 26, 2016.

22. Robert Anglen, "Taser's Lawsuits Challenge Coroners," *Arizona Republic*, May 3, 2008.

23. Interviews with Matt Masters, May 25 and 26, 2016.

24. Jim Johnson, "Taser Held Responsible in Salinas Death," *Monterey Herald*, June 7, 2008.

25. Thomas R. Braidwood, *Restoring Public Confidence: Restricting the Use of Conducted Energy Weapons in British Columbia*, Braidwood Commission on Conducted Energy Weapon Use (Vancouver, BC: Braidwood Commission, 2009), 15.

26. Documents released by the U.S. Securities and Exchange Commission via Freedom of Information Act request. See officialpolicebusiness.com for complete set of e-mails and related documents.

27. Interviews with Mike Leonesio during the week of July 19, 2016.

28. Ibid.

29. Recording of Taser International law enforcement conference call, October 2009. For audio, more information on the recording, and related documents, visit officialpolicebusiness.com.

30. Ryan Felton and Oliver Laughland, "Officers at Sam DuBose Scene Involved in Death of Another Unarmed Black Man," *Guardian*, July 30, 2015.

31. *Kelly Brinson II and Derek Brinson et al. v. University Hospital, Inc. et al.* (U.S. District Court of the Southern District of Ohio, filed November 11, 2011).

32. "Taser Lawsuit Against University of Cincinnati Police and University Hospital Settled for $638,000.00 and Reforms," Gerhardstein & Branch Co. LPA, accessed August 1, 2018, www.gbfirm.com/taser-lawsuit-against-university -of-cincinnati-police-and-university-hospital-settled-for-638000-00-and -reforms/.

33. Securities and Exchange Commission, "Form 8-K: Current Report Pursuant to Section 13 or 15(d) of the Exchange Act of 1934," November 27, 2013, accessed August 1, 2018, https://www.sec.gov/Archives/edgar/data /1069183/000119312513456977/d635668d8k.htm.

34. Securities and Exchange Commission, "Form 10-K: Annual Report Pursuant to Section 13 or 15(d) of the Exchange Act of 1934," December 31, 2009, accessed August 1, 2018, https://www.sec.gov/Archives/edgar/data/1069183 /000095012310024799/c97679e10vk.htm.

35. Securities and Exchange Commission, "Form 10-K: Annual Report Pursuant to Section 13 or 15(d) of the Exchange Act of 1934,"December 31, 2016, accessed August 1, 2018, https://www.sec.gov/Archives/edgar/data/1069183 /000106918317000042/a10ktasr123116.htm.

36. Peter Eisler, Grant Smith, and Jason Szep, "How Reuters Tracked Fatalities and Taser Incidents," Reuters, August 22, 2017.

7: THE GOOD SHEPHERD WATCHING OVER THE FLOCK

1. New York Police Department, Intelligence Division, Intelligence Analysis Unit, "US-Iran Conflict: The Threat to New York City," May 15, 2006.

2. Matt Apuzzo and Adam Goldman, "Document Shows NYPD Eyed Shiites Based on Religion," Associated Press, February 3, 2012.

3. John Logie Baird, dir., *The First Television Picture with a Greyscale Image*, 1925.

4. Walter Dornberger, *V-2* (New York: Ballantine Books, 1954), 14.

5. Albert Abramson, *The History of Television, 1942–2000* (Jefferson, N.C.: McFarland & Company, 2003), 6.

6. Tim Moriarty, "$1 Million Policy on Champ," *Desert Sun*, May 25, 1965.

7. "Enforcement of Security Laws Will Test New Spirit of Reform," *New York Times*, January 28, 1966.

8. "Electronic Setup Helping Hospital," *New York Times*, February 27, 1966.

9. Chris Kelly, "Herbert Balmer," Liverpool City Police, accessed November 7, 2017, liverpoolcitypolice.co.uk/balmer/4551685029.

10. David Scott, "Television Eyes Catch Criminals in the Act," *Popular Science* 187, no. 6 (December 1965): 102–3.

11. Theodore Jones, "Subway Stations to Test TV Units as Curb on Crime," *New York Times*, May 2, 1965.

12. "A History of Listening In," *Scientific American*, September 2008.

13. *Olmstead v. United States*, 277 U.S. 438 (1928).

14. Ibid.; President's Commission on Law Enforcement and Administration of Justice, "The Challenge of Crime in a Free Society," 1967, 117.

15. *Olmstead v. United States*, 277 U.S. 438 (1928); President's Commission on Law Enforcement and Administration of Justice, 202.

16. Ralph Michael Stein, "*Laird v. Tatum*: The Supreme Court and a First Amendment Challenge to Military Surveillance of Lawful Civilian Political Activity," *Hofstra Law Review* 1 (1973): 244–75.

17. *Laird v. Tatum*, 408 U.S. 1, 10 (1972).

18. "VIDEO SURVEILLANCE: Information on Law Enforcement's Use of Closed-Circuit Television to Monitor Selected Federal Property in Washington, D.C," Government Accountability Office, June 2003.

19. John Darnton, "Theater of the Observed," *New York Times*, September 30, 1973.

20. Richard Haitch, "Follow-Up on the News," *New York Times*, October 12, 1975.

21. Richard Haitch, "Policing by TV," *New York Times*, December 15, 1985.

22. Tsutomu Shimomura, "Catching Kevin," *Wired*, February 1, 1996.

23. Ibid.

24. Tsutomu Shimomura with John Markoff, *Takedown: The Pursuit and Capture of Kevin Mitnick, America's Most Wanted Computer Outlaw—By the Man Who Did It* (New York: Hyperion, 1996).

25. Scott D. Easterling, Michael O. Linden, and John C. Voelkel, U.S. Patent 5428667, 1996.

26. Benjamin Dangl, "An Interview with Evo Morales," *Upside Down World*, December 8, 2003.

27. Maude Barlow, "The Free Trade Area of the Americas and the Threat to Social Programs, Environmental Sustainability and Social Justice in Canada and the Americas," Council of Canadiens, February 2001, accessed July 25, 2018, https://ratical.org/co-globalize/MBonFTAA.html.

28. "Section #5 Emergency Purchases," Miami Police Department, accessed November 2017, https://cdn.arstechnica.net/wp-content/uploads/2013/09/miami-dade.pdf.

29. *Beau Hodai, an investigative reporter, Plaintiff/Petitioners, v. The City of Tucson, a municipal corporation, and the Tucson Police Department, a municipal agency*, Court of Appeals of Arizona, Division 2, Decided January 7, 2016.

30. Curtis Waldman, "Here's How Much a StingRay Cell Phone Surveillance Tool Costs," *Motherboard*, December 8, 2016.

31. Ryan Gallagher, "Meet the Machines That Steal Your Phone's Data," *ArsTechnica*, September 25, 2013.

32. Detective M. J. Pusatere, "Bomb Threat," Palm Bay Police Department, May 1,

2007, accessed August 1, 2018, https://www.documentcloud.org/documents /1676253-03-05-2014-pbpd-stingray-records-excerpt-redacted.html.

33. Ibid.

34. Nathan Freed Wessler, "ACLU-Obtained Documents Reveal Breadth of Secretive Stingray Use in Florida," American Civil Liberties Union, February 22, 2015.

35. Michael Morisy, "Requester's Voice: Lucy Parsons Labs' Freddy Martinez [on] How the Lab Used Public Records to Open Up Chicago's Secret $4.7 Million Surveillance Program," *Muckrock*, October 7, 2016.

36. Jon Campbell, "LAPD Spied on 21 Using StingRay Anti-Terrorism Tool," *Los Angeles Weekly*, January 24, 2013.

37. Robert Patrick, "Controversial Secret Phone Tracker Figured in Dropped St. Louis Case," *St. Louis Post-Dispatch*, April 19, 2015.

38. Elizabeth E. Joh, "The Undue Influence of Surveillance Technology Companies on Policing," *N.Y.U. Law Review Online*, 2017.

8: TRANSPARENCY AND OPENNESS

1. Taser International, Inc., "Form 10-K, Annual Report Pursuant to Section 13 or 15(D) of the Securities Exchange Act of 1934," U.S. Securities and Exchange Commission, accessed July 31, 2018, https://www.sec.gov /Archives/edgar/data/1069183/000119312514091839/d652561d10k.htm.

2. "Implementing a Body-Worn Camera Program Recommendations and Lessons Learned," U.S. Department of Justice, Office of Community Oriented Policing Services, 2014.

3. "Obama Requests $263 Million for Police Body Cameras, Training," NBC News, December 1, 2014.

4. "Movie Camera in Police Car Puts Evidence on Film," *Popular Science*, September 1939.

5. "What Happened in 1968: Important News and Events, Key Technology and Popular Culture," The People History, accessed November 21, 2017, www.thepeoplehistory.com/1968.html.

6. "Smile and Don't Lie—You're on Copper's Camera," United Press International, June 10, 1983.

7. "Nielsen Ratings: Top Programs of 1990–1991," accessed August 1, 2018, https://library.uoregon.edu/sites/default/files/data/guides/english /television_almanac.pdf.

8. Debra Seagal, "Tales from the Cutting-Room Floor," *Harper's Magazine*, November 1993.

9. See chapter 7 for more on Taser Cam.

10. Matt Stroud, "Cop-Cams: Taser's Last Shot at Getting Beyond the Stun Gun," *Bloomberg Businessweek*, May 7, 2015.

11. Interview with Patrick W. Smith, February 17, 2015.

12. *Taser International, Inc. v. Ward*, 231 P.3d 921 (Arizona Court App. 1 2010).

13. Matt Stroud, "Police Commander's Relationship with Axon Raises Questions about Pittsburgh's No-Bid Contract for Body Cameras," *PublicSource*, September 25, 2017.

14. Pennsylvania Wiretapping and Electronic Surveillance Control Act, 18 Pa. C.S.A. §§5701 et seq., 1978, accessed July 31, 2018, http://www.legis.state .pa.us/cfdocs/legis/LI/consCheck.cfm?txtType=HTM&ttl=18&div =0&chpt=57.

15. Liz Reid, "Wiretap Laws Complicate Deployment of Body Cameras to Pittsburgh Police Officers," WESA, November 9, 2015.

16. Matt Stroud, "Breaking Down Trapp-Axon Ties over Time," *PublicSource*, September 25, 2017.

17. Angela Couloumbis and Karen Langley, "Senate Amends Pa. Wiretap Act to Protect Evidence Gathered by Police Body Cameras," *Pittsburgh Post-Gazette*, October 20, 2016.

18. Matt Stroud, "How an Impromptu Meeting between a Body Camera Vendor and a Pittsburgh Police Official Led to a $1.5 Million Deal," *Public-Source*, September 26, 2017.

19. Jaimy Jones, "New MVPD Chief of Police Named, Will Focus on Technology to Enhance Performance," *Houston Chronicle*, January 5, 2017.

20. Martin Salazar, "City Council Votes 5–3 to Approve Taser Contract," *Albuquerque Journal*, May 2, 2017.

21. Ryan J. Foley, "Taser Has Financial Ties to Police Chiefs, Including Halstead," Associated Press, March 4, 2015.

22. *Digital Ally, Inc. v. Taser International, Inc.*, 2:16-cv-02032, 2016.

23. Kashmir Hill, "Weapons of Documentation: Taser Is Pushing Police Body Cameras, Wants to Be Dropbox for Cops," *Forbes*, November 5, 2014.

24. Ibid.

25. Stephen Nellis, "Taser Changes Name to Axon in Shift to Software Services," Reuters, April 5, 2017.

26. "Safariland Acquires VIEVU, a Leader in Body Worn Video Cameras for Law Enforcement Officers," Safariland Group, June 29, 2015.

27. Ashley Southall, "Police Department's Body Camera Contract Fuels a Fierce Rivalry," *New York Times*, October 13, 2016.

28. Alex Pasternack, "NYC Mayor Defends Police Body Camera Buy, Decrying a Competitor's 'Smear' Campaign," *Fast Company*, February 9, 2017.

29. "VIEVU, a Subsidiary of Safariland, to Be Acquired by Axon Enterprise, Inc.," Safariland Group, May 4, 2018.
30. *Digital Ally, Inc. v. Taser International, Inc.*, 2:16-cv-02032-CM-TJJ.
31. Ryan Kocian, "Taser Competitor Loses Fight Over Body-Camera Bid," *Courthouse News Service*, April 6, 2017.
32. Justin Fenton and Kevin Rector, "Body Camera Footage Shows Officer Planting Drugs, Public Defender Says," *Baltimore Sun*, July 19, 2017.
33. Gretchen Parsons, "Weiser Body Cam Footage Reveals Questionable Encounter," KTVB, November 16, 2016.
34. Albert Samaha, "Blue Lies Matter," *Buzzfeed*, January 17, 2017.
35. Michael Levenson and Evan Allen, "Boston Police Union Challenges Body Camera Program," *Boston Globe*, August 26, 2016.
36. Julie Bosman, "Hollywood-Style Heroism Is Latest Trend in Police Videos," *New York Times*, May 28, 2017.
37. Chuck Wexler et al., "Implementing a Body-Worn Camera Program Recommendations and Lessons Learned," Police Executive Research Forum, 2014.
38. Joshua C. Hausman, "Smile, You're on Body Camera! Pennsylvania's New Law Clears Hurdles for Wider Adoption of Police Body Cameras, and Changes How Requests for Recordings Will Be Handled," Campbell, Durrant, Beatty, Palombo, and Miller, P.C., July 14, 2017.

CONCLUSION: THE PROBLEM WITH SOLUTIONISM

1. Evgeny Morozov, *To Save Everything, Click Here: The Folly of Technological Solutionism* (New York: PublicAffairs, 2013), 5.
2. "Chicago to Expand Police Body Camera Program," NBC 5 Chicago, November 29, 2015.
3. Jessica D'Onofrio, "Chicago Police to Receive 780 More Tasers," ABC 7 Chicago, February 4, 2016.
4. "Randomized Controlled Trial of the Metropolitan Police Department Body-Worn Camera Program," *The Lab @ DC*, October 2017; Nell Greenfieldboyce, "Body Cam Study Shows No Effect on Police Use of Force or Citizen Complaints," NPR, October 20, 2017.
5. Patti Gillman, "1043+ Dead after Taser Use," TNT—Truth . . . Not Tasers, truthnottasers.blogspot.com, accessed July 31, 2018.
6. "Reuters Finds 1,005 Deaths in U.S. Involving Tasers, Largest Accounting to Date," Reuters, August 22, 2017.
7. Peter Eisler, Grant Smith, and Jason Szep, "How Reuters Tracked Fatalities and Taser Incidents," Reuters, August 22, 2017.

8. Annie Gilbertson, "LA Police Expand Taser Use, Even Though It's Effective Only Half the Time," KPCC, March 4, 2016.

9. Kate Mather, "Tasers Often Don't Work, Review of LAPD Incidents Finds," *Los Angeles Times*, April 1, 2016.

10. Emma Discher, "Baton Rouge Police Receive Long-Awaited Body Cameras Thursday, Friday," *Advocate*, August 24, 2017.

11. Erik Ortiz, "Walter Scott Shooting: North Charleston Orders 250 Body Cameras for Officers," NBC News, April 8, 2015.

12. Michael Daly, "'Taser Town' and the Shots Heard 'Round the World,'" *Daily Beast*, April 8, 2015.

13. Emily Ekins, "Policing in America: Understanding Public Attitudes Toward the Police. Results from a National Survey," Cato Institute, December 7, 2016.

14. Gene E. Carte, "August Vollmer and the Origins of Police Professionalism" (Ph.D. diss., University of California at Berkeley, 1972).

15. Ibid.

16. Glen Martin, "Black Cop, White Cop: What Can Two Berkeley Police from the Century Before Tell Us about Race Relations in America Today?" *California*, Fall 2015.

ACKNOWLEDGMENTS

In addition to working a full-time job of her own, my wife, Kylie, allowed me the time during early morning hours, late nights, and weekends to read, write, and take over our home's basement. Kylie nurtured two of our very energetic kids, Evy and Cori—and gave birth to a third, Charlie—while I wrote this book. There is no way that it would have come into existence without her patience and love and support. Thank you, Kylie.

Thank you, also, to my parents—Nancy and David Stroud—who offered counsel as I rambled on and on during Sunday morning breakfasts about policing cultures and technologies that, I'm sure, couldn't have been further away from their interests.

Kylie's parents, Nancy and Tom Butler, and her siblings, Matt and Marissa—and their wonderful spouses and children—also helped to make our lives joyful.

Thanks to Jesse Hicks, too, who is perhaps the smartest writer, editor, and thinker I've had the privilege of meeting and calling a friend. He assisted with interviews surrounding the Taser's early history and helped to scan hundreds of documents, drawings, and contracts in the San Clemente garage of Ginny Cover, Jack Cover's widow. Ginny was exceedingly generous with her time and with her recollections about Jack, his personality, and his work developing his most famous invention—clearly one of dozens he developed over decades in his garage. Thank you, Ginny.

The filmmaker Nick Berardini helped to conduct some of the interviews in this book and taught me a lot of what I know about Taser International and Axon Enterprise through his incredible documentary film *Killing Them Safely* and his general knowledge and dogged investigative reporting. Nick also connected me to Matt Masters, a cop with the Kansas City Police Department who is the kind of cop everyone should know—someone who's thoughtful and empathetic and wants to do right by the people he serves and protects. Matt's son, Bryce, is still recovering from a Taser shock that nearly killed him, and his wife, Stacy, helps to keep their family centered. The entire Masters family has been inspirational throughout my reporting on this project.

Lauren Sharp, a phenomenal agent with writing chops that far exceed mine, helped to mold a vague idea into a solid book proposal and usher it to life. Her guidance—along with the guidance of her colleagues at Aevitas—has been indispensable.

Connor Guy, my editor, made this book happen. He's been my closest writing confidant throughout this process and knows more about my tendencies in print than anyone. If you need an editor, he's who you want in the role. Thank you to Connor and to Metropolitan Books for taking a chance on a first-time author.

Thanks also to *CityLab*'s Brentin Mock for guidance and knowledge, and to Carmen Gentile for friendship and letting me borrow your motorcycle indefinitely. Thanks to Mila Sanina and Halle Stockton at *PublicSource* for supporting investigative journalism in Pittsburgh; Josh Dzieza and Michael Zelenko at the *Verge* for publishing "Official Police Business"; Stephen Greenwood for *not* getting Tasered in Scottsdale; Kevin Friess for being a good cop and a great friend; Rick Smith and Steve Tuttle for making my job interesting; Roger Hodge at the *Intercept* for supporting an odd journalistic collaboration; and Esther Kaplan at the Investigative Fund for being open to just about any pitch from any eager journalist.

And thanks to Evy, Cori, and Charlie for being goofballs and for making every day worth living.

INDEX

ABOUT THE AUTHOR

MATT STROUD is an investigative reporter with a focus on companies that do business with police departments and prisons. Formerly on staff at the Associated Press, Bloomberg News, and *The Verge*, he has also written for publications such as *The Atlantic*, *Politico*, *Buzzfeed*, and *The Intercept*. He lives in Pittsburgh.